KEN HOM
TRAVELS WITH A HOT WOK

KEN HOM

TRAVELS WITH A HOT WOK

160 QUICK AND EASY DISHES WITH EAST–WEST FLAVOURS

PHOTOGRAPHS BY SANDRA LANE

BBC BOOKS

In Memory of My Chinese Grandparents

Acknowledgements

I have always been fortunate to have a solid team assisting me in my cookbooks. Their work is reflected in this book. I appreciated their constant questioning and prodding and, under intense pressure, they also remained cool and calm. First I must thank Gordon Wing, my right hand in the kitchen and a keen observer of every step in each recipe; Gerry Cavanaugh, for his insightful editing of my rough words and suggestions; and Andrew Walton Smith (Drew), who checks every detail of the manuscript for inconsistency – to them I am truly indebted. We were assisted superbly by Eric Litzky and Storm Thomas.

Of course, my thanks must also go to all the hardworking team at BBC Books, including my publisher, Chris Weller; the project editor who supervised the book, Khadija Manjlai; the copy-editor, Deborah Savage; Vivien Bowler, the senior commissioning editor; Jane Parsons, her assistant; and the imaginative art director, Frank Phillips, and designer Isobel Gillan for their masterful design. To them I make a deep bow.

For the enticing and mouthwatering photographs, only humble gratitude can be offered to Sandra Lane and her stylist Mary Norton, and her home economist Sarah Ramsbottom.

Both my producer, Kate Kinninmont, and executive producer, Tom Kinninmont, were a source of inspiration; as were Carole Blake and Julian Friedmann, my indispensable advisers.

Thank you all.

This book is published to accompany the television series
Ken Hom Travels with a Hot Wok which was produced by
Independent Image Ltd for BBC Independent Commissions.

Executive Producer for Independent Image Ltd: Tom Kinninmont
Series Producer for Independent Image Ltd: Kate Kinninmont

Published by BBC Books, BBC Worldwide Limited,
Woodlands, 80 Wood Lane, London W12 0TT

First published in 1998

ISBN 0 563 38394 1

Edited by Deborah Savage
Designed by Isobel Gillan
Home economist for photography: Sarah Ramsbottom
Stylist for photography: Mary Norton

Set in Futura by BBC Books
Printed and bound in Great Britain by Butler & Tanner Ltd, Frome and London
Colour separations by Radstock Reproductions Ltd, Midsomer Norton
Jacket printed by Lawrence Allen Ltd, Weston-super-Mare

Page 2: *Grilled Pork Chops with Chinese Spices* (page 110)

CONTENTS

INTRODUCTION

The global village is upon us and with it has come the global kitchen and the emergence of a global cuisine. It has been called 'East meets West cuisine', 'Pacific Rim cuisine' and, more recently, 'fusion cookery'. We need only look at the menus of popular and upmarket restaurants throughout the world to discover the extensive and marvellous blending of foods, ingredients and techniques from the many different cultures that are at the heart of this new cuisine.

Moreover, in home kitchens worldwide, the new spices, seasonings, foods and techniques are becoming staple items. Today's home-cooked meals quite often reflect an easy and eclectic cosmopolitanism that was impossible and even unthinkable just twenty years ago. Today, formerly exotic eastern ingredients – such as bok choy, five-spice powder, or soy sauce – are to be found in shops and home pantries, nestling comfortably and familiarly alongside traditional western foodstuffs.

Of course, throughout history, every culture has assimilated foreign influences and every cuisine worthy of the name has adopted new techniques and accepted exotic ingredients into its repertoire. The venerable Chinese culinary traditions, for example, are notable for their readiness to assimilate new and appropriate foods and ideas. French cuisine, in all its glory, owes much to Italian and other influences. And these cuisines have reciprocally and profoundly influenced their neighbours.

Historically, though, foods from one culture moved only gradually to another. For example, French historians have calculated that when the tomato (a New World plant) was first introduced into southern France over four hundred years ago its integration into the French countryside moved initially at a rate of about one mile every ten years. Potatoes, too, were but slowly naturalized into the European diet. The process worked the same way, east and west. Maize, peanuts and sweet potatoes (again, New World plants) were introduced into China in the sixteenth century and spread very slowly, although much more rapidly than ten miles every century!

What is new about 'fusion' cookery is the speed with which its tenets and techniques have spread. This, of course, is primarily due to the remarkable advances in transport and communication that have characterized modern times. We have moved from horseback to jet planes and 'real time' communication in one hundred and fifty years: cultures and peoples are joined together as never before. 'Fusion cuisine' is a natural accompaniment of this process.

Another effect of the transport and communication revolutions is that global travel has rocketed, while vicarious experience and awareness of other cultures has deepened. Insularity, parochialism and ignorance of those other cultures are becoming things of the past. Travel has always been mind-broadening, but today it also widens one's culinary horizons.

Among the blessings of this new global mobility – of people and of products – has been the proliferation, in metropolitan districts throughout the world, of restaurants serving ethnic cuisines. They have become especially prominent in western cities. Japanese, Thai, Vietnamese, Mexican, Latin American, Korean and other cuisines are now generally available in most urban centres. The already familiar Chinese restaurants, which once offered only westernized pseudo-Cantonese fare, now serve authentic Sichuan, Hunan, Shanghai, Taiwanese and other regional cuisines, along with truly authentic Cantonese cookery. The popularity of these ethnic restaurants, together with cookery books and television programmes on ethnic foods, has led supermarkets and other outlets to stock the basic ingredients of these cuisines. Consumers have led the way in developing their own fusion tastes and recipes.

Another factor encourages the adoption of fusion cuisine and that is a heightened awareness of how one's general health is based on one's diet. Today, medical and health experts are warning us about a global epidemic in the so-called 'diseases of affluence', especially in the West. These maladies, especially cardiovascular disease and cancer, may stem mainly from recent changes in people's diets. And there is irony here, because these diseases are most closely linked to greater consumption of meat and dairy products, foods which have come to symbolize prosperity and health.

As westerners have discovered the dangers of over-relying on fatty meats, butter and cream, they have found at hand eastern substitutes to calm and satisfy their beleaguered palates. Asian cuisines have never been based primarily on meat and dairy products, and compensate for the absence or reduction of those rich western foods. They lighten the diet but also add refreshing and satisfying flavours, thus making the new fusion tastes appealing as well as wholesome. As the eastern nations 'modernize' and emulate certain aspects of the western lifestyle – I am thinking here of the over-consumption of fatty hamburgers and other 'junk' foods – it is to be hoped that fusion cookery will at least lessen the impact of such unhealthy diets in both the East and West.

Finally, we must note the economic benefits of a global food market, which have allowed a greater selection of foods to be available than ever before. The expansion of trade, improvements in the preparation and preservation of all ingredients, rapid transport, and innovative marketing and advertising have all come together to create the consumer awareness, the possibilities, the needs and the capabilities required to sustain a global cuisine. The availability and the variety of the earth's bounty, combined with a natural tendency to experiment, to try something new and pleasing, has contributed to the rise of fusion cookery.

Although fusion cuisine appears to have caught on relatively quickly, in retrospect one may see the first stirring of the fusion approach about thirty years ago. The introduction of the French *nouvelle cuisine* may be taken as the earliest manifestation of the new, cosmopolitan, thoughtfully eclectic spirit at work in the kitchen. Its essentials included shortened cooking times, which the food writers Henri Gault and Christian Millau quickly perceived as a Chinese technique. The great *nouvelle cuisine* chef, Paul Bocuse, noted a Japanese influence, drawn from the work of the many Japanese apprentice cooks then learning their craft in France. This new way of cooking emphasized fresh foods, lightness, inventiveness and an eager acceptance of whatever produced nutritious, imaginative, palate-pleasing menus.

Gault and Millau summed up the accomplishments of *nouvelle cuisine* and presciently described the coming emergence of fusion cookery: 'There are still thousands of dishes to be invented – and probably one hundred of them will be memorable. [The new cooks] don't disdain special condiments, products and recipes from the East. Bocuse brings saffron from Iran for his mussel soup; Oliver is learning to lacquer ducks; Guerard mixes together duck and grapefruit.' Inventiveness was a crucial factor. As Craig Claiborne, the doyen of American food writers, put it: 'The soul of the new cuisine depends upon the inspiration and improvisations of a cook or chef. *Nouvelle cuisine* is not doctrinaire.'

Today, Asian ingredients are at home in French cookery, having achieved what Florence Fabricant, a food writer for the *New York Times*, calls 'a tantalizing revolution that is transforming the formal bastions of French cuisine'. And this is not limited to France itself. Hubert Keller, the chef at the Fleur de Lys restaurant in San Francisco, notes that, 'Ten years ago, with our reputation as a traditional French restaurant, we might have been criticized for blending cuisines if we added ingredients like ginger and coconut milk. Now, times have changed.'

From France this trend moved to California. During the 1960s, partially as a result of the influence of *nouvelle cuisine* and partially because California is so bountifully supplied both with fresh foods and with vibrant ethnic cultures, a 'new California cuisine' sprouted and flowered profusely. It soon became the 'new American cuisine'. This approach to cookery, to the preparation of nutritious and tasty foods, incorporates the essence of *nouvelle cuisine*: freshness of ingredients; undercooking (or, more accurately, the avoidance of overcooking); respect for but not slavish adulation of traditions; inventiveness, innovation, imagination. California cuisine added its own virtues to this splendid list: a purposeful, thoughtful introduction of 'exotic' foods and flavourings from Latin America and from Asia, an openness to innovation, a receptivity to different tastes and textures, and an almost unprecedented readiness to assimilate aspects of other culinary cultures. With its multicultural population and strategic location on the Pacific Rim, California was destined to become a leader in the new, global fusion style of cookery.

I must mention one of the great chefs who has been a leader of this transformation. I refer to Alice Waters. Her now famous restaurant, Chez Panisse, is deservedly renowned as a showcase of all that is best in California cuisine. But, as the name indicates, she reveres her French cooking traditions. Keeping the best of the old and adding the best of the new and different sums up the best of fusion cookery. Alice Waters has enticed, beguiled and trained an entire generation of people who care about good, fresh, delicious foods: 'fusion cookery' before that term was coined.

Alice Waters was a pioneer and Chez Panisse became a model that has been emulated throughout the world. Or, rather, I should say that many chefs and cooks everywhere were thinking and acting along the same lines and reacting imaginatively to the globalization of the world economy and the interpenetration of cultures and cuisines. In Hong Kong, for example, chefs were aware of the cosmopolitan nature both of their patrons and of the foodstuffs that passed through the bustling port city. They seized upon the opportunities before them and imaginatively 'invented' a new Hong Kong cuisine, a fusion of Chinese and other cultures' foods and techniques, all the while emphasizing the same virtues to be found in *nouvelle* and California cuisine. It was all inspired by the spirit of the age (and of the communication/transport revolution).

And, of course, this happened not only in Hong Kong, California and France. Chefs and food writers in cosmopolitan centres of Australia, Britain, Germany, Thailand, Singapore – even (or especially) those who had been trained in their native classical cuisines – eagerly and innovatively adopted the flexible and imaginative approaches inherent in fusion cookery. So today, from Adelaide and Sydney to London and Paris, and from Bangkok and Hong Kong to San Francisco, Los Angeles, Chicago and New York – and back again, with many worthwhile detours north and south – fusion restaurants and fusion home-cooking have come to stay, to our benefit and pleasure.

I have been a most fortunate beneficiary of (and participant in) the culinary revolution or reformation over the past quarter-century. My Chinese–American heritage, with the grand traditions of its glorious cuisine; my childhood in ethnically diverse Chicago; my youthful experience working in the family restaurant; my coming of age in San Francisco and Berkeley, in France and Italy – all of these contributed to my natural tendency

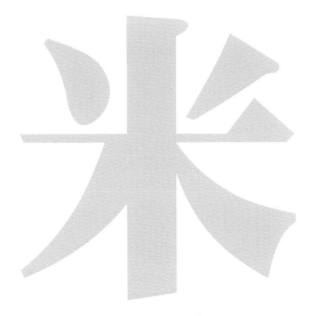

towards, and advocacy of, fusion cuisine. For example, I have always believed that 'western' butter worked better than Chinese lard (in small amounts), and that, for many purposes, white potatoes can serve as well as rice.

But the fundamentals have always been the same: freshness, clarity and balance of tastes and textures, lightness, simplicity, a reliance upon grains, vegetables, fruits and seafood, with other animal products mainly as a garnish or in a sauce. (A note on 'freshness': until the jet age, this always meant local or regional supplies, but today the term may include practically every popular food in the world.) And taste, of course, with spices, condiments and seasonings to enhance, to accentuate and never to overwhelm the natural tastes of good food. Such are the characteristics of all fine cuisines and, therefore, of fusion cookery.

The goal of fusion cookery, as with all good cookery, is to provide delicious, wholesome food that is enjoyable to eat. It is a goal attainable with but a little care, concern and application. For two decades, I have been practising the fusion style, both professionally and in my home, for family and friends. This book is filled with ideas and recipes drawn from that practice, tested in the kitchen and refined over many years. Remember that fusion cookery is not doctrinaire. It is an approach to cookery whose distinguishing characteristics are flexibility, experimentation, innovation and imagination – all informed, of course, by proper regard for what is necessary and appropriate in the matter of taste and appearance.

A recipe is not a rigid formula – *you* can determine what is 'necessary and appropriate'. Cooking is an art more than a science, it is creative as well as imitative, and is, or should be, more play than work. Follow the few simple, basic rules and then experiment, and discover the tastes and virtues of the various ingredients, some subtle, some assertive, and how they mix and match and mutually enhance your foods. Use your imagination, listen to your palate. You will be rewarded with dishes that are both familiar and exotic, and deliciously satisfying as well. You will discover your own fusion cooking.

EQUIPMENT

A wonderful aspect of fusion cooking is that it can easily be done with your ordinary kitchen tools. Traditional Asian and Chinese cooking equipment is not essential for the preparation of fusion food, but there are some tools which will make it very much easier. Moreover, there is a gain when one relies upon implements that have been tested over many centuries.

WOK

A most useful and versatile piece of equipment that is popular with fusion cooks and chefs, the wok may be used for stir-frying, blanching, deep-frying, steaming and even smoking foods. Its shape, with deep sides and either a tapered or a slightly flattened but still round bottom, allows for fuel-efficient, quick and even heating and cooking. In the stir-frying technique, the deep sides prevent the food and oils from spilling over; in deep-frying, much less oil is required because of the shaped concentration of the heat and ingredients at the wok's base. You can even use a well-seasoned wok for simple omelettes or bacon and eggs.

There are two basic wok types: the traditional Cantonese version, with short, rounded handles on either side of the edge or lip of the wok; and the *pau* or Peking wok, which has one handle about 30–35 cm (12–14 in) long. The long-handled wok keeps you safely distanced from the possible splashing of hot oils or water.

You should know that the round-bottomed wok can be used only on gas hobs. Woks are now available with flatter bottoms, designed especially for electric hobs. Although this shape really defeats the purpose of the traditional design, which is to concentrate intense heat at the centre, it does have the advantage over ordinary frying-pans in that it has deeper sides to allow deep-frying and prevent spillage.

Choosing a Wok

Choose a large wok – preferably about 30–35 cm (12–14 in) in diameter, with deep sides. It is easier, and safer, to cook a small batch of food in a large wok than a large quantity in a small one. Be aware that some modernized woks are too shallow or too flat-bottomed and thus no better than a frying-pan. A heavier wok, preferably made of carbon steel, is superior to the lighter stainless steel or aluminium type, which cannot take very high heat and tends to blacken, as well as scorching the food. There are now on the market good, non-stick, carbon-steel woks that maintain the heat without sticking. However, these woks need special care to prevent scratching. In recent years, the non-stick technology has improved vastly, so that now they can be safely recommended. They are especially useful when cooking foods that have a high acid level, such as lemons.

Seasoning a Wok

All woks (except non-stick ones) need to be seasoned. Many need to be scrubbed first as well, to remove the machine oil which is applied to the surface by the manufacturer to protect the wok in transit. This is the only time you will ever scrub your wok – unless you let it rust up. Scrub it with a cream cleanser and water, to remove as much of the machine oil as possible. Then dry it and put it on the hob on a low heat. Add 2 tablespoons of cooking oil and, using kitchen paper, rub it over the inside of the wok until the entire surface is lightly coated with oil. Heat the wok slowly for about 10–15 minutes and then wipe it thoroughly with more kitchen paper. The paper will become blackened. Repeat this process of coating, heating and wiping until the kitchen paper comes away clean. Your wok will darken and become well seasoned with use, which is a good sign.

Cleaning a Wok

Once your wok has been seasoned, it should never be scrubbed with soap and water. Plain, clear water is all that is needed. The wok should be thoroughly dried after each use. Putting the cleaned wok over low heat for a minute or two should do the trick. If it does happen to rust a bit, then it must be scrubbed with a cream cleanser and re-seasoned.

Wok Accessories

Wok Stand This is a metal ring or frame, designed to keep a conventionally shaped wok steady on the hob, and it is essential if you want to use your wok for steaming, deep-frying or braising. Stands come in two designs. One is a solid metal ring punched with about six ventilation holes. The other is a circular, thin-wire frame. If you have a gas cooker, use only the latter type, as the more solid design does not allow for sufficient ventilation and may lead to a build-up of gas which could put the flame out completely.

Wok Lid This light and inexpensive domed cover, usually made from aluminium, is used for steaming. The lid normally comes with the wok but, if not, it may be purchased from Chinese or Asian grocers, or you may use any domed pot-lid that fits snugly.

Spatula A long-handled metal spatula, shaped rather like a small shovel, is ideal for scooping and tossing food in a wok. Alternatively, any good, long-handled spoon can be used.

Rack When steaming foods in your wok, you will need a wooden or metal rack or trivet, to raise the food to be cooked above the water level. Wok sets usually include a rack, but, if not, Asian and Chinese grocers sell them separately. Department stores and hardware shops also sell wooden and metal stands, which can serve the same purpose. Any rack, improvised or not, that keeps the food above the water so that it is steamed and not boiled, will suffice. You will find a wire rack very practical for smoking food in the wok.

Bamboo Brush This bundle of stiff, split bamboo is used for cleaning a wok without scrubbing off the seasoned surface. It is an attractive, inexpensive implement, but not essential. A soft washing-up brush will do just as well.

DEEP-FAT FRYERS

These are very useful and you may find them safer and easier to use for deep-frying than a wok. The quantities of oil given in the recipes are based on the amount required for deep-frying in a wok. If you are using a deep-fat fryer instead, you will need about double that amount, but never fill the deep-fryer more than half-full with oil.

CLEAVERS

To Chinese and Asian cooks, the cleaver is an all-purpose cutting instrument that makes all other knives unnecessary. Once you gain facility with a cleaver, you will see how it can be used on all types of food, to slice, dice, chop, fillet, shred, crush or whatever. In practice, most chefs rely upon three different sizes of cleaver – light, medium and heavy – to be used appropriately. Of course, you may use your own familiar kitchen knives but, if you decide to invest in a cleaver, choose a good-quality stainless steel model and keep it sharpened.

CHOPPING BOARD

One decided improvement over the traditional implements of Asian and Chinese cooking is the modern chopping board made of hardwood or white acrylic. The typical Asian and Chinese chopping board is of soft wood, which is not only difficult to maintain but, being soft, also provides a fertile surface for bacteria. A hardwood or white acrylic board is easy to clean, resists bacterial accumulation and lasts much longer. Fusion cookery entails much chopping, slicing and dicing, so it is essential to have a large, dependable, steady chopping board. For reasons of hygiene, never place cooked meat on a board on which raw meat or poultry has been prepared. For raw meats, always use a separate board and clean it thoroughly after each use.

STEAMERS

Steaming is not a very popular cooking method in the West. This is unfortunate because it is the best method for preparing many foods of delicate taste and texture, such as fish and vegetables. Steaming is a method well worth learning. In Asia, bamboo steamers have been in use for thousands of years. Bamboo steamers come in several sizes, of which

the 25 cm (10 in) one is the most suitable for home use. The food is placed in the steamer and that in turn is placed above boiling water in a wok or pan. To prevent the food from sticking to the steamer as it cooks, clean damp muslin may be used under the food itself. A tight-fitting bamboo lid prevents the steam from escaping; several steamers, stacked one above the other, may be used at the same time. Of course, any kind of wide metal steamer can be used, if you prefer. Before using a bamboo steamer for the first time, wash it and then steam it, empty, for about 5 minutes.

RICE COOKERS

Electric rice cookers are increasing in popularity. They cook rice perfectly and keep it warm throughout a meal. A rice cooker also has the advantage of freeing a burner or element, making for a less cluttered hob. They are relatively expensive, however, so unless you eat rice frequently I do not think they are worth the expense.

MISCELLANEOUS

Stainless-steel bowls of different sizes, along with strainers and colanders, round out the list of basic implements. They will be very useful because you will be doing much mixing of wonderful foods and you will often have to drain or strain oils and juices. It is better to have one too many tools than one too few.

BARBECUE

This is a convenient cooking tool to have for fusion cooks as many recipes can be cooked on a barbecue. Nothing beats the outdoor, smoky flavours of cooking on a barbecue.

Barbecues come in all sizes and prices. However, I highly recommend a good solid one which can last for years. It needs to be cleaned and covered during the wet season. This is, of course, an optional piece of cooking equipment and you can always use your oven grill as a substitute.

INGREDIENTS

Asian ingredients have become an integral part of eating at home and in restaurants. This is not only a trendy dining fashion; these ingredients are now part of home cooks' and chefs' repertoires. This has been driven partly by heath consciousness – most Asian cookery is light and clean, with very little added animal fat (such as cream, cheese or butter). Also, as Asian emigration expands throughout the West, cooking becomes ever more cross-pollinated. Greater exposure to Asian cooking techniques through books and television programmes has broadened the appeal of Asian culture. Formerly exotic Asian ingredients are becoming familiar and widely available.

The following is a brief guide to authentic ingredients which I have used in this book. I have added a few comments on common European ingredients which I have fused with Asian techniques and flavours. In the recipes themselves, I have added page references to the less familiar items.

AUBERGINES

These pleasing, purple-skinned vegetables range in size from the larger plump ones, easy to find in all produce stores, to the small thin variety which the Chinese prefer for their more delicate flavour. Look for those with smooth, unblemished skin.

Chinese people normally do not peel aubergines, since the skin preserves texture, taste and shape. Large western-variety aubergines should be cut according to the recipe, sprinkled with a little salt and left to sit for 20 minutes. They should then be rinsed and blotted dry with kitchen paper. This process, called degorging, extracts bitter juices and excess moisture from the vegetable before it is cooked, giving a truer taste to a dish. The aubergines also absorb less fat if you do this. Degorging is unnecessary if you are using Chinese aubergines.

BEAN SPROUTS

Now widely available, these are the sprouts of the green mung bean, although some Chinese stores also stock yellow soya bean sprouts, which are much larger. Bean sprouts should always be very fresh and crunchy. They will keep for several days when loosely wrapped in kitchen paper inside a plastic bag in the vegetable compartment of a refrigerator. It is ironic that bean sprouts, now so common in the West, have become a luxury in China, where keeping the bean sprouts fresh is difficult because they are so perishable and refrigeration is so expensive. However, this refreshing, nutritious food has enjoyed a revival in China's more highly priced restaurants.

BEANCURD

Beancurd is also known by its Chinese name *doufu* or, in Japanese, *tofu*. It has played a crucial role in Chinese cookery for over a thousand years, since it is highly nutritious and rich in protein. Beancurd has a distinctive texture but a bland taste. It is made from yellow soya beans, which are soaked, ground, mixed with water and then cooked briefly before being solidified. In the West, it is usually sold in two forms: as firm cakes or as a thick junket. It is also available in several dried forms and in a fermented version. The soft, junket-like variety (sometimes called silken tofu) is used for soups, while the solid type is used for stir-frying, braising and poaching. Solid beancurd 'cakes' are white in colour and are sold in supermarkets and by Chinese stores, as well as in many health-food shops. They are packed in water in plastic containers and may be kept refrigerated in this state for up to five days, provided the water is changed daily. To use solid beancurd, cut the amount required into cubes or shreds using a sharp knife. Do this with care as it is delicate. It also needs to be cooked carefully as too much stirring can cause it to crumble. Whatever its shape or texture, beancurd remains highly nutritious.

BLACK BEANS

These small black soya beans, also known as salted black beans, are preserved by being fermented with salt and spices. They have a distinctive, slightly salty taste and a rich pleasant smell. Thus prepared, they are a tasty seasoning, especially when used in conjunction with garlic or fresh ginger. They are inexpensive and can be obtained from Chinese grocers, usually in tins labelled 'Black Beans in Salted Sauce', but you may also see them packed in plastic bags. You can rinse them before use, though this is an optional step; I prefer to chop them slightly, too, as it helps to release their pungent flavour. Transfer any unused beans and liquid to a sealed jar and the beans will keep indefinitely if stored in the refrigerator.

CHINESE CHIVES

The taste of Chinese chives is much stronger and more garlic-like than western chives; their flowers can be used as well as the blades. They have an earthy, onion taste and are delicious by themselves or cooked with other foods. They can be substituted for regular chives but adjust the quantity to allow for their stronger chives but adjust the quantity to allow for their stronger flavour. Rinse and dry the chives, wrap them in slightly damp kitchen paper and store them in a plastic bag in the refrigerator. Use as soon as possible.

Chinese yellow chives are Chinese chives which have been grown in the dark and are pale yellow in colour – like endive – and have a more subtle flavour than the green Chinese chives. Select the freshest leaves possible. Trim any decaying parts. Wash and dry thoroughly and store between kitchen paper in the lower part of your refrigerator; as they are highly perishable, they will keep for only one or two days. They possess a rich, earthy taste and yet are delicate and fragile at the same time.

CHINESE GREENS

They are available all year and can be treated like cabbage and kept for a week or so in the vegetable crisper of the refrigerator.

Chinese Flowering Cabbage

Chinese flowering cabbage, or *choi sum*, is part of the wide mustard-green cabbage family. This cabbage has green leaves and may have small yellow flowers, which are eaten along with the leaves and stems. In China, this is one of the most common and popular leafy vegetables and it is delicious as a stir-fry dish. When buying, look for bright leaves and firm, moist-looking stalks.

Chinese Leaves

Chinese leaves, also known as Peking Cabbage, comes in various sizes, from long, compact, barrel-shaped ones to short, squat-looking types. They are also tightly packed with firm, pale green (or in some cases slightly yellow), crinkled leaves. This versatile vegetable is used for soups and added to stir-fried meat dishes. Its sponge-like ability to absorb flavours and its sweet pleasant taste and texture make it a favourite for chefs, who match it with rich foods. This is a delicious crunchy vegetable with a mild but distinctive taste. Store it as you would ordinary cabbage.

Chinese White Cabbage

There are many varieties of this. The most common, bok choy, is the one with a long, smooth, milky-white stem and large, crinkly, dark green leaves. The size of the plant indicates how tender it is; the smaller, the better. Bok choy has a light, fresh, slightly mustardy taste and requires little cooking. It is now widely available in supermarkets. Look for firm, crisp stalks and unblemished leaves. Store bok choy in the vegetable crisper of your refrigerator.

CHINESE WHITE RADISH

Also known as *mooli*, Chinese icicle radish or *daikon*, it is long and white and like a carrot in shape but larger. It is a winter radish or root and can withstand long cooking without disintegrating. It thus absorbs the flavours of other foods while retaining its distinctive radish taste and texture. Look for firm, heavy, solid, unblemished ones. They should be slightly translucent inside, solid and not fibrous. Always peel before use. Store mooli in a plastic bag in the vegetable crisper of your fridge where they will keep for over a week.

CHILLIES

Chillies are used extensively in western China and, somewhat less frequently, in the south. They are the seed pods of the capsicum plant and can be obtained fresh, dried or ground. One must differentiate between the various types because, for one thing, they vary greatly in taste and strength.

Chilli-Bean Sauce (see Sauces and Pastes, page 22)

Chilli Oil/Chilli Dipping Sauce

Chilli oil is sometimes used as a dipping condiment as well as a seasoning in China. Of course, as chillies vary, so do the oils vary in strength and flavour. You can purchase chilli oil from Chinese grocers. The Thai and Malaysian versions are especially hot; the Taiwanese and Chinese versions are more subtle. Such commercial products are quite acceptable, but I include the following recipe because the home-made version is the best. Remember that chilli oil is too dramatic to be used directly as the sole cooking oil; it is best used as part of a dipping sauce or as a condiment, or combined with other milder oils. I include pepper and black beans in this recipe for additional flavours so that I can also use it as a dipping sauce.

Once made, put the chilli oil in a tightly sealed glass jar and store in a cool, dark place, where it will keep for months.

Chilli Oil/Chilli Dipping Sauce

2 tablespoons chopped dried red chillies
1 tablespoon whole unroasted Sichuan peppercorns (page 20)
2 tablespoons whole black beans (page 14)
150 ml (5 fl oz) groundnut oil

Heat a wok over a high heat and add the oil and the rest of the ingredients. Continue to cook over a low heat for about 10 minutes. Allow the mixture to cool undisturbed and then pour it into a jar. Let the mixture sit for two days and then strain the oil. It will keep indefinitely.

Chilli Powder

Chilli powder is made from dried red chillies and is also known as cayenne pepper. It is pungent and aromatic and ranges from hot to very hot; it is thus widely used in many spicy dishes. You will be able to buy it in any supermarket. As with chillies in general, your own palate will determine the acceptable degree of 'hotness' to be added to each dish by this spice.

Dried Red Chillies

Dried red chillies are small, thin and about 1 cm (½ in) long. They are commonly employed to season the oil used in stir-fried dishes, in sauces and in braising. They are left whole or cut in half lengthways with the seeds left in, or may be flaked. The Chinese like to blacken them and leave them in the dish during cooking, but, as they are extremely hot and spicy, you may choose to remove them immediately after using them to flavour the cooking oil. They can be found in Chinese and Asian grocers as well as in most supermarkets, and will keep indefinitely in a tightly covered jar. When eating out, most diners carefully move the blackened chillies to one side of their plates.

Fresh Chillies

Fresh chillies can be distinguished by their small size and elongated shape. They should look fresh and bright, with no brown patches or black spots. There are several varieties. Red chillies are generally milder than green ones because they sweeten as they ripen.

To prepare fresh chillies, first rinse them in cold water. Then, using a small sharp knife, slit them lengthways. Remove and discard the seeds. Rinse the chillies well under cold running water and then prepare them according to the recipe's instructions. Wash your hands, knife and chopping board before preparing other foods, and be careful not to touch your eyes until you have washed your hands thoroughly with soap and water. The seeds are especially pungent and 'hot' to a fault.

Thai Chillies

They are small, pointed and very hot and they come in orange, red, green and white.

CINNAMON STICKS OR BARK

Cinnamon sticks are curled, paper-thin pieces of the bark of the cinnamon tree. Chinese cinnamon comes as thicker sticks of this bark. The latter is highly aromatic and more pungent than the cinnamon sticks commonly found in the West. Try to obtain the Chinese version but, if you cannot find it, the western sticks are an adequate substitute. They add a refreshing taste to braised dishes and are an important ingredient of five-spice powder. Store cinnamon bark or sticks in a tightly sealed jar to preserve their aroma and flavour. Ground cinnamon is not a satisfactory substitute.

COCONUT MILK

In south-east Asia, coconut milk is widely used. It has some of the properties of cow's milk: the 'cream' (fatty globules) rises to the top when the milk sits; it must be stirred as it comes to a boil; and its fat is closer in chemical composition to butterfat than to vegetable fat. The milk itself is the liquid wrung from the grated and pressed coconut meat, combined with water.

Coconut milk is not unknown in southern China. That region has for centuries been open to the influences emanating from south-east Asia – from places, that is, where curries and stews made with coconut milk are common. The milk is used as a popular cooling beverage and in puddings and candies. In Hong Kong and parts of southern China today, one will find many coconut-milk dishes and desserts, directly inspired by Thai and other south-east Asian cuisines.

In Chinese grocers, it may be possible to find freshly made coconut milk, especially near areas where there is a large south-east Asian population. Fortunately, however, an inexpensive tinned version can be found in supermarkets. Many of the available brands are of high quality and can be recommended. Look for the ones from Thailand or Malaysia. You can find them at Asian speciality grocers. They are usually in 400 ml (14 fl oz) or 425 ml (15 fl oz) tins. Be sure to shake the tin well before opening.

CORIANDER

Fresh coriander (also known as Chinese parsley or Cilantro) is one of the most popular herbs used in fusion cookery. It looks like flat parsley but its pungent, musky, citrus-like flavour gives it a distinctive character that is unmistakable. That is to say, it is an acquired taste for many people. Its feathery leaves are often used as a garnish or they can be chopped and mixed into sauces and stuffings.

Many Asian and Chinese grocers stock it, as do some greengrocers and, increasingly, supermarkets. When buying fresh coriander, look for deep green, fresh-looking leaves. Yellow and limp leaves indicate age and should be avoided.

To store coriander, wash it in cold water, drain it thoroughly (use a salad spinner to spin the fresh coriander dry) and wrap it in kitchen paper. Store it in the vegetable compartment of your refrigerator, where it should keep for several days.

CORIANDER, GROUND

Ground coriander has a fresh, lemon-like sweet flavour. Widely used in curry mixes, it can be purchased already ground. However, the best method is to dry-roast whole coriander seeds and then finely grind the seeds.

CUMIN, GROUND

This common spice adds a touch of fragrance to many fusion recipes. I prefer to oven-roast whole cumin seeds and grind them as I need them.

CURRY POWDER, MADRAS

Although this western-style powder is quite different from those used by the Indian community, there are many reliable commercial brands used by fusion cooks for their exotic and subtle aroma and flavour.

FISH SAUCE (see Sauces and Pastes, page 22)

FIVE-SPICE POWDER

Five-spice powder is less commonly known as five-flavoured powder or five-fragrance spice powder, and it is becoming a staple in the spice section of supermarkets. Chinese grocers always keep it in stock. This brown powder is a mixture of star anise, Sichuan peppercorns, fennel seeds, cloves and cinnamon. A good blend is pungent, fragrant, spicy and slightly sweet at the same time. The exotic fragrance it gives to a dish makes the search for a good mixture well worth the effort. It keeps indefinitely in a well-sealed jar.

GINGER

Fresh root ginger is an indispensable ingredient in authentic Chinese cookery and is one of the most common ingredients adopted by fusion cooks. Its pungent, spicy and fresh taste adds a subtle but distinctive flavour to soups, meats and vegetables. It is also an important seasoning for fish and seafood since it neutralizes fishy smells. Root ginger looks rather like a gnarled Jerusalem artichoke and can range in size from 7.5 cm (3 in) to 15 cm (6 in) long. It has pale brown, dry skin, which is usually peeled away before use. Select fresh ginger which is firm, with no signs of shrivelling. It will keep in the refrigerator, well wrapped in cling film, for up to two weeks. Fresh ginger can now be bought at most Chinese and Asian grocers as well as at many greengrocers and supermarkets. Dried powdered ginger has a quite different flavour and should not be substituted for fresh root ginger.

GINGER JUICE

Ginger juice is made from fresh ginger and is used in marinades to give a subtle ginger taste without the bite of fresh chopped pieces. Here is a simple method of extracting ginger juice: cut unpeeled fresh ginger into 2.5 cm (1 in) chunks and drop them into a running food processor. When the ginger is finely chopped, squeeze out the juice by hand through a cotton or linen towel. Alternatively, mash some fresh ginger with a kitchen mallet or the side of a cleaver or knife until most of the fibres are exposed. Then simply squeeze out the juice by hand through a cotton or linen towel.

HOISIN SAUCE (see Sauces and Pastes, page 22)

LEMON GRASS

Originally from south-east Asia, this plant is little used in China and then usually in dried form for making tea. Its subtle, lemony fragrance and flavour impart a very special cachet to delicate foods and it is a standard ingredient in Thai and Vietnamese dishes. As is typical in Asian cuisine, the herb is considered a medicinal agent as well as a spice and is often prescribed for digestive disorders. Lemon grass is closely related to citronella grass. The latter plant has a stronger oil content and is more likely to be used commercially in perfumes and as a mosquito repellent. The two plants should not be confused.

Fresh lemon grass is sold in stalks that can be 60 cm (2 ft) long – it looks like a very long spring onion. It is a fibrous plant but this is no problem because what is wanted is its fragrance and taste. The lemon grass pieces are always removed after the dish is cooked. Some recipes may call for lemon grass to be finely chopped or pounded into a paste, in which cases it becomes an integral aspect of the dish.

Get the freshest possible, usually found in Chinese grocers or other Asian grocers and in some supermarkets. Avoid dried lemon grass for cooking; it is more suited to herbal tea.

It can be kept, loosely wrapped, in the bottom part of your refrigerator for up to one week.

Lemon is not a substitute for the unique flavour of lemon grass.

LIME

This small, green, citrus fruit has a delicate, tart taste that is widely used in Asia to impart a zing to food or as a base for sauces. The refreshing juice and the peel have been used by fusion cooks and chefs to impart a unique taste to many dishes.

LOTUS ROOT

This well-known, perennial aquatic plant, with its beautiful white and pink water-lily flowers, is a native of Asia. Although all the lotus plant is edible, the root or stems are the parts most commonly available. They are buff-coloured, wooden-looking and are quite long, divided into sausage-like segments, each up to 12 cm (5 in) long. Air passages run the length of the root, giving them a beautiful, paper-chain cross-section. They have a crisp fibrous texture with a mild, distinctive flavour (some say they resemble artichokes). They may be cooked in many ways: stir-fried, mixed with other vegetables, used in vegetarian dishes, dried, steamed in soup, fried or candied. They are also used raw in salads and cut into slices, to make a most attractive appearance. They also provide a speciality starch. Look for lotus roots that are firm and free of bruises. Uncut, they can be kept in the bottom part of your refrigerator for up to three weeks.

Fusion chefs love to deep-fry lotus roots because they make a wonderful-looking garnish.

MIRIN

This is a heavy, sweet Japanese rice wine with a light, syrupy texture. It is used only in cooking to add a mild sweetness to sauces or foods. It is especially delicious with grilled foods as, once the alcohol is burned off, only the sweet essence of the mirin remains. There is no fully satisfactory substitute for this unique item but in this book I have suggested dry sherry as an alternative. Mirin can be found in many Chinese or Asian supermarkets or Japanese speciality food shops. One bottle will last quite a long time and is well worth the search.

MUSHROOMS, CHINESE DRIED

There are many varieties of these, which add a particular flavour and aroma to Chinese dishes. They can be black or brown in colour. The very large ones with a lighter colour and a cracked surface are the best. They are usually the most expensive, so use them with a light touch. They can be bought in boxes or plastic bags from Chinese grocers. Store them in an air-tight jar. They have a rich, smoky aroma that fusion cooks prize.

To use Chinese dried mushrooms: soak the mushrooms in a bowl of warm water for about 20 minutes, or until they are soft and pliable. Squeeze out the excess water and cut off and discard the woody stems. Only the caps are used.

The soaking water can be saved and used in soups and as rice water. Strain the liquid through a fine sieve to separate any sand or residue from the dried mushrooms.

MUSTARD GREENS, PICKLED (see Sichuan Preserved Vegetables, page 23)

NOODLES/PASTA

Noodles provide a nutritious, quick, light snack and are usually of good quality. Several styles of Chinese noodle dishes have now made their way to the West, including the fresh, thin, egg noodles which are browned on both sides, and the popular thin rice noodles. Both kinds can be bought fresh and dried in Chinese grocers. Below is a listing of the major types of noodles which are used by fusion cooks and chefs.

Bean Thread (Transparent) Noodles

These noodles, also called cellophane noodles, are made from ground mung beans and not from a grain flour. They are available dried and are very fine and white. Easy to recognize, packed in their neat, plastic-wrapped bundles, they are stocked by Chinese grocers and supermarkets. They are never served on their own, instead being added to soups or braised dishes or being deep-fried and used as a garnish. They must be soaked in warm water for about 5 minutes before use. As they are rather long, you might find it easier to cut them into shorter lengths after soaking. If you are frying them, they do not need soaking beforehand, but they do need to be separated. A good technique for separating the strands is to pull them apart in a large paper bag, which stops them from flying all over the place.

Chinese Wheat Noodles and Egg Noodles

These are made from hard or soft wheat flour and water. If egg has been added, the noodles are usually labelled as egg noodles. Supermarkets and delicatessens also stock both the dried and fresh varieties. Flat noodles are usually used in soups, while rounded noodles are best for stir-frying or pan-frying. The fresh ones freeze nicely if they are well wrapped. Thaw them thoroughly before cooking.

To Cook Wheat and Egg Noodles Noodles are very good blanched and served with main dishes, instead of plain rice. I think dried wheat or fresh egg noodles are best for this. If you are using fresh noodles, immerse them in a pan of boiling water and cook them for 3–5 minutes or until you find their texture to your taste. If you are using dried noodles, either cook them according to the instructions on the packet, or cook them in boiling water for 4–5 minutes. Drain and serve.

If you are cooking noodles ahead of time, or before stir-frying them, toss the cooked and drained noodles in 2 teaspoons of sesame oil and put them into a bowl. Cover this with cling film and refrigerate. The cooked noodles will remain usable for about 2 hours.

Rice Noodles

These dried noodles are opaque white and come in a variety of shapes. One of the most common examples is rice-stick noodles, which are flat and about the length of a chopstick. They can also vary in thickness. Use the type called for in each recipe. Rice noodles are very easy to prepare. Simply soak them in warm water for 20 minutes until they are soft. Drain them in a colander or a sieve, and then they are ready to be used in soups or to be stir-fried.

Somyun noodles

These Korean wheat noodles are different from egg noodles in that they are whiter and contain no egg. The noodles are made of wheat flour, salt and water (or sometimes mixed with rice flour), kneaded to a dough and then rolled and cut. In the West, they are usually available dried.

OILS

Oil is the most commonly used cooking medium in China as well as many other parts of Asia. The favourite is groundnut oil. Animal fats, usually lard and chicken fat, are also used in some areas, particularly in northern China. I always use groundnut oil, since I find animal fats too heavy.

Throughout this book I have indicated where oils can be re-used. Where this is possible, simply cool the oil after use and filter it through muslin or a fine strainer into a jar. Cover it tightly and keep in a cool, dry place. If you keep it in the refrigerator, it will become cloudy, but it will clarify again when the oil returns to room temperature. I find oils are best re-used just once, and this is healthier, since constantly re-used oils increase in saturated fat.

Corn Oil

Corn or maize oil is also quite suitable for Chinese cooking. It has a high heating point although I find it to be rather bland and with a slightly disagreeable smell. It is high in polyunsaturates and is, therefore, one of the healthier oils.

Groundnut Oil

This is also known as peanut oil or arachide oil. I prefer to use this for Chinese cookery because it has a pleasant, unobtrusive taste. Although it has a higher saturated fat content than some oils, its ability to be heated to a high temperature without burning makes it perfect for stir-frying and deep-frying. Most supermarkets stock it, but if you cannot find it, use corn oil instead.

OTHER VEGETABLE OILS

Some of the cheaper vegetable oils available include soya bean, safflower and sunflower oils. They are light in colour and taste, and can also be used in Chinese cooking, but they smoke and burn at lower temperatures than groundnut oil, so care must be used when cooking with them.

Sesame Oil

This thick, rich, golden brown oil made from sesame seeds has a distinctive, nutty flavour and aroma. It is widely used in Chinese cookery as a seasoning but is not normally used as a cooking oil because it heats rapidly and burns easily. Therefore, think of it more as a flavouring than as a cooking oil. It is often added at the last moment to finish a dish. Sold in bottles, it can be obtained in Chinese grocers and many supermarkets.

OYSTER SAUCE (see Sauces and Pastes, page 22)

PEPPERCORNS

Black Peppercorns

Black peppercorns are unripe berries from a vine of the Piperaceae family, which are picked, fermented and dried until they are hard and black. They are best when freshly ground.

Sichuan Peppercorns

Sichuan peppercorns are known throughout China as 'flower peppers' because they look like flower buds opening. They are reddish-brown in colour and have a strong, pungent odour, which distinguishes them from the hotter black peppercorns. They are actually not from peppers at all; they are the dried berries of a shrub which is a member of the citrus family. Their smell reminds me of lavender, while their taste is sharp and mildly spicy. They can be ground in a conventional peppermill and are very often roasted before they are ground, to bring out their full flavour. They are inexpensive and sold wrapped in cellophane or plastic bags in Chinese grocers. They will keep indefinitely if stored in a well-sealed container.

To Roast Sichuan Peppercorns Heat a wok or heavy frying-pan to a medium heat. Add the peppercorns (you can cook about 150 g/5 oz at a time) and stir-fry them for about 5 minutes, until they brown slightly and start to smoke. Remove the pan from the heat and let them cool. Grind the peppercorns in a pepper mill, clean coffee grinder or with a mortar and pestle. Seal the mixture tightly in a screw-topped jar until you need some. Alternatively, keep the whole roasted peppercorns in a well-sealed container and grind them when required.

White Peppercorns

White peppercorns are made from the largest of the ripe berries, which are suspended in running water for several days. The berries swell, making the removal of the outer skin easier; the pale-coloured inner seeds are sun-dried, which turns them a pale beige colour.

Five-pepper Mixture

Five-pepper or five-peppercorn mixture is a fragrant aromatic mixture of whole black, white, pink and green peppercorns and allspice berries. Available in supermarkets, this mix, freshly ground, gives food a wonderful tasty touch. It is popular with fusion cooks and chefs because it bestows an added dimension to recipes.

PRAWNS, RAW

Most prawns previously available in Britain were sold cooked, either shelled or unshelled. However, large uncooked prawns, known as Pacific or king prawns, are increasingly available and are, for the most part, found frozen. These are most suitable for recipes used in this book. Most Chinese grocers and many fishmongers and some supermarkets stock them frozen and in the shell, and they are quite reasonably priced. Fresh prawns are, on occasion, available. In any case, the frozen uncooked prawns are preferable to cooked prawns, which in most cases are already overcooked. Thus, any sauce you cook them in will not permeate to flavour the prawns.

To Peel Prawns First twist off the head and pull off the tail. It should then be quite easy to peel off the shell and with it the tiny legs. If you are using large, uncooked king prawns, make a shallow cut down the back of each prawn and remove the fine digestive cord, which runs the length of each prawn. Wash the prawns before you use them.

Chinese Trick for Frozen Uncooked Prawns After peeling and preparing the uncooked prawns as instructed above, rinse them twice in 1 tablespoon of salt and 1.2 litres (2 pints) cold water, changing the mixture of salt and water each time. This process helps to firm the prawns and gives them a crystalline clean taste as well as a crisp texture.

RICE, BASMATI

This fragrant rice from the subcontinent of India and Pakistan is prized for its aromatic and nutty flavour. Widely available in supermarkets, this popular rice is much favoured by fusion cooks and chefs.

RICE FLOUR

This flour is made from raw rice and is used to make fresh rice noodles. Store it as you would wheat flour.

RICE PAPER

Made from a mixture of rice flour, water and salt and rolled out by a machine to paper thinness, rice paper, or *bánh tráng* as is it known, is then dried on bamboo mats in the sun, giving it a beautiful cross-hatch pattern. It is available only in dry form, in a round or triangular shape that is semi-transparent, thin and hard. It is used extensively for wrapping Vietnamese spring rolls of pork and seafood, which are then fried and wrapped with crisp fresh lettuce and herbs and, finally, dipped in a sweet, sour hot sauce. Although more identified with Vietnamese cooking, rice paper has nevertheless become quite popular and is often used by restaurants in Hong Kong, Taiwan and parts of southern China.

Available from many Chinese grocers and supermarkets, it is inexpensive and comes in packets of 50–100 sheets. All brands are good, especially the ones from Vietnam and Thailand. Choose white-looking rice paper; a yellowish colour may be a sign of age. Broken pieces in the packet may also indicate age.

Store rice paper in a dry cool place. After use, wrap the remaining rice papers carefully in the package they came in and put this in another plastic bag and seal well before storing.

RICE WINE, SHAOXING

An important component in Chinese cookery, rice wine is used extensively for cooking and drinking throughout China, but I believe the finest of its many varieties to be from Shaoxing in Zhejiang Province in eastern China. It is made from glutinous rice, yeast and spring water. Chefs use it for cooking as well as in marinades and sauces. Now readily available in Chinese grocers and in some wine shops in the West, it should be kept tightly corked at room temperature. A good-quality, dry pale sherry can be substituted but cannot equal its rich, mellow taste. Do not confuse this wine with sake, which is the Japanese version of rice wine and quite different. Western grape wines are not an adequate substitute, either.

SAUCES AND PASTES

Chinese and Asian cookery involves a number of thick, tasty sauces and pastes. They are essential to the authentic taste of Chinese cooking, and it is well worth making the effort to obtain them. Most are sold in bottles or tins by Chinese grocers and some supermarkets. Tinned sauces, once opened, should be transferred to screw-topped glass jars and kept in the refrigerator, where they will last indefinitely.

Chilli-bean Sauce

This thick, dark sauce or paste, which is made from soya beans, chillies and other seasonings, is very hot and spicy. It is usually available in jars from Chinese grocers. Be sure to seal the jar tightly after use and store in the larder or refrigerator. Do not confuse it with chilli sauce (see page 15) which is a hotter, redder, thinner sauce made without beans and used mainly as a dipping sauce for cooked dishes.

Fish Sauce

Fish sauce is also known as fish gravy or *nam pla* and is a thin brown sauce made from fermented, salted, fresh fish. It is sold bottled and has a very fishy odour and salty taste. However, cooking greatly diminishes the 'fishy' flavour, and the sauce simply adds a special richness and quality to dishes. The Thai brands are especially good.

Hoisin Sauce

This is a thick, dark, brownish-red sauce, which is made from soya beans, vinegar, sugar, spices and other flavourings. It is sweet and spicy. Hoisin sauce (sometimes called barbecue sauce) is sold in tins and jars and is available from Chinese grocers and supermarkets. If refrigerated, it can keep indefinitely.

Oyster Sauce

This thick, brown sauce is made from a concentrate of oysters cooked in soy sauce and brine. Despite its name, oyster sauce does not taste fishy. It has a rich flavour and is used in cooking and as a condiment, diluted with a little oil, for vegetables, poultry and meats. It is usually sold in bottles and can be bought in Chinese grocers and supermarkets. Best kept refrigerated. There is also an oyster-flavoured version for vegetarians.

Sesame Paste

This rich, thick, creamy, light or dark brown paste is made from sesame seeds. It is sold in jars by Chinese grocers and is used in both hot and cold dishes. If you cannot obtain it, use peanut butter which resembles it in texture. Avoid using the Middle Eastern sesame paste, which is less flavourful.

Soy Sauce

Soy sauce is an essential ingredient in Chinese cooking. It is made from a mixture of soya beans, flour and water, which is then fermented naturally and aged for some months. The liquid finally distilled is soy sauce. There are two main types.

Light Soy Sauce

As the name implies, this is light in colour, but it is full of flavour and is the better one to use for cooking. It is saltier than dark soy sauce and is known in Chinese grocers as 'Superior Soy'.

Dark Soy Sauce

This sauce is aged for much longer than light soy sauce, hence its darker, almost black colour. It is slightly thicker, stronger and less salty than light soy sauce and is more suitable for stews. I prefer it to light soy as a dipping sauce. It is known in Chinese grocers as 'Soy Superior Sauce'.

Most soy sauces sold in supermarkets are dark soy. Chinese grocers sell both types and the quality is excellent. Be sure you buy the correct one, as the names are very similar.

Thai curry paste

An intensely flavoured paste of herbs and spices, this is used to flavour coconut curries and soups, as well as other dishes. The red curry paste is made with red dried chillies, while the green curry paste is made with fresh green chillies. Home-made curry paste is time-consuming to prepare; however, ready-made curry pastes of high quality are available in supermarkets.

Whole Yellow-bean Sauce

This thick, spicy, aromatic sauce is made of yellow beans, flour and salt, which are fermented together. It is quite salty, but it adds a distinctive flavour to Chinese sauces. There are two forms: whole beans in a thick sauce and mashed or puréed beans (sold as 'crushed yellow bean sauce'). I prefer the whole-bean variety because it is slightly less salty and has a better texture.

SESAME SEEDS

These are dried seeds of the sesame herb. Unhulled, the seeds range from greyish-white to black in colour but, once the hull is removed, the sesame seeds are found to be tiny, somewhat flattened, cream-coloured and pointed at one end. Keep them in a glass jar in a cool, dry place; they will last indefinitely.

To Make Toasted Sesame Seeds Heat a frying-pan or skillet until hot. Add the sesame seeds and stir occasionally. Watch them closely and, when they begin to brown lightly (about 3–5 minutes), stir them again and pour them onto a plate. When cold, store them in a glass jar in a cool, dark place.

Alternatively, you could pre-heat the oven to 160°C/325°F/gas mark 3. Spread the sesame seeds on a baking sheet and roast them in the oven for about 10–15 minutes until they are nicely toasted and lightly browned. Allow them to cool and place in a glass jar until you are ready to use them.

SICHUAN PRESERVED VEGETABLES

The root of the mustard green, pickled in salt and hot chillies. Sold in tins in Chinese grocers, it gives a pleasantly crunchy texture and spicy taste to dishes. Before using it, rinse in cold water and then slice or chop as required. any unused vegetable should be transferred to a covered jar and stored in the fridge where it will keep indefinitely.

STAR ANISE

The star anise is a hard, star-shaped spice and is the seed-pod of a bush. It is similar in flavour and fragrance to common anise, but is more robust and liquorice-like. Star anise is an essential ingredient of five-spice powder and is widely used in braised dishes, to which it imparts a rich taste and fragrance. It is sold in plastic packs by Chinese grocers and should be stored in a tightly covered jar in a cool, dry place.

SUGAR

Sugar has been used – sparingly – in the cooking of savoury dishes in China for a thousand years. Properly employed, it helps balance the various flavours of sauces and other dishes. Chinese sugar comes in several forms: as rock or yellow lump sugar, as brown sugar slabs, and as maltose or malt sugar. I particularly like to use rock sugar, which is rich and has a more subtle flavour than that of refined granulated sugar. It also gives a good lustre or glaze to braised dishes and sauces. You can buy it in Chinese grocers, where it is usually sold in packets. You may need to break the lumps into smaller pieces with a wooden mallet or rolling pin. If you cannot find it, use white sugar or coffee sugar crystals (the amber, chunky kind) instead.

TARO ROOT

An ancient food cultivated for a long time, taro was a starch used in China and south-east Asia, long before rice. These tubers vary in shape, but they are roughly spherical, anything from tennis-ball size to about 23 cm (9 in) in diameter, and often covered with a rough skin and brownish hairs. They are starchy, with a sweet flavour and doughy texture and a whitish flesh, often with purple streaks. They can be cooked like potatoes and are sometimes used to make flour. They are often combined with meats in braised dishes. However, they are versatile enough to be used in desserts and as a paste for *dim sum*, as well as deep-fried. They must be peeled before using. Buy firm-looking taro without bruises.

Store in a dark, cool place (like potatoes or onions) but use within a week.

TEA, CHINESE BLACK

Chinese black tea is a full-bodied, fragrant and smooth tea, with a rich aroma and a superb bouquet. There are various kinds, of which Keemun

is one of the most well known. Tea is used in smoked dishes or in sauces. You can purchase Chinese black teas in Chinese grocers, delicatessens and in many supermarkets. I prefer to store tea in tins, since these keep the tea in the freshest possible condition.

VINEGAR

Vinegars are widely used in Chinese cooking. Unlike western vinegars, they are usually made from rice. There are many varieties, ranging in flavour from the spicy and slightly tart to the sweet and pungent. The following vinegars can be bought in Chinese grocers and supermarkets. They are sold in bottles and will keep indefinitely. If you cannot get Chinese vinegars, I suggest you use cider vinegar. Malt vinegar can be used, but its taste is stronger and more acidic.

White Rice Vinegar

White rice vinegar is clear and mild in flavour. It has a faint taste of glutinous rice and is used for sweet and sour dishes. The Japanese white rice vinegar is milder in flavour than its Chinese counterpart.

Black Rice Vinegar

Black rice vinegar is very dark in colour and rich, though mild, in taste. It is used for braised dishes, sauces and sometimes as a dipping sauce for crab.

Red Rice Vinegar

Red rice vinegar is sweet and spicy in taste and is usually used as a dipping sauce for seafood.

WATER CHESTNUTS

Water chestnuts are a sweet root vegetable or bulb, about the size of a walnut. They are white and crunchy. In China, they are eaten as a snack, having first been boiled in their skins, or peeled and then simmered in rock sugar. They are also used in cooked dishes, especially in southern China.

In the West, fresh water chestnuts can sometimes be obtained from Chinese grocers or good supermarkets. They are tastier than tinned ones and will keep, unpeeled, in a paper bag in the refrigerator for up to two weeks. Peel them before use, and, if you have any left over, put them back in the refrigerator, covered with cold water. Tinned water chestnuts are sold in many supermarkets and Chinese grocers. They have a good texture but little taste. Rinse them well in cold water before you use them, and store any unused ones in a jar of cold water. They will keep for several weeks in the refrigerator if you change the water daily.

WONTON SKINS

Wonton skins are made from egg and flour and can be bought, fresh or frozen, from Chinese grocers. They are thin, pastry-like wrappings, which can be stuffed with minced meat and fried, steamed or used in soups. They are sold in little piles of 8 cm (3¼ in) yellowish squares, wrapped in plastic. The number of squares or skins in a packet varies from about 30 to 36, depending upon the supplier. Fresh wonton skins will keep for about five days if stored in cling film or a plastic bag in the refrigerator. If you are using frozen wonton skins, just peel off the number you require and thaw them thoroughly before you use them.

COMMONLY USED EUROPEAN INGREDIENTS

BUTTER

Although butter is rarely used by Asian cooks or chefs, in fusion recipes good-quality unsalted butter adds a delicate, slightly rich flavour and sheen to sauces. Unlike in western cooking, the butter is used sparsely in fusion recipes.

CAUL FAT

Caul fat (or *crépine*) is a lacy membrane, often used by European and Chinese cooks to encase stuffings and to keep food moist while cooking. Actually the lower stomach of a pig or cow, caul fat melts during cooking and keeps meats and fillings moist and delicious. It is highly perishable, so buy it in small quantities and use quickly. For longer storage, wrap the caul fat carefully and freeze it. To defrost, rinse in cold water. I find that soaking caul fat in cold water helps to separate the fat, without tearing its lacy and fragile webs. You can order caul fat from your butcher.

CREAM

Like butter, cream is not normally used in Asia. However, in fusion recipes it adds an overtone of richness to the sharp taste of spices, rounding out the overall flavour of the dish, uniting it.

CRÈME FRAÎCHE

This sour cream is prized for its wonderful tangy taste and, like cream, adds another dimension of flavours to sauces.

GARLIC

This common flavouring is used by fusion cooks in numerous ways: whole, finely chopped, crushed and pickled. It is used to flavour oils as well as spicy sauces, and it is often paired with other, equally pungent, ingredients, such as sun-dried tomatoes, spring onions, black beans or fresh ginger.

Select fresh garlic that is firm and, preferably, pinkish in colour. It should be stored in a cool, dry place but not in the refrigerator, where it can easily become mildewed or begin sprouting.

HERBS: basil, chives, rosemary, thyme, marjoram, sage

These herbs, common in European cookery but relatively unknown in Asia, give fusion dishes a liveliness that is delicate at the same time.

HONEY

Used in fusion cookery to give food a rich, deep-colour sheen.

LEMON

Both the zest and juice of this common fruit are used to give fusion dishes a tart accent. Lemon is usually used to balance rich tastes and flavours.

MUSTARD, DIJON

This delectable condiment combines well with Asian flavours, such as soy sauce, to create a union of aromatic fragrances that gives meat a special fusion taste.

OIL, EXTRA VIRGIN OLIVE

Use the best quality extra virgin olive oil to cook fusion dishes. Its rich, fruity seasoning combines well with the exotic spices of the East.

ORANGE

Like lemon, this tangy fruit is used to balance the sharp spices of Asia.

PEPPERS

Used by many fusion cooks and chefs for their bright colours as well as their delicate taste.

RICE (ARBORIO)

This is the Italian rice that is perfect for making risotto. It is a round, plump rice that absorbs large quantities of liquid without the rice turning into a mush. The starch in the rice makes the dish creamy.

SHALLOTS

Shallots are mild-flavoured members of the onion family. They are small – about the size of pickling onions – with copper-red skins. They have a distinctive onion taste, without being as strong or as overpowering as ordinary onions. Readily available, they make an excellent substitute for Chinese shallots, which are difficult to find even in Chinese grocers. In China, you will find them fresh or pickled, and they are paired with preserved eggs as a snack. They are expensive, but their sweet flavour permeates food; a few go a long way. Keep them in a cool, dry place (not the refrigerator) and peel, slice or chop them as you would an onion.

SPINACH

Western varieties of spinach are quite different from those used in China. Nevertheless, they make satisfactory substitutes for the Chinese variety. Spinach is most commonly stir-fried, so frozen spinach is, obviously, unsuitable, since it is so moist. Chinese water spinach is the type most frequently cooked in China and is available in Chinese grocers in the West. It has hollow stems and delicate, green, pointed leaves; it is also lighter in colour than common spinach and has a milder taste. It should be cooked when it is very fresh, preferably on the day it is bought.

TOMATOES: fresh, tinned, sun-dried, puréed

Fresh tomatoes are prized by fusion cooks for their refreshing taste as well as flavour. Tinned tomatoes are a convenience and perfectly acceptable. Sun-dried tomatoes are pungent, tangy, dried tomatoes preserved in olive oil. Their intense flavours are a perfect foil for strong Asian spices. Puréed tomatoes are used to enrich sauces.

VANILLA

This common, sweet, fragrant spice marries well with other fusion flavours. Used in desserts, the vanilla pod is split in half and the small dark seeds are scraped out and used.

COOKING TECHNIQUES

A number of cooking techniques are referred to in this book. Here is a short explanation for your reference.

BLANCHING

Putting food into a pan filled with hot water or into moderately hot oil for a few minutes will cook it briefly but not entirely. It is a sort of softening-up process, to prepare the food for final cooking. Chicken is often blanched in oil or water after being velveted (that is, coated in egg white and cornflour). Meat is sometimes blanched to rid it of unwanted gristle and fat and in order to ensure a clean taste and appearance. Blanching in water is common with hard vegetables, such as broccoli or carrots. The vegetable is plunged into boiling water for several minutes; it is then drained and plunged into cold water to arrest the cooking process. In such cases blanching usually precedes stir-frying.

BRAISING AND RED-BRAISING

This technique is most often applied to tougher cuts of meat and certain vegetables. The food is usually browned and then put into flavoured stock and brought to the boil. It is then simmered gently until cooked. Red-braising is simply the technique by which food is braised in a dark liquid, such as soy sauce. This gives food a reddish-brown colour, hence the name. This type of braising sauce can be saved and frozen for re-use. It can be re-used many times and becomes richer in flavour.

DEEP-FRYING

Deep-frying is also popular. The trick is to regulate the heat so that the surface of the food is sealed but does not brown so fast that the food is uncooked inside. As with any technique, mastery comes with practice. Although deep-fried food must not be greasy, the process does require a lot of oil. Using a wok for deep-frying makes a great deal of sense, as it requires less oil to achieve the depth needed for properly deep-fried foods.

Some points to bear in mind when deep-frying are:

• Wait for the oil to get hot enough before adding the food to be fried. The oil should give off a haze and almost produce little wisps of smoke when it is the right temperature, but you can test it by dropping in a small piece of food. If it bubbles all over then the oil is sufficiently hot. Adjust the heat as necessary to prevent the oil from actually smoking or overheating. You should use only groundnut oil for deep-frying as it is relatively odourless.
• To prevent splattering, use kitchen paper to thoroughly dry the food to be deep-fried. If the food is in a marinade, remove it with a slotted spoon and let it drain before putting it into the oil. If you are using batter, make sure all the excess batter drips off before adding the food to the hot oil.
• Oil used for deep-frying can be re-used. Cool it and then strain it into a jar through several layers of muslin or through a fine mesh to remove any particles of food which might otherwise burn if re-heated and give the oil a bitter taste. Label the jar according to what food you have cooked in the oil and only re-use it for the same thing. Oil can be used up to twice before it begins to lose its effectiveness.

GRILLING

Next to stir-frying, perhaps the most popular method of cooking fusion foods is barbeque or oven grilling. High heat from charcoals is used to seal juices in and give foods a rich, smoky flavour, with a crisp coating and moist inside. Allow grilled meats and chicken to rest for at least 15 minutes before carving.

POACHING

This is a method of simmering food gently in a pan until it is partially cooked. It is then put into soup or combined with a sauce and the cooking process continued. Delicately flavoured and textured foods, such as eggs and chicken, are often poached.

SHALLOW-FRYING

This wok technique is similar to sautéing in a frying-pan and is just as effective. It involves more oil than stir-frying but less than deep-frying. Food is fried first on one side and then on the other. Sometimes, the excess oil is then drained off and a sauce added to complete the dish.

SLOW SIMMERING AND STEEPING

These processes are similar. In slow simmering, food is immersed in liquid, which is brought almost to the boil, and then the temperature is reduced so that it simmers, cooking the food to the desired degree. This is the technique used for making stock. In steeping, food is similarly immersed in liquid (usually stock) and simmered for a time. The heat is then turned off and the remaining heat of the liquid finishes off the cooking process.

SMOKING

Smoked foods are popular with fusion cooks. The wok is also useful for smoking foods. Simply line the inside of the wok and its lid with aluminium foil. Add the smoking ingredients (usually black tea leaves, sugar and spices). Place your marinated food on an oiled rack. Slowly heat the ingredients and, when they begin to burn and smoke, cover the wok tightly. Turn the heat to low and slowly smoke according to the instructions in the recipe.

STEAMING

Steaming has been used by the Chinese for thousands of years. Along with stir-frying and deep-frying it is the most widely used technique. Steamed foods are cooked by a gentle, moist heat, which must circulate freely in order to cook the food. It is an excellent method for bringing out subtle flavours and so is particularly appropriate for fish. Bamboo steamers are used by the Chinese but you could use any one of several utensils.

• *Using a bamboo steamer in a wok* For this, you need a large bamboo steamer about 25 cm (10 in) wide. Put about 5 cm (2 in) of water in a wok. Bring it to a simmer. Put the bamboo steamer containing the food into the wok, where it should rest safely perched on the sloping sides. Cover the steamer with its matching lid and steam the food until it is cooked. Replenish the water as required.

• *Using a wok as a steamer* Put about 5 cm (2 in) of water into a wok. Then put a metal or wooden rack into the wok. Bring the water to a simmer and put the food to be steamed on to a heatproof plate. Lower the plate on to the rack and cover the wok tightly with a wok lid. Check the water level from time to time and replenish it with hot water, when necessary. The water should never make direct contact with the food.

• *Using a large roasting pan or pot as a steamer* (if your wok is not large enough to use as a steamer). Put a metal or wooden rack into the pan or pot and pour in about 5 cm (2 in) of water. Bring it to a simmer and put the food to be steamed on to a plate. Lower the plate on to the rack and cover the pan or pot with a lid, or with aluminium foil. Replenish the water as necessary.

• *Using a European steamer* If you have a metal steamer which is wide enough to take a plate of food, this will give you very satisfactory results. Make sure of the level of the water in the base: it must not all evaporate, nor should it be so high as to touch the food.

If you do not have a metal or wooden rack, you could use a small, empty tin can to support the plate of food. Remember that the food needs to remain above the water level and must not get wet. The water level should always be at least 2.5 cm (1 in) below the edge of the food plate. (Be sure to use a heatproof plate.)

STIR-FRYING

This is the most famous of all Chinese cooking techniques and is a favourite with fusion cooks and chefs around the world. It is possibly the trickiest, since success depends on having all the required ingredients prepared, measured out and immediately at hand, and on having a good source of fierce heat. Its advantage is that, if stir-frying is properly executed, the stir-fried foods can be cooked in minutes in very little oil, so they retain their natural flavours and textures. It is very important that stir-fried foods are not overcooked or made greasy. Using a wok is definitely an advantage when stir-frying; its shape conducts the heat well and its high sides enable you to toss the contents rapidly, keeping them constantly moving while cooking. Having prepared all the ingredients for stir-frying, the steps are:

• Heat the wok or frying-pan until it is very hot before adding the oil. This prevents food from sticking and will ensure an even heat. Groundnut oil and olive oil are my favourites. Add the oil and, using a metal spatula or long-handled spoon, distribute it evenly over the surface. It should be very hot indeed – almost smoking – before you add the next ingredient, unless you are going on to flavour the oil (see next step).

• If you are flavouring the oil with garlic, spring onions, ginger, dried red chilli or salt, do wait for the oil to get so hot that it is almost smoking; however, you will need to work very quickly so that these ingredients do not burn and become bitter. Toss them quickly in the oil for a few seconds. In some recipes, these flavourings will then be removed and discarded before cooking proceeds.

• Now add the food to be cooked, and stir-fry by tossing it around the wok or pan with the metal spatula or long-handled spoon. If you are stir-frying meat, let each side rest for just a few seconds before continuing to stir. Keep moving the food from the centre of the wok to the sides. Stir-frying is a noisy business and is usually accompanied by quite a lot of splattering because of the high temperature at which the food must be cooked, hence my preference for the long-handled wok.

• Some stir-fried dishes are thickened with a mixture of cornflour and cold water. To avoid getting a lumpy sauce, be sure to remove the wok or pan from the heat for a minute before you add the cornflour mixture, which must be thoroughly blended before it is added. The sauces can then be returned to the heat and thickened.

Stir-frying Vegetables

It is easy to use the wok to cook vegetables; however, you need to remember these few hints:

• Never add all the vegetables at once: you must sort them out according to their proper cooking time. Hard vegetables must go in first; then in go softer vegetables and, lastly, leafy ones.
• Hard vegetables, such as carrots, baby corn, broccoli and fennel, have very little moisture. They need to be cooked first and require a longer cooking time. You can either blanch them in salted, boiling water for a few minutes to soften them, or you must cook them longer in the wok with a little liquid. Cover the wok to speed up the cooking.
• Softer vegetables, such as red or green peppers, asparagus or mushrooms, should be added after the hard vegetables have cooked for a few minutes. These vegetables do not need as much cooking as the hard ones.
• Leafy vegetables, such as Chinese bok choy, spinach and lettuce, are full of moisture and should be added at the last moment and cooked only briefly.
• If, when stir-frying vegetables, the wok becomes dry, do NOT add oil as this will make the vegetables greasy and fatty; add a tablespoon or so of either water or Shaoxing rice wine instead.
• Covering the wok can speed the cooking; however, be careful of overcooking.

Although these are just some of the many techniques used with the wok, you will find the wok is just as useful for cooking any type of food. You can even use it for a good fry up. In other words, use your wok and you will find what an essential tool it can become in your kitchen.

BASICS

基本食譜

BASICS ≈

Basic or 'foundation' recipes refer to those combinations of ingredients that recur frequently throughout this book. They include stocks which provide the basis for many different fusion dishes. Good stocks support the flavours of the other ingredients and enhance the overall taste and aromas of the completed ensemble. They can also be used as clear soups.

These stocks are best when home-made and every kitchen should keep a supply of frozen stock on hand. Of course, reliable good commercial stocks may be used for convenience.

I have given recipes for three types of stock: chicken, fish and vegetable. The chicken stock is an all-purpose one: I find that the richer stocks – made with ham or pork bones – are heavier and do not quite fit my eating preferences. This simple recipe reflects what I believe works best for any dish, fusion or otherwise.

The vegetables and the herbs in the fish stock help boost its flavour without overwhelming the natural taste of the fish dish.

The vegetable stock solves the problem presented by vegetarian cooking when it comes to stocks: in the absence of poultry, fish or meat, it is difficult to prepare a truly rich stock, the foundation of any cuisine, but having a greater vegetables-to-water ratio will help give the stock a certain robustness.

Stocks do take time to prepare but it is easy to make your own. Your first step on the path to success with fusion cooking must be to prepare and maintain an ample supply of good stocks, as many recipes in this book rely on them for just the right finish. I prefer to make large quantities at a time and freeze them. (They keep their flavour for at least three months.) Once you have a supply of stock available, you will be able to prepare any number of soups or sauces very quickly.

Here are several important points to keep in mind when making stock:

● The stock should never boil. If it does, it will turn cloudy and any fat will be incorporated into the liquid. Flavours and digestibility come with a clear stock and clarity is essential for good-looking soups and sauces.

● Use a tall, heavy pan so the liquid covers all the solids and evaporation is slow.

● Simmer slowly and skim the stock regularly, which also helps to keep the stock clear and the flavour clean. Be patient: you will reap the rewards each time you prepare one of these tasty fusion dishes. Do not cover the pan.

● Strain the finished stock well through several layers of muslin or a fine-meshed strainer.

● Let the stock cool thoroughly, refrigerate it and remove any fat before freezing it.

I have included steamed rice in this chapter as it goes well with many other dishes. Rice is so subtle and congenial that it is perfect for fusion cookery, and it stores well. Experiment with as many different types of rice as you can.

Infused flavoured oils are other basics that are much used in fusion cookery. Their use was pioneered by Jean-Georges Vongerichten, a young and very talented chef who first made his mark in New York and who has since opened a very successful restaurant, Vong, in London. Jean-Georges came into his own while working at the Oriental Hotel in Bangkok, where he discovered and created his personal fusion cookery. Infused oils are like flavour bridges that bring together subtle and apparently disparate flavours while at the same time enhancing in surprising ways the entire spectrum of tastes. A splash of these aromatic oils provides fragrance with a minimum of fat – an important factor for fusion cooks and chefs. Once made, they keep well in the refrigerator.

HOME-MADE CHICKEN STOCK ≈

MAKES ABOUT 3.4 LITRES
(6 PINTS)

2 kg (4½ lb) uncooked
   chicken bones, such as
   backs, feet, wings
750 g (1½ lb) chicken
   pieces, such as wings,
   thighs, drumsticks, etc.
3.4 litres (6 pints) cold water
6 diagonal 5 x 1 cm
   (2 x ½ in) slices of
   fresh ginger (page 17)
9 spring onions, green tops
   removed
1 whole head garlic, cloves
   separated but unpeeled
2 teaspoons salt
1 teaspoon whole black
   peppercorns

CHICKEN STOCK IS THE ALL-PURPOSE BASE FOR SOUPS AND SAUCES. ITS CHIEF INGREDIENT IS INEXPENSIVE, IT IS LIGHT AND DELICIOUS AND IT MARRIES WELL WITH OTHER FOODS, ENHANCING AND SUSTAINING THEM. I HAVE FOUND THIS BASIC, HOME-MADE, CHINESE-INSPIRED CHICKEN STOCK IS PRECISELY THAT: THE ESSENCE OF CHICKEN, WITH FUSION COMPLEMENTS OF GINGER AND SPRING ONIONS ADDED. COMBINED WITH FRESH HERBS, BUTTER, INFUSED OILS OR OLIVE OIL, THIS STOCK GIVES FUSION DISHES THEIR DISTINCTIVE FLAVOUR. GOOD STOCK CAPTURES THE ESSENTIAL AND BEST TASTE OF EAST AND WEST.

GOOD STOCK GENERALLY REQUIRES MEAT TO GIVE IT RICHNESS AND FLAVOUR. IT IS THEREFORE NECESSARY TO USE AT LEAST SOME CHICKEN MEAT, IF NOT A WHOLE BIRD, AND NOT JUST THE CARCASS. REMEMBER TO SAVE ALL YOUR UNCOOKED CHICKEN BONES AND CARCASSES FOR STOCK. THEY CAN BE FROZEN UNTIL YOU ARE READY TO MAKE IT.

IF YOU FIND THIS RECIPE MAKES TOO MUCH STOCK FOR YOUR NEEDS, MAKE HALF THE QUANTITY.

Put the chicken bones and chicken pieces into a very large pan. (The bones can be put in either frozen or defrosted.) Cover them with the cold water and bring it to a simmer, uncovered.

Using a large, flat spoon, skim off the scum as it rises from the bones. Watch the heat, as the stock should never boil. Keep skimming until the stock looks clear. This can take 20–40 minutes. Do not stir or disturb the stock.

Now turn the heat down to a low simmer. Add the ginger, spring onions, garlic cloves, salt and peppercorns. Simmer the stock on a very low heat for between 2 and 4 hours, skimming any fat off the top at least twice during this time. The stock should be rich and full-bodied, which is why it needs to be simmered for such a long time. This way the stock (and any soup you make with it) will have plenty of taste.

Strain the stock through several layers of dampened muslin or through a very fine-meshed strainer; then let it cool thoroughly. Remove any fat that has risen to the top. It is now ready to be used or transferred to containers and frozen for future use.

ⓥ Home-made Vegetable Stock ≈

One of the best vegetarian stocks I have ever sampled was that of Chef Norbert Kostner, the Executive Chef of the famed Oriental Hotel in Bangkok. He kindly shared with me some of his ideas for this superb stock and I have made a simpler version suitable for our home kitchens. To get assertive flavours, a ratio of 3 litres (5½ pints) of water to at least 5 kg (11 lb) of vegetables is needed. (Although such a quantity of vegetables may sound extravagant, remember we are distilling essences here and the cost is a fraction of what it would be to make a meat stock.) Browning the vegetables in the oven *before* simmering helps to impart flavours to the stock.

Experiment with different vegetable combinations and always aim to suit your own taste. If you find this recipe makes too much stock for your needs, cut the quantities in half or freeze some. It keeps, frozen, for up to three months.

Soak the dried mushrooms in warm water for 20 minutes. Drain them, saving the liquid. Then squeeze out any excess liquid, saving it also. Now coarsely chop the caps and stems. Strain the mushroom liquid through a fine sieve and set aside.

Coarsely chop the carrots, celery, onions and mooli. Discard the green part of the leeks and wash and coarsely chop the white. Peel the shallots but leave them whole. Coarsely chop the cucumber and tomatoes.

Pre-heat the oven to 220°C/450°F/gas mark 8. On a baking tray, put the spring onions, ginger, garlic, shallots, mushrooms, carrots, celery, onions, mooli and leeks, and brown for 20 minutes. Add the cucumber and tomatoes and brown for another 8 minutes. Place the contents of the tray in a large pan; add the peppercorns, salt, water and light soy sauce. Cover and bring the mixture to a simmer.

Using a large, flat spoon, skim off any foam as it rises to the top; this will take about 10–20 minutes. Bring the stock to a fast simmer. Now turn the heat down to a moderate simmer and cook for about 2 hours.

Strain the stock through a large colander and then through a very fine-meshed strainer; let it cool thoroughly. It is now ready to be used or transferred to containers and frozen for future use.

Makes about 2.75 litres (5 pints)

50 g (2 oz) dried Chinese black mushrooms (page 19)
1 kg (2¼ lb) carrots, peeled
4 celery sticks
1 kg (2¼ lb) onions
1 kg (2¼ lb) Chinese white radish (page 15), peeled
4 leeks
225 g (8 oz) shallots
225 g (8 oz) cucumber, peeled and seeded
1 kg (2¼ lb) tomatoes, halved
6 spring onions
6 slices of fresh ginger (page 17)
10 unpeeled garlic cloves, crushed
2 tablespoons black peppercorns
1 tablespoon Sichuan peppercorns (page 21) (optional)
2 tablespoons salt
2.75 litres (5 pints) water
3 tablespoons light soy sauce (page 23)

HOME-MADE FISH STOCK ≈

2.75 kg (6 lb) fish bones
    from any firm-fleshed, white
    fish, such as halibut, sea
    bass, sole, monkfish or cod
3.4 litres (6 pints) cold water
225 g (8 oz) leeks
225 g (8 oz) onions,
    coarsely chopped
450 g (1 lb) carrots,
    coarsely chopped
100 g (4 oz) shallots,
    coarsely chopped
8 sprigs of fresh parsley
4 sprigs of fresh thyme or
    2 teaspoons dried thyme
2 bay leaves
5 garlic cloves, unpeeled,
    crushed
2 teaspoons salt
1 tablespoon whole black
    peppercorns

FISH STOCK EXISTS IN ORIENTAL COOKERY MAINLY FOR LIGHT FISH SOUPS, RATHER THAN AS A BASIC KITCHEN INGREDIENT. HOWEVER, I HAVE DISCOVERED THE VIRTUES OF FISH STOCK WHILE WORKING AND LIVING IN FRANCE. IT IS EASIER TO MAKE THAN CHICKEN STOCK AND GIVES AN INTENSE TASTE AND FLAVOUR TO FISH AND SEAFOOD DISHES AS WELL AS TO SAUCES THAT ACCOMPANY THOSE DISHES. ONCE MADE, IT KEEPS WELL, FROZEN, FOR AT LEAST THREE MONTHS. IF YOU FIND THE RECIPE MAKES TOO MUICH STOCK FOR YOUR NEEDS, HOWEVER, CUT THE QUANTITIES IN HALF.

Rinse the fish bones under running cold water until there is no sign of blood; the water should run clear. Put the fish bones in a very large pan. Cover them with the cold water and bring it to a simmer.

Meanwhile, trim the leeks and discard any yellow parts. Cut the leeks at the point where they begin to turn green and discard the green parts. Then split the white parts in half and rinse them well in cold running water until there is no trace of dirt. Coarsely chop the leeks.

Using a large, flat spoon, skim off the scum as it rises from the bones. Watch the heat, as the stock should never boil. Keep skimming, until the stock looks clear. This can take 20–30 minutes. Do not stir or disturb the stock.

Now turn the heat down to a low simmer. Add the rest of the ingredients and simmer, uncovered, for 1 hour.

Remove the bones and other ingredients with a large, slotted spoon and strain the stock through several layers of dampened muslin or through a very fine-meshed strainer; then let it cool thoroughly. It is now ready to be used or transferred to containers and frozen for future use.

ⓋSteamed Rice ≈

Serves 4

400 ml (14 fl oz) long-grain
   white rice
600 ml (1 pint) water

Steaming is the simple, direct and efficient technique for cooking rice. I prefer to use Indian basmati rice. It is a superior, long-grain white rice, which is dry and fluffy when cooked. Don't use pre-cooked or 'easy-cook' rice for fusion cookery, as they have insufficient flavour, lack texture and have a starchy taste.

The secret of preparing rice without it being sticky is to cook it first in an uncovered pan at a high heat, until most of the water has evaporated. Then the heat should be turned very low, the pan covered and the rice cooked slowly in the remaining steam.

Here is a good trick to remember: if you make sure that you cover the rice with about 2.5 cm (1 in) of water, it should always cook properly, without sticking. Many packet recipes for rice use too much water and result in a gluey mess. Follow my method and you will have perfect steamed rice.

For the rice recipes in this book, the required rice is simple, long-grain rice, of which there are many varieties. As well as Basmati, I particularly like Thai fragrant rice, which is widely available. Here are the rules with regard to successful cooking of long-grain rice.

• Use volume, rather than weight, to measure the rice: pour it into a clear measuring jug to the required level.

• The water should be at a level 2.5 cm (1 in) above the surface of the rice; too much water means gummy rice.

• Never uncover the pan once the simmering process has begun; time the process and wait.

Put the rice into a large bowl and wash it in several changes of water until the water becomes clear. Drain the rice, put it in a heavy pan with the water and bring it to the boil. Continue boiling until most of the surface liquid has evaporated; this should take about 15 minutes. The surface of the rice should have small indentations, like pitted craters. At this point, cover the pan with a very tight-fitting lid, turn the heat as low as possible and let the rice cook, undisturbed, for 15 minutes. There is no need to 'fluff' the rice. Let it rest for 5 minutes before serving it.

ⓥBASIL-FLAVOURED OLIVE OIL ≈

**MAKES 300 ML
(10 FL OZ)**

Bunches of fresh basil,
including stems, weighing
about 100 g (4 oz)
300 ml (10 fl oz) extra virgin
olive oil

Blanch the basil in a large pan of boiling water for 15 seconds.
Remove immediately and plunge into icy-cold water. Drain well and
pat dry with kitchen paper.

Combine the blanched basil with the olive oil in a blender or food
processor and purée them. Remove and let stand overnight.

Strain the oil through a fine sieve. Use at once or store, tightly
covered, in the refrigerator for up to two weeks. Bring to room
temperature and shake before using.

ⓥCORIANDER-FLAVOURED OLIVE OIL ≈

**MAKES 300 ML
(10 FL OZ)**

Bunches of fresh coriander,
including stems, weighing
about 100 g (4 oz)
300 ml (10 fl oz) extra virgin
olive oil

Blanch the coriander in a large pan of boiling water for 15 seconds.
Remove immediately and plunge into icy-cold water. Drain well and
pat dry with kitchen paper.

Combine the blanched coriander with the olive oil in a blender or
food processor and purée them. Remove and let stand overnight.

Strain the oil through a fine sieve. Use at once or store, tightly
covered, in the refrigerator for up to two weeks. Bring to room
temperature and shake before using.

ⓋCHIVE-FLAVOURED OLIVE OIL ≈

Put the chives in a juice extractor, blender or food processor, with the water, and extract the juice. Strain though a fine sieve, if using a blender or processor. You should have about 135 ml (4½ fl oz) of juice.

Combine the chive juice with the olive oil in a blender and mix well. Use at once or store, tightly covered, in the refrigerator for up to three days. Bring to room temperature and shake before using.

MAKES 400 ML
(14 FL OZ)

Bunches of fresh chives, weighing about 100 g (4 oz)
2 tablespoons water
300 ml (10 fl oz) extra virgin olive oil

ⓋWATERCRESS-FLAVOURED OLIVE OIL ≈

Put the watercress in a juice extractor, food processor or blender, with the water, and extract the juice. If using a processor or blender, sieve the juice. You should have about 135 ml (4½ fl oz) of juice.

Combine the watercress juice with the olive oil in a blender and mix well. Use at once or store, tightly covered, in the refrigerator for up to three weeks. Bring to room temperature and shake before using.

MAKES 400 ML
(14 FL OZ)

Bunches of fresh watercress, including stems, weighing about 100 g (4 oz)
2 tablespoons water
300 ml (10 fl oz) extra virgin olive oil

ⓥ ORANGE-FLAVOURED OIL ≈

MAKES 200 ML (7 FL OZ)

6 tablespoons grated orange
zest (4 small oranges)
200 ml (7 fl oz) groundnut or
vegetable oil

Combine the orange zest and oil in a blender or food processor and mix for 1 minute. Let stand for two days.

Strain the mixture through a fine sieve. Use at once or store, tightly covered, in the refrigerator for up to six months. Bring to room temperature and shake before using.

ⓥ LEMON-FLAVOURED OIL ≈

MAKES 200 ML (7 FL OZ)

3 tablespoons grated lemon
zest (2 small lemons)
200 ml (7 fl oz) groundnut or
vegetable oil

Combine the lemon zest and oil in a blender or food processor and mix for 1 minute. Let stand for two days.

Strain the mixture through a fine sieve. Use at once or store, tightly covered, in the refrigerator for up to six months. Bring to room temperature and shake before using.

ⓥ CURRY-FLAVOURED OIL ≈

MAKES 300 ML (10 FL OZ)

300 ml (10 fl oz) groundnut
or vegetable oil
6 tablespoons Madras curry
powder (page 17)

Heat a wok or large frying-pan over a high heat until it is hot. Add the oil and, when it is very hot and slightly smoking, remove from the heat. Then add the curry powder. Stir to mix well. Allow the mixture to cool thoroughly. Let stand overnight.

Strain the mixture through a fine sieve. Use at once or store, tightly covered, in the refrigerator for up to six months. Bring to room temperature before using.

ⓥ Garlic, Ginger and Spring Onion Oil ≈

Heat a wok or large frying-pan over a high heat until it is hot. Add the oil and, when it is very hot and slightly smoking, add the garlic, ginger and spring onions. Cook in the hot wok until the vegetables turn brown. Remove immediately from the heat and allow to cool thoroughly. Let stand overnight.

Strain the mixture through a fine sieve. Use at once or store, tightly covered, in the refrigerator, for up to six months. Bring to room temperature before using.

Makes 300 ml (10 fl oz)

300 ml (10 fl oz) groundnut or vegetable oil
6 tablespoons peeled, thinly sliced garlic
12 slices of fresh ginger (page 17), 5 x 1 cm (2 x ½ in)
6 spring onions

ⓥ Sesame and Chilli Oil ≈

Heat a wok over a high heat, add the groundnut or vegetable oil and, when the oil is moderately hot, add the chillies and Sichuan peppercorns. Lower the heat and continue to cook over a low heat for about 10 minutes. Stir in the sesame oil and allow the mixture to cool thoroughly.

Strain the mixture through a fine sieve. Use at once or store, tightly covered, in the refrigerator for up to six months. Bring to room temperature before using.

Makes 150 ml (5 fl oz)

150 ml (5 fl oz) groundnut or vegetable oil
3 tablespoons chopped dried red chillies (page 15)
2 tablespoons whole unroasted Sichuan peppercorns (page 21)
3 tablespoons sesame oil

ⓥ TOMATO-FLAVOURED OLIVE OIL ≈

MAKES 300 ML (10 FL OZ)

2 tablespoons plus 300 ml
(10 fl oz) extra virgin olive oil

3 tablespoons chopped garlic

1 tablespoon finely chopped
fresh ginger (page 17)

100 g (4 oz) onions, chopped

100 g (4 oz) celery, finely
chopped

3 tablespoons coarsely
chopped fresh basil

1 tablespoon chopped fresh
oregano or 2 teaspoons
dried oregano

2 bay leaves

6 tablespoons tomato purée

8 tablespoons finely chopped
tinned tomatoes

Heat a non-stick wok or large non-stick frying-pan until it is hot, then add the 2 tablespoons of olive oil. Add the garlic, ginger, onions, celery, basil, oregano and bay leaves and stir-fry for 5 minutes. Then add the tomato purée and chopped tomatoes. Lower the heat and simmer for 15 minutes.

Now add the remaining olive oil and simmer for another 20 minutes. Remove from the heat and allow to cool thoroughly. Let stand overnight.

Strain the mixture through a fine sieve (the vegetable mixture can be saved and used with pasta). Use at once or store, tightly covered, in the refrigerator for up to two weeks. Bring to room temperature before using.

HOME-MADE OVEN-DRIED TOMATOES ≈

MAKES 350 G (12 FL OZ)

450 g (1 lb) tomatoes,
preferably Roma

2 teaspoons salt

1 teaspoon freshly ground five-
pepper mixture (page 21)
or black pepper

1 teaspoon sugar

1 tablespoon extra virgin olive
oil, plus extra for storing

ALTHOUGH SUN-DRIED TOMATOES IN OLIVE OIL ARE WIDELY AVAILABLE IN SUPERMARKETS, IT IS JUST AS EASY TO MAKE YOUR OWN. YOU CAN ALSO FLAVOUR THEM WITH 1 TABLESPOON EACH OF MIXED CHOPPED FRESH HERBS, CHOPPED GARLIC AND OLIVE OIL BEFORE THEY ARE PLACED IN THE OVEN.

Pre-heat the oven to 110°C/225°F/gas mark ¼.

Slice the tomatoes in half lengthways. Place them sliced side up on a baking tray and sprinkle with salt, pepper, sugar and olive oil. Put in the oven and leave overnight. The tomatoes should be dry, but not crispy or hard. They are now ready to use or you can put them in a clean, sterilized jar and cover them with olive oil. Store in the refrigerator, where they will last up to two weeks.

APPETIZERS 開胃品

ⓥ CRISP RICE-PAPER PRAWN ROLLS ≈

SERVES 4–6 (MAKES 8–9
PRAWN ROLLS)

For the Filling:

25 g (1 oz) dried bean-
    thread (transparent)
    noodles (page 19)
225 g (8 oz) raw prawns
2 tablespoons plus
    1½ teaspoons salt
½ teaspoon freshly ground
    five-pepper mixture
    (page 21)
1½ tablespoons extra virgin
    olive oil
3 tablespoons finely
    chopped fresh chives
2 tablespoons finely
    chopped spring onions
1 tablespoon finely chopped
    fresh coriander
3 tablespoons finely
    chopped sun-dried
    tomatoes

For the Sealing Mixture:

5 tablespoons plain flour
5 tablespoons water

One packet dried rice paper
    in 22 cm (8½ in) rounds
    (page 21)
450 ml (15 fl oz) oil,
    preferably groundnut, for
    deep-frying

THESE CRACKLING, PAPER-THIN WRAPPERS, ASSERTIVELY FLAVOURED WITH
PIQUANT SUN-DRIED TOMATOES, ARE A PERFECT CONTRAST IN TEXTURE TO THE
EXPLOSIVE FUSION FILLING OF CHINESE NOODLES WITH WESTERN, AS WELL AS
ASIAN, HERBS; THEY NEED NO DIP AND MAKE A PERFECT STARTER.

Soak the noodles in a large bowl of warm water for 15 minutes.
When soft, drain and discard the water. Cut the noodles in 7.5 cm
(3 in) lengths, using scissors or a knife.

Peel the prawns and discard the shells. Using a small, sharp knife,
remove the fine digestive cords. Wash the prawns in cold water with
a tablespoon of salt. Drain and repeat. Rinse well and pat dry with
kitchen paper.

Combine the prawns with the remaining salt, pepper, olive oil,
chives, spring onions, fresh coriander, sun-dried tomatoes and the
noodles. Mix well and let the mixture sit in the refrigerator for about
1 hour, covered with cling film.

Make the sealing mixture by mixing the flour and water together.

When you are ready to make the prawn rolls, fill a large bowl
with warm water. Dip a round of rice paper in the water and let it
soften for a few seconds. Remove and drain on a clean tea-towel.

Place one prawn, with about 1 teaspoon of noodles, on the edge
of the rice paper. Roll the edge over the prawn and noodles at once,
fold up both ends of the rice paper, and continue to roll to the end.
Seal the end with a little of the flour-paste mixture. The roll should be
compact and tight, like a short, thick cigar, about 7.5 cm (3 in) long.
Set it on a clean plate and continue the process until you have used
up all the mixture. The prawn rolls can be made ahead to this point;
cover loosely with a dry tea-towel and refrigerate for up to 4 hours.

Heat a wok or large frying-pan over a high heat until it is hot.
Add the oil and, when it is very hot and slightly smoking, turn the heat
to medium and deep-fry the prawn rolls until golden brown. Fry only a
few at a time and, should they stick together, do not break them apart
until they have been removed from the oil. Drain them on kitchen
paper and serve at once.

GRILLED PRAWNS WITH SPICY SOUTH-EAST ASIAN PESTO ≈

THIS IS AN EASY BUT SPECTACULAR GRILLED PRAWN STARTER THAT IS VERY TASTY. THE PRAWNS ARE SIMPLY GRILLED, COOKED IN A MATTER OF MINUTES AND THEN DRIZZLED WITH A SAUCE MADE FROM GARLIC, CHILLI, BASIL, GINGER AND FRESH CORIANDER, GIVING THEM A RICH GREEN COLOUR AS WELL AS A DELECTABLE BITE. THE INSPIRATION IS FROM BOTH ASIA AND EUROPE; THE COMBINATION IS WHAT MAKES FUSION COOKING SO EXCITING AND NEW.

Soak some bamboo skewers in water for a quarter of an hour or so to prevent them from burning during cooking.

Peel the prawns and discard the shells. Using a small, sharp knife, remove the fine digestive cords. Wash the prawns in cold water with a tablespoon of salt. Drain and repeat. Rinse well and pat dry with kitchen paper. Mix the prawns with the remaining salt and the pepper and olive oil and skewer them on the bamboo.

Combine the pesto ingredients in a food processor or blender and mix until smooth, like a paste. Set this aside.

Pre-heat the oven grill to high or make a charcoal fire in the barbecue. When the grill is very hot or the charcoal is ash-white, grill the prawns on each side for about 2 minutes. Arrange on a warm platter. Drizzle with the pesto and serve at once.

SERVES 4

450 g (1 lb) raw prawns
2 tablespoons plus
   1 teaspoon salt
½ teaspoon freshly ground
   five-pepper mixture (page
   21) or black pepper
1½ tablespoons extra virgin
   olive oil

For the Pesto Sauce:
3 tablespoons coarsely
   chopped fresh basil
2 tablespoons coarsely
   chopped fresh coriander
1 tablespoon coarsely
   chopped fresh mint
2 tablespoons coarsely
   chopped garlic
1 tablespoon finely chopped
   fresh ginger (page 17)
1 tablespoon seeded and
   finely chopped fresh red
   chillies (page 16)
2 teaspoons salt
½ teaspoon freshly ground
   five-pepper mixture (page
   21) or black pepper
3 tablespoons extra virgin
   olive oil
1 teaspoon sesame oil
3 tablespoons mirin
   (Japanese sweet rice wine)
   (page 18)
2 tablespoons lemon juice

TWO-MINUTE COCONUT PRAWN STARTER ≈

SERVES 4

225 g (8 oz) large raw
   prawns (about 8)
2 tablespoons plus
   1 teaspoon salt
2 teaspoons sugar
Freshly ground five-pepper
   mixture (page 21) or black
   pepper
3 tablespoons lime juice
4 tablespoons tinned
   coconut milk (page 16)

To Garnish:
3 tablespoons finely sliced
   shallots
2 small fresh red Thai chillies
   (page 16), coarsely
   chopped

MY FIRST EXPERIENCE WITH THIS DELECTABLE STARTER WAS AT THE
LEMONGRASS RESTAURANT IN BANGKOK. I WAS DETERMINED TO FIND OUT
HOW IT WAS MADE AND WAS PLEASED TO LEARN HOW QUICK AND EASY IT
IS. THE CHEFS USED COCONUT MILK MADE FROM SCRATCH BUT I HAVE
FOUND TINNED COCONUT MILK PERFECTLY ACCEPTABLE. IMAGINE MY SURPRISE
WHEN I WAS TOLD IT WAS MADE IN THE MICROWAVE! TRULY AN EAST-MEETS-
WEST DISH.

Peel the prawns and discard the shells. Using a small, sharp knife,
remove the fine digestive cords. Rinse the prawns in cold water
with a tablespoon of salt. Drain and repeat. Rinse well and pat dry
with kitchen paper.

   Combine the prawns with the remaining salt, sugar, pepper and
lime juice. Mix well. Arrange the prawns on a small platter. Pour the
coconut milk over the prawns. Microwave at full power for 2 minutes.
If you don't have a microwave, set up a steamer or put a rack into a
wok or deep pan and pour in 5 cm (2 in) of water. Bring the water to
the boil or a high heat and lower the prawns into the steamer or onto
the rack. Steam for 3–4 minutes, while heating the coconut milk in a
separate pan.

   Remove the prawns, pour over the coconut milk if you have
steamed them, garnish with shallots and chillies and serve immediately.

PEAR WITH SCALLOPS TREAT ≈

SERVES 4–6

225 g (8 oz) prawns

2 tablespoons plus
 ½ teaspoon salt

225 g (8 oz) large sea
 scallops, without corals

50 g (2 oz) Italian pancetta
 or bacon

1 large pear-apple or bosch
 pear, if available, or
 1 comice or conference
 pear

Fresh coriander leaves,
 rinsed and dried

Potato flour or plain flour,
 for dusting

3 egg yolks, beaten with
 1 tablespoon water

75 g (3 oz) dried
 breadcrumbs

300 ml (10 fl oz) ground-
 nut oil

AMONG THE MOST INNOVATIVE FUSION-STYLE CHINESE RESTAURANTS IS THE LAI CHING HEEN, LOCATED IN HONG KONG'S REGENT HOTEL. THE FOUNDATION OF ITS MENU IS CLASSICAL CHINESE CUISINE BUT THE CHEFS THERE HAVE IMAGINATIVELY REWORKED AND ADAPTED THE TRADITIONAL CANON, TO PRODUCE A FUSION OR COSMOPOLITAN CUISINE WHICH ITS DISCRIMINATING LOCAL AND INTERNATIONAL PATRONS FIND QUITE DELECTABLE.

I HAVE ENJOYED MANY TREATS AT THAT RESTAURANT AND THIS RECIPE EXEMPLIFIES THE VIRTUES OF FUSION COOKING. WE SEE AND TASTE INNOVATIONS THAT ENHANCE TRADITIONAL AND CLASSICAL CUISINES, RETAINING ALL THEIR EXCELLENCE WHILE ADDING EVEN GREATER DIMENSIONS TO THEM.

HERE, THE CHEF HAS CLEVERLY COMBINED CRUNCHY, SLIGHTLY SWEET CHINESE PEAR-APPLES WITH SOFT, SUCCULENT SCALLOPS. WITHIN THE SCALLOPS, ONE DISCOVERS A FILLING OF FRESHLY MADE PRAWN PURÉE, AND THE ENSEMBLE IS CROWNED WITH HAM AND FRESH CORIANDER, RESTING ON A SLICE OF THE PEAR-APPLE. THE COMBINATION IS DELICIOUS, WITH ALL THE TASTES AND CONTRASTING TEXTURES COMING TOGETHER IN A DELIGHTFUL AND UNEXPECTED FASHION.

YOU COULD MODIFY THE RECIPE BY USING HAM INSTEAD OF PANCETTA OR BACON AND PLACING IT WITH THE CORIANDER, SLICED PEAR AND PRAWN PURÉE INSIDE THE SPLIT SCALLOP. THE WONDERFUL TASTE OF THE TREAT IS UNALTERED.

Peel the prawns and discard the shells. Using a small, sharp knife, remove the fine digestive cords. Wash the prawns in cold water with a tablespoon of salt. Drain and repeat. Rinse well and pat dry with kitchen paper. Put the prawns in a food processor, with the remaining salt, and chop finely until it is a firm, but sticky, paste.

Cut the scallops in half. Finely slice the pancetta or bacon into eight pieces about the size of the scallops. Peel and core the pear and slice lengthways into discs about the size of the scallops. I find using a 4 cm (1½ in) biscuit cutter helpful for getting neat circular slices. Spoon about 1 tablespoon of the prawn mixture on eight scallop halves, then cover with a pear-apple slice, one slice of pancetta or bacon and two fresh coriander leaves. Finish by placing

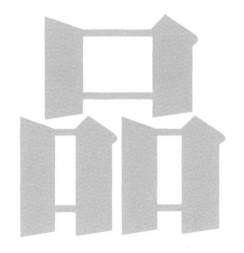

the other half of the split scallop on top so that it resembles a sandwich. Continue until you have used up the scallops and prawn mixture.

Dust each scallop 'sandwich' in potato flour or plain flour, dip them in the egg mixture and, finally, roll them in the breadcrumbs.

Heat a wok or deep frying-pan until it is hot, add the oil and, when it is hot, add four of the scallop sandwiches and cook them for 3 minutes or until they are golden brown. Drain on kitchen paper. Now fry the remaining scallop sandwiches. Arrange on a warm platter and serve at once, with the lemon juice and salt and pepper mixture.

To serve:
25 ml (1 fl oz) fresh lemon juice
1 tablespoon roasted and ground Sichuan peppercorns (page 21), mixed with 1½ tablespoons salt

CRACKLING RICE-PAPER-WRAPPED FISH ≈

SERVES 4

450 g (1 lb) boneless,
skinless cod, halibut or sea
bass
1 teaspoon salt
½ teaspoon freshly ground
five-pepper mixture
(page 21)
2 teaspoons Madras curry
powder (page 17)
2 tablespoons plain flour
2 tablespoons water
1 packet dried rice paper
(page 21) in 22 cm
(8½ in) rounds
8 fresh coriander leaves
3 tablespoons chopped
fresh chives
2 tablespoons groundnut oil
Tomato-flavoured Olive Oil
(page 40) and Chive-
flavoured Olive Oil
(page 37), to serve

THIS DISH IS A TYPICAL EXAMPLE OF FUSION COOKING. I USE RICE PAPER
(A VERY ASIAN INGREDIENT) TO WRAP COD (A VERY EUROPEAN FISH), AND
SEASON IT AT THE SAME TIME WITH FRESH ASIAN AND WESTERN HERBS, AND
A TOUCH OF MADRAS CURRY POWDER. IT IS SURPRISINGLY EASY TO MAKE
AND THE RESULTS ARE A DELIGHTFUL CRACKLING AND STUNNING-LOOKING
APPETIZER THAT WILL SURELY IMPRESS YOUR FAMILY, FRIENDS AND GUESTS. YOU
CAN USE HALIBUT OR SEA BASS INSTEAD OF COD.

Divide the cod into four equal pieces, about 7.5 x 7.5 cm (3 x 3 in).
Combine the salt, pepper and curry powder. Sprinkle the mixture
evenly over the fish pieces.

Make the sealing mixture by mixing the flour and water together.
Fill a large bowl with hot water and dip one of the rice paper rounds
in the water to soften; this will take but a few seconds. Remove and
drain on a clean tea-towel. In the centre of the round, layer two
coriander leaves, a piece of fish and 2 teaspoons of chives on top.
Fold the first edge over the ingredients, then fold in the sides. Fold the
remaining side over and seal with a little flour-paste mixture to secure
the parcel. Repeat for the other three rounds to form four parcels.

Heat a large, heavy frying-pan over a high heat until it is hot; then
add the oil. When the oil is hot, add the four parcels and pan-fry on
the seamless side for about 3 minutes or until golden brown. Turn over
to the other side and continue to cook until golden brown.

Now arrange the packages on a platter. Drizzle with the tomato-
flavoured and chive-flavoured olive oils and serve at once.

STEAMED SCALLOPS IN SPICED BUTTER SAUCE ≈

SERVES 4

450 g (1 lb) fresh scallops,
including corals

2 fresh red chillies (page
16), seeded and chopped

1 tablespoon finely chopped
orange zest

2 teaspoons finely chopped
fresh ginger (page 17)

1 tablespoon Shaoxing rice
wine (page 22) or dry
sherry

1 teaspoon five-spice
powder (page 17)

½ teaspoon roasted and
ground Sichuan
peppercorns (page 20)

1 teaspoon salt

50 ml (2 fl oz) Home-made
Fish (page 34) or Chicken
(page 32) Stock

2 tablespoons (25 g/1 oz)
unsalted butter, cut in small
pieces

1 tablespoon finely chopped
fresh chives, to garnish

FRESH SCALLOPS ARE BEST COOKED BY THE SIMPLE CHINESE TECHNIQUE OF STEAMING. USING HOT WET VAPOURS, THIS METHOD BRINGS OUT THE SUCCULENT TEXTURE OF SCALLOPS WITHOUT OVERCOOKING THEM. I COMBINE THEIR NATURAL JUICES WITH FISH STOCK TO MAKE A TASTY DISH THAT IS BOTH SIMPLE AND ELEGANT. THE SMALL AMOUNT OF BUTTER ADDS A TOUCH OF RICHNESS. THIS RECIPE IS IDEAL FOR A QUICK AND EASY SNACK AND I THINK IT MAKES A PERFECT APPETIZER FOR ANY DINNER PARTY.

Place the scallops evenly on a heatproof platter. Then sprinkle evenly the chillies, orange zest, ginger, rice wine or sherry, five-spice powder, Sichuan peppercorns and salt.

Next, set up a steamer or put a rack into a wok or deep pan and pour in 5 cm (2 in) of water. Bring the water to the boil over a high heat. Carefully lower the scallops into the steamer or onto the rack. Turn the heat to low and cover the wok or pan tightly. Steam gently for 5 minutes.

Remove the platter and pour any scallop juices into a saucepan. Add the stock and reduce by three-quarters. Slowly mix in the butter.

Return the scallops to the sauce to warm, garnish with the chives and serve at once.

LEMON GRASS AND PRAWN QUICHE ≈

Although quiche has fallen out of fashion, it is a simple but delicious dish. The conception is brilliant: rich egg and cream baked in pastry. It lends itself to any type of food you wish to add to it. Here, I have used two eastern spices to give a new twist to a traditional theme. This quiche makes a perfect starter or a delightful light lunch treat.

Put all the pastry ingredients in a food processor and mix to a dough. Roll the dough into a ball on a lightly floured board. Cover with cling film and refrigerate for 30 minutes.

Pre-heat the oven to 180°C/350°F/gas mark 4.

Roll out the pastry to 3 mm (⅛ in) thick and press the pastry into a 20 cm (8 in) tart tin. Place a sheet of foil over the surface of the pastry and put about 350 g (12 oz) of dried beans on the foil to weigh it down. Bake the pastry in the oven for 12 minutes. Remove the beans and foil. Lightly mark tiny holes in the pastry surface with a fork. Return the pastry to the oven and continue to bake for 10 minutes. Remove and allow to cool thoroughly.

Pour the cream into a small saucepan, add the lemon grass and ginger and simmer for about 15 minutes over a very low heat. Strain through a fine sieve, discard the lemon grass and ginger and allow the infused cream to cool.

Pre-heat the oven to 200°C/400°F/gas mark 6.

Peel the prawns and discard the shells. Using a small, sharp knife, remove the fine digestive cords. Wash the prawns in cold water with a tablespoon of salt. Drain and repeat. Rinse well and pat dry with kitchen paper.

Coarsely chop the prawns and combine them with the cream, eggs, remaining salt and the pepper, spring onions and chives. Pour this mixture into the cooked pastry.

Bake the quiche for 25 minutes or until the egg has set. Serve warm or at room temperature.

SERVES 4–6

For the Pastry:
150 g (5 oz) plain flour
4 tablespoons (50 g/2 oz) butter
½ teaspoon salt
2 tablespoons cold water
2 tablespoons single cream

For the Filling:
350 ml (12 fl oz) single cream
3 tablespoons finely chopped lemon grass (page 18)
1 tablespoon finely chopped fresh ginger (page 17)
250 g (8 oz) raw prawns
2 tablespoons plus 1 teaspoon salt
3 eggs, beaten
¼ teaspoon freshly ground five-pepper mixture (page 21) or black pepper
2 tablespoons finely chopped spring onions
2 tablespoons finely chopped fresh chives

Salmon Dumplings ≈

Makes 30–32
DUMPLINGS

1 packet wonton skins (about
40 skins) (page 25)
Curry-flavoured Oil (page
38) and Tomato-flavoured
Olive Oil (page 40),
to serve

For the Stuffing:

450 g (1 lb) boneless,
skinless salmon fillets
2 tablespoons finely
chopped Parma ham or
lean smoked bacon
3 tablespoons cream cheese
3 tablespoons finely
chopped spring onions
2 tablespoons finely
chopped fresh chives
2 teaspoons finely chopped
fresh ginger (page 17)
1 teaspoon salt
½ teaspoon freshly ground
five-pepper mixture (page
21) or black pepper
2 teaspoons paprika
1 teaspoon finely chopped
lemon zest
1 egg

THIS IS A FUSION VERSION OF THE POPULAR SOUTHERN CHINESE DUMPLING
SNACK. FRESH SALMON IS COMBINED WITH MILD CREAM CHEESE, WRAPPED
IN WONTON SKINS AND THEN STEAMED FOR A SUBTLE APPETIZER. THIS MAKES
A DELIGHTFUL STARTER FOR ANY MEAL. I LIKE TO SERVE IT DRIZZLED WITH
CURRY-FLAVOURED OIL AND TOMATO-FLAVOURED OLIVE OIL.

Start by preparing the stuffing. Finely chop the salmon and combine it
with the ham or bacon, cream cheese, spring onions, chives, ginger,
salt, pepper, paprika, lemon zest and egg.

Place a portion of filling on each wonton skin. Bring up the sides
and press them around the filling mixture. Tap the dumpling on the
bottom to make a flat base. The top should be wide open, exposing
the fish filling.

Set up a steamer or put a rack inside a wok or large, deep pan.
Pour in about 5 cm (2 in) of water and bring it to the boil. Put the
dumplings on a heatproof plate and carefully place this in the steamer
or on the rack.

Cover the pan tightly, turn the heat low and steam gently for about
5–6 minutes. (You may have to do this in several batches. Keep the
first batches warm by covering the dumplings with foil and placing
them in a warm but switched-off oven.) Serve the dumplings hot, with
the curry and tomato oils drizzled over them.

TUNA CARPACCIO ≈

Named after a Venetian Renaissance painter, *carpaccio* is an Italian first course of thin, pounded slices of raw beef which are then drizzled with a creamy vinaigrette sauce, made with olive oil. It is said to have originated at the famed Harry's Bar in Venice. Here is a lighter version, with fusion flavours from East and West. Get the best quality tuna you can afford; it is worth it. This starter is easy to make and can be made hours in advance if kept refrigerated. Simply drizzle the dressing over when you're ready to serve. It is especially refreshing during warm weather.

Divide the tuna into four equal fillets. Place one fillet between two sheets of cling film and, with a mallet or empty bottle, lightly pound the tuna until it is thin. It should be transparent enough to see through. Put the fillet on a large serving plate. Do the same to the remaining fillets. You should now have four thin tuna sheets on four plates.

In a small bowl, combine the spring onions, coriander and ginger. Sprinkle this mixture evenly over the tuna sheets.

In another bowl, combine the salt, pepper and lemon zest with the vinegar. Then add the mustard and slowly beat in the olive oil. Drizzle the dressing over the tuna and serve at once.

Serves 4

450 g (1 lb) boneless tuna fillet

3 tablespoons finely chopped spring onions

1 tablespoon finely chopped fresh coriander

2 teaspoons finely chopped fresh ginger (page 17)

For the Dressing:

1 teaspoon salt

½ teaspoon freshly ground five-pepper mixture (page 21) or black pepper

1 teaspoon finely chopped lemon zest

2 tablespoons Chinese white rice vinegar (page 24) or cider vinegar

1 tablespoon Dijon mustard

6 tablespoons extra virgin olive oil

ⓥ Spring Salad with Sesame Oil and Shallot Dressing ≈

Serves 4–6

For the Caramelized Pecans:
225 g (8 oz) pecans, shelled
100 g (4 oz) caster sugar
450 ml (15 fl oz) oil, preferably groundnut

For the Salad:
350 g (12 oz) tender salad greens
3 tablespoons finely chopped shallots, squeezed dry
2 tablespoons Chinese white rice vinegar (page 24) or cider vinegar
salt and freshly ground black pepper
2 teaspoons sesame oil
2 tablespoons oil, preferably groundnut

GREEN SALADS, SO POPULAR THESE DAYS, ARE NOT SOMETHING I GREW UP WITH. THE CHINESE NEVER EAT RAW GREENS AS SUCH. SALADS WERE DISCOVERED BY ME WHEN I WENT OUT INTO THE WESTERN CULINARY WORLD AND THEY ARE A FOOD I HAVE LEARNED TO LOVE. NOTHING BEATS THE CRISP FLAVOURS OF YOUNG, TENDER SALAD GREENS. A SALAD IS A REFRESHING STARTER OR CAN BE A CLEAN ENDING TO ANY MEAL. HERE, I HAVE COMBINED THE GREENS WITH CARAMELIZED PECANS, AN AMERICAN NUT THAT IS A DELICIOUS SNACK ON ITS OWN. THE CARAMELIZED NUTS CAN BE MADE DAYS AHEAD. THE DRESSING IS ASIAN, WITH A TOUCH OF SESAME OIL. IF YOU ARE IN A RUSH, YOU CAN BYPASS THE CARAMELIZED PECANS AND JUST MAKE THE SALAD.

Bring a pan of water to the boil. Add the pecans and blanch them for about 5 minutes. Drain the nuts in a colander or sieve, then pat dry with kitchen paper and spread them on a baking tray. Let the pecans dry for 40 minutes.

Sprinkle the sugar over the pecans and roll them around in it to cover them completely. Place the tray of sugared pecans in a cool, draughty place. Let them dry overnight. (The recipe can be done ahead to this point.)

Heat a wok or large frying-pan over a high heat until it is hot. Add the oil and, when it is hot, turn the heat to medium and deep-fry a batch of the pecans for about 2 minutes, or until the sugar melts and the pecans turn golden. (Watch the heat to prevent burning.) Remove the pecans from the oil with a slotted spoon or strainer. Lay them on a cake rack to cool. (Do not drain them on kitchen paper or the sugar will stick to it when it dries.) Deep-fry and drain the rest of the pecans in the same way. Once cooled, the caramelized pecans can be kept in a sealed glass jar for about two weeks.

Wash and thoroughly spin-dry the salad greens. In a large salad bowl, combine the shallots with the vinegar and salt and pepper to taste. Slowly beat in the sesame and groundnut oils. Add the greens and toss thoroughly. Add the pecans, mix and serve at once.

ⓋREFRESHING WATERCRESS SALAD WITH JAPANESE SESAME DRESSING ≈

WATERCRESS IS AN ANCIENT AND VENERABLE PLANT AND HAS BEEN A FAVOURITE IN EUROPE AND ASIA FOR CENTURIES, PRIZED FOR ITS PIQUANT, PUNGENT, MUSTARD-LIKE TASTE. WATERCRESS QUICKLY STIR-FRIED WITH AN ARRAY OF SPICES AND CONDIMENTS WAS A FAMILIAR AND MUCH-FAVOURED AROMATIC TREAT IN MY MOTHER'S KITCHEN AS I GREW UP. HOWEVER, WHEN I LIVED IN EUROPE, I DISCOVERED THE REFRESHING, TART FLAVOUR OF THIS PLANT EATEN FRESH FROM THE GARDEN AND UNCOOKED IN A SALAD. I INCLUDE HERE A SUGGESTED ASIAN DRESSING AS AN ALTERNATIVE TO THE USUAL EUROPEAN STYLE.

Wash the watercress thoroughly and remove any tough stems. Then spin-dry it in a salad spinner or drain it well in a colander and dry thoroughly with a clean tea-towel.

Combine all the dressing ingredients in a small bowl and mix thoroughly. Combine the watercress and dressing, sprinkle the toasted sesame seeds on top and serve at once.

SERVES 4

450 g (1 lb) watercress
2 teaspoons sesame seeds, toasted (page 23), to serve

For the Dressing:
½ teaspoon salt
A pinch of freshly ground five-pepper mixture (page 21) or black pepper
1 tablespoon light soy sauce (page 23)
1 teaspoon sugar
2 teaspoons Chinese white rice vinegar (page 24) or cider vinegar
2 teaspoons oil, preferably groundnut
2 teaspoons sesame oil

ⓥBILL MEGALOS' COLD BEANCURD SALAD ≈

SERVES 4

450 g (1 lb) silky Japanese beancurd (page 13)
6 tablespoons chopped fresh coriander
6 tablespoons chopped spring onion tops
1 teaspoon salt
½ teaspoon freshly ground black pepper
3 tablespoons extra virgin olive oil

WHILE WE WERE FILMING THE *HOT WOK* BBC TV SERIES, OUR CAMERAMAN, BILL MEGALOS, CONTRIBUTED THIS DELICIOUS AND SIMPLE TOFU DISH. ('TOFU' IS THE POPULAR NAME FOR BEANCURD.) THE WEATHER WAS HOT AND DUSTY AND THIS COLD DISH WAS THE PERFECT LUNCHEON FARE.

HE SIMPLY CHOPPED FRESH CORIANDER AND COMBINED IT WITH AN EQUAL AMOUNT OF SPRING ONION TOPS, SALT AND PEPPER, AND THEN ADDED OLIVE OIL INSTEAD OF THE USUAL SESAME OIL. THE RESULT WAS DELECTABLE; A NUTRITIOUS AND TASTY VEGETARIAN DISH THAT LITERALLY TOOK ONLY MINUTES TO PREPARE.

THE SECRET, I DISCOVERED, WAS THE USE OF SOFT, SILKY JAPANESE BEANCURD, AN INGREDIENT THAT ENSURES SUCCESS. THIS DELICATE VERSION OF BEANCURD IS AKIN TO A SEMI-SOFT PUDDING, BUT WHAT MAKES IT WORK IS ITS CONGENIALITY, ITS ABILITY TO TAKE ON AMBIENT AROMAS AND FLAVOURS. DEFINITELY A FUSION RECIPE TO TRY.

Allow the beancurd to drain for 10 minutes. Place it on a platter and sprinkle evenly with the coriander, spring onions, salt and pepper. Drizzle with olive oil and serve at once.

ⓥ Alice Chen's Ginger Green Bean Salad ≈

Serves 4

450 g (1 lb) Chinese long
  beans, runner beans or
  French beans, trimmed
3 tablespoons finely
  chopped fresh ginger
  (page 17)
1 teaspoon salt
2 tablespoons oil, preferably
  groundnut
2 teaspoons sesame oil
2 tablespoons light soy
  sauce (page 23)

One of the best cooks I know is Alice Chen. Originally from Chengdu, the capital of Sichuan province in western China, Alice now makes her home in California.

Sichuan is a region famous for its spicy cuisine. When Alice made this tasty ginger green bean salad for me one Sunday, I was not surprised at how spicy and stimulating it was to the palate. What did surprise me was how simple and easy it is to make. Alice told me that it was a dish typical of popular 'small eats' snacks in Sichuan.

Although Alice used Chinese long beans (which are also known as yard-long beans because they grow to such a long length), I have found that runner or French beans work just as well. The sauce is an excellent alternative to the European oil and vinegar dressing.

If you are using Chinese long beans or runner beans, cut them into 5 cm (2 in) pieces. If you are using French beans, leave them whole. Blanch the beans in a large pan of salted, boiling water for 2 minutes and then immerse them in cold water. Drain thoroughly and set aside.

Combine the ginger and salt and put in a heatproof bowl.

Heat a wok or large frying-pan over a high heat until it is hot. Add the groundnut and sesame oils and, when very hot and slightly smoking, pour the hot oils over the ginger mixture. Mix in the soy sauce.

Add the beans to the mixture and toss well. Serve the salad immediately or refrigerate it and serve the next day.

Ⓥ PICKLED YOUNG GINGER ≈

FEW FOODS ARE MORE REFRESHING TO THE PALATE THAN PICKLED YOUNG GINGER. ONCE MADE, IT CAN BE EATEN RAW AS A SNACK OR APPETIZER, OR STIR-FRIED WITH OTHER VEGETABLES. AS ITS NAME SUGGESTS, IT ADDS A PIQUANT, SPICY TASTE TO DISHES.

PICKLED GINGER IS EASY TO MAKE. BECAUSE THE ROOT IS YOUNG, IT IS LESS FIBROUS AND HAS A MILDER TANG THAN MATURE GINGER ROOT. BUT IT HAS THE AUTHENTIC FRESH AND FRAGRANT GINGER APPEAL AND IT CAN BE SLICED AND EATEN AS A VEGETABLE.

WITH IT, YOU CAN TURN A SALAD INTO SOMETHING SPECIAL. IF NECESSARY, YOU CAN USE ORDINARY FRESH GINGER BUT THE YOUNG GINGER IS PREFERABLE. RUBBING THE GINGER WITH SALT DRAWS OUT ITS EXCESS MOISTURE, GIVING IT MORE TEXTURE.

THIS SIMPLE DISH CAN BE MADE WELL IN ADVANCE AND IT WILL KEEP FOR AS LONG AS THREE MONTHS IN THE REFRIGERATOR. THE PICKLING PROCESS NEEDS ABOUT A WEEK, AND THEN THE GINGER IS READY TO EAT AS A REFRESHING APPETIZER OR TO USE AS AN ACCOMPANIMENT TO GRILLED FOODS.

MAKES 450 G (1 LB)

450 g (1 lb) fresh young
   ginger (page 17)
2 tablespoons salt

For the Pickling Liquid:
600 ml (1 pint) Chinese
   white rice vinegar
   (page 24) or cider vinegar
1 teaspoon salt
6 large garlic cloves, peeled
   and lightly crushed
450 g (1 lb) sugar

Wash the ginger well under cold running water. Trim and peel the ginger. Cut the ginger into large (7.5–10 cm/3–4 in) chunks. Blanch the ginger in boiling water for 2 minutes. Remove and rub with the salt and set aside for 1 hour.

Rinse well in cold running water. Dry thoroughly with kitchen paper and set aside.

Bring the vinegar, salt, garlic and sugar to the boil in a large enamel or stainless steel saucepan. Put the ginger into a heatproof bowl. Pour the vinegar mixture over, making sure that the liquid completely covers the ginger. When cool, pack the ginger and the liquid into a glass jar and refrigerate.

The ginger will turn slightly pink in about a week, ready to be used.

Ⓥ Asian-flavoured Aubergine Crostini ≈

Serves 4–6

900 g (2 lb) Chinese or
  ordinary aubergines
  (page 13)
3 garlic cloves
225 g (8 oz) fresh tomatoes
1½ tablespoons groundnut oil
1 onion, finely chopped
1 tablespoon finely chopped
  fresh ginger (page 17)
2 tablespoons finely
  chopped fresh coriander
2 tablespoons finely
  chopped spring onions
2 teaspoons finely chopped
  orange zest
2 teaspoons chilli-bean sauce
  (page 22)
1 teaspoon light soy sauce
  (page 23)
2 tablespoons black rice
  vinegar (page 24)
1 teaspoon sesame oil
¼ teaspoon salt
¼ teaspoon freshly ground
  black pepper
1 tablespoon sesame seeds,
  toasted (page 23)
1 teaspoon sugar
French bread, thinly sliced
  diagonally and toasted,
  to serve

Aubergine dips are popular in Mediterranean countries. During one of my many East–West vegetarian cookery promotions at the famed Oriental Hotel in Bangkok, I offered this spicy dip. We served it on toasted bread and it proved to be quite popular. The aubergines are first roasted in the oven and then combined with tasty Asian spices to create an unusual East–West treat. You will note that aubergines can work congenially with many robust spices. Since the dip is served at room temperature, it can easily be made in advance.

Pre-heat the oven to 240°C/475°F/gas mark 9.

If you are using Chinese aubergines, roast them for 20 minutes; if you are using ordinary large aubergines, roast them for about 30–40 minutes, or until they are soft and cooked through. Halfway through the roasting, add the garlic and tomatoes. Allow them to cool and then peel the aubergines, tomatoes and garlic. Put them in a colander and let them drain for 30 minutes. This procedure can be done hours in advance.

Combine the aubergines, tomatoes and garlic in a food processor with the rest of the ingredients and process until well blended. Serve with toasted bread slices.

ⓥ STIR-FRIED PEANUTS WITH CHILLIES ≈

SERVES 4–6

225 g (8 oz) raw peanuts
1½ tablespoons oil,
    preferably groundnut
2 small fresh red chillies
    (page 16), seeded and
    finely chopped
2 tablespoons coarsely
    chopped garlic
2 teaspoons sugar
1 teaspoon salt

FULL OF FLAVOUR AND TEXTURE, THE HUMBLE PEANUT IS A VALUABLE SOURCE OF NUTRITION IN A VEGETARIAN DIET. HERE WE HAVE AN UNUSUAL WAY TO PAY OUR RESPECTS TO PEANUTS, AND STIR-FRYING THEM WITH CHILLIES GIVES THEM A WONDERFUL PIQUANT KICK. SERVE THIS DISH AS A SNACK WITH DRINKS OR AS A NOTABLE ADDITION TO ANY MEAL.

Pick over and remove any loose skins from the peanuts.

Heat a wok or large frying-pan over a high heat until it is hot; then add the oil. When the oil is hot and slightly smoking, stir-fry the peanuts for 2 minutes, until they are lightly brown. Then add the chillies and garlic and stir-fry for 2 minutes. Sprinkle in the sugar and salt. Continue to stir-fry for 2 minutes, mixing well. Turn out onto a serving dish and serve warm.

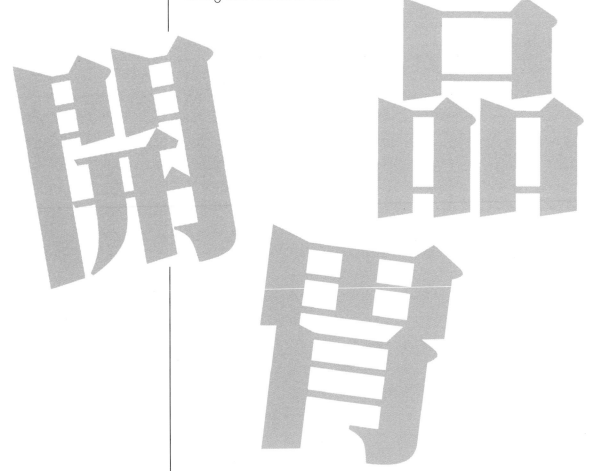

Fresh *Foie Gras* with Ginger and Five-spice Apples ≈

Foie gras is as French or western as can be, while ginger and five-spice seasoning are distinctly Chinese or eastern. As for apples or apple relatives, surely they are universally appreciated? Put them nicely together, as in this fusion recipe, and you have a delightfully cosmopolitan appetizer, combining the unique taste and texture of *foie gras* with the zesty flavours of apple and Chinese spices.

The apples may be prepared well ahead of time and reheated; the *foie gras* cooks very quickly. This is an elegant and impressive starter for any special occasion.

Pre-heat the oven to 240°C/475°F/gas mark 9.

Cut the *foie gras* into 1 cm (½ in) slices.

Slice the apples into 1 cm (½ in) slices and put in cold water with the lemon juice. This will prevent the apples from turning brown.

Heat a wok or large frying-pan. Drain and dry the apples and add to the pan with the butter and ginger. Stir-fry gently for 2 minutes. Then sprinkle on the five-spice powder, sugar, salt and pepper and add the chicken stock. Cook for 1 minute. Remove with a slotted spoon and keep warm on a platter. Reserve the juices.

Season the *foie gras* generously with salt and pepper. In a heavy roasting tin or pan, arrange the *foie gras* slices in one layer. Place in the oven and roast for 4 minutes on one side; then turn and roast for another 4 minutes until the *foie gras* is golden and almost caramelized on the outside.

Remove the roasting tin or pan from the oven and drain off *all* the fat. Place the pan with the *foie gras* still in it over a moderate heat, add the apple liquid and reduce to a glaze.

Put the apples on the warm platter, place the *foie gras* slices on top, garnish with salt, pepper, chives and spring onions and serve at once.

Serves 4–6

350 g (12 oz) fresh duck
  foie gras
450 g (1 lb) apples, cored
  and peeled
Juice of 1 lemon
3 tablespoons (35 g/1½ oz)
  unsalted butter
2 tablespoons finely
  chopped fresh ginger
  (page 17)
1 teaspoon five-spice
  powder (page 17)
1 teaspoon sugar
Salt and freshly ground black
  pepper
3 tablespoons Home-made
  Chicken Stock (page 32)

To Garnish:
Coarse sea salt and coarse
  freshly ground white
  pepper
2 tablespoons finely
  chopped fresh chives
1 tablespoon finely chopped
  spring onions

SOUPS

MUSSEL AND LEMON GRASS SOUP ≈

THIS IS MY FUSION VERSION OF A CLASSIC FRENCH MUSSEL SOUP WHICH IS MADE FROM THE BROTH IN WHICH THE MUSSELS HAVE BEEN COOKED. THE BRINY SEA FLAVOUR, COMBINED WITH ZESTY LEMON GRASS, MAKES THIS EASY-TO-MAKE SOUP AN ELEGANT START TO ANY MEAL.

Peel the lemon grass stalks to the tender, whitish centres and crush them with the flat of a knife. Then cut them into 7.5 cm (3 in) pieces.

Put the lemon grass, mussels, onions, shallots, ginger, fish stock, rice wine or sherry, parsley, coriander, butter, bay leaf, thyme, salt and pepper in a large pan and cook over a high heat for 8 minutes or until all the mussels have opened. Discard any that do not open.

Strain the liquid through muslin or a fine-meshed sieve and discard the solids. Remove the mussels from their shells and set aside.

Bring the strained liquid to a simmer and slowly drizzle in the cream, stirring all the while. Adjust the seasoning, if necessary. Return the mussels to the liquid to warm, sprinkle with chives and serve at once.

SERVES 4–6

3 lemon grass stalks (page 18)

1.5 kg (3 lb) fresh live mussels, well scrubbed

2 small onions, quartered

3 tablespoons coarsely chopped shallots

2 teaspoons finely chopped fresh ginger (page 17)

250 ml (8 fl oz) Home-made Fish Stock (page 34)

3 tablespoons Shaoxing rice wine (page 22) or dry sherry

3 sprigs of flatleaf parsley

3 sprigs of fresh coriander

2 tablespoons (25 g/1 oz) butter

1 bay leaf

3 sprigs of fresh thyme or 1 teaspoon dried thyme

1 teaspoon salt

¼ teaspoon freshly ground five-pepper mixture (page 21) or white pepper

250 ml (8 fl oz) double cream

1 tablespoon finely chopped fresh chives, to garnish

GINGER FISH SOUP ≈

SERVES 2–4

450 g (1 lb) fresh, flat,
white fish fillets, such as
plaice or sole

225 g (8 oz) tomatoes, peeled
and seeded if fresh, drained
if tinned

1.2 litres (2 pints)
Home-made Fish (page 34)
or Chicken (page 32) Stock

2 teaspoons salt

1 teaspoon freshly ground five-
pepper mixture (page 21)
or black pepper

2 teaspoons Shaoxing rice wine
(page 22) or dry sherry

2 teaspoons finely shredded
fresh ginger (page 17)

2 tablespoons finely chopped
spring onions

1 tablespoon finely chopped
fresh coriander

1 tablespoon finely chopped
fresh chives

1 tablespoon extra virgin
olive oil

ONE OF THE BEST CHINESE TECHNIQUES FOR COOKING DELICATE FOODS SUCH AS FISH IS TO STEEP THEM, THAT IS, TO ADD THE FISH PIECES TO HOT BROTH AND TURN THE HEAT OFF. THE GENTLE HEAT OF THE BROTH COOKS THE FISH PERFECTLY – RESULTING IN MOIST AND FLAVOURFUL FISH – WITHOUT OVERCOOKING IT OR DRYING IT OUT. IN THIS RECIPE, I USE THE TECHNIQUE TO MAKE A LOVELY, ELEGANT FISH SOUP. THIS TYPE OF SOUP IS POPULAR IN FUSION COOKING BECAUSE ONE CAN COMBINE TASTES FROM MANY CULTURES TO CREATE A DELECTABLE, AROMATIC DISH. INFUSED WITH GINGER, WIDELY USED IN ASIAN FISH DISHES, THIS EASY SOUP IS SURE TO BECOME ONE OF YOUR FAVOURITES.

Remove the skins from the fish and then cut the fillets into pieces about 5 cm (2 in) square and set aside. If you are using fresh tomatoes, cut them into 2.5 cm (1 in) cubes. If you are using tinned tomatoes, chop them into small chunks.

Pour the stock into a wok or large pan and bring it to a simmer. Add the salt, pepper, rice wine or sherry and ginger and simmer for 5 minutes. Then add the fish, remove the pan from the heat and let it sit for 5 minutes or just until the fish turns white. Using a slotted spoon, transfer the fish to individual bowls or a soup tureen. Stir the spring onions, coriander, tomatoes, chives and olive oil into the soup. Ladle the soup over the fish and serve at once.

Thai Consommé with Seafood and Spices ≈

Serves 4

175 g (6 oz) raw prawns
2 tablespoons plus
  1 teaspoon salt
175 g (6 oz) salmon fillets,
  skinned
2 lemon grass stalks
  (page 18)
1.2 litres (2 pints)
  Home-made Fish
  (page 34) or Chicken
  (page 32) Stock
1 fresh red chilli (page 16),
  seeded and finely
  shredded
¼ teaspoon freshly ground
  five-pepper mixture
  (page 21) or black pepper
2 spring onions, finely
  shredded
2 tablespoons lime juice
5 sprigs of fresh coriander

Thai spices and herbs are so fragrant and aromatic that they can easily transform any dish into an explosion of tastes. In this savoury soup, I use the Chinese steeping technique to cook the seafood, while seasoning the broth with Thai essence. I think it makes a sensational beginning for any meal.

Peel the prawns and discard the shells. Using a small, sharp knife, remove the fine digestive cords. Wash the prawns in cold water with a tablespoon of salt. Drain and repeat. Rinse well and pat dry with kitchen paper. Cut the salmon into 2.5 cm (1 in) cubes.

Peel the lemon grass stalks to the tender, whitish centres and crush them with the flat of a knife. Then cut them into 7.5 cm (3 in) pieces.

In a large pan, bring the stock to a simmer and add the lemon grass. Turn the heat to low, cover and cook for 10 minutes. Remove the lemon grass with a slotted spoon and discard. Then add the chilli, the remaining salt and the pepper, prawns and salmon to the liquid. Cover the pan and remove from the heat. Let it sit for 10 minutes.

Finally, stir in the spring onions, lime juice and coriander sprigs. Ladle into a large soup tureen or individual bowls and serve immediately..

CRAB WONTONS IN AROMATIC BROTH ≈

WONTON SKINS ARE SUCH A GREAT CONVENIENCE: THEY ARE INEXPENSIVE, BECOMING EASIER TO FIND AND ARE WELL MADE. THIS RECIPE TAKES ADVANTAGE OF THESE VERSATILE, FLEXIBLE PASTRY SHEETS – POPULAR AMONG FUSION CHEFS. TASTY WONTONS ARE FILLED WITH CRAB AND WESTERN AS WELL AS EASTERN HERBS, AND THEN MATCHED WITH A THAI-FLAVOURED, INFUSED BROTH. AN EAST–WEST DISH THAT IS EASY TO MAKE, THIS IS A WONDERFUL LIGHT STARTER FOR ANY ELEGANT MEAL.

Peel the lemon grass stalks to the tender, whitish centres and crush them with the flat of a knife. Then cut them into 7.5 cm (3 in) pieces.

Bring the stock to a simmer in a large pan, add the lemon grass pieces, lime zest, salt and pepper and leave to simmer for 25 minutes. Remove and discard the lemon grass stalks.

Meanwhile, put the crabmeat in a large bowl, add the olive oil, chives, chervil, shallots, coriander, spring onions, lemon zest, salt and pepper and mix well.

When you are ready to stuff the wontons, put 1 tablespoon of the filling in the centre of the first wonton skin. Dampen the edges with a little water and bring up the sides of the skin around the filling. Pinch the edges together at the top so that the wonton is sealed. It should look like a small drawstring bag. Repeat the process until all the filling has been used.

In another pan, bring salted water to the boil and poach the wontons for 1 minute, or until they float to the top (you may have to do this in batches – there is no need to keep the wontons warm as they will warm up in the soup). Remove them immediately and transfer them to individual, flat soup plates. Ladle a small amount of the stock into each soup plate, garnish with chives and serve at once.

SERVES 6 (MAKES 30–35 WONTONS)

For the Broth:
3 lemon grass stalks (page 18)
2.25 litres (4 pints) Home-made Fish (page 34) or Chicken (page 32) Stock
1 teaspoon finely chopped lime zest
Salt and freshly ground pepper

For the Wontons:
350 g (12 oz) cooked fresh crabmeat
2 teaspoons extra virgin olive oil
3 tablespoons finely chopped fresh chives
2 tablespoons finely chopped fresh chervil
2 tablespoons finely chopped shallots, squeezed dry
1½ tablespoons finely chopped fresh coriander
2 tablespoons finely chopped spring onions
1 teaspoon finely chopped lemon zest
1 teaspoon salt
¼ teaspoon freshly ground five-pepper mixture (page 21) or black pepper
225 g (8 oz) wonton skins (page 25)
1½ tablespoons finely chopped fresh chives, to garnish

Oxtail Wonton Soup ≈

Serves 4–6 (makes
about 30 wontons)

750 g (1½ lb) oxtail, jointed
2.75 litres (5 pints)
   Home-made Chicken Stock
   (page 32)
1 teaspoon sesame oil
1½ tablespoons capers,
   rinsed and chopped
1 tablespoon Dijon mustard
½ teaspoon salt
¼ teaspoon freshly ground
   five-pepper mixture
   (page 21) or black pepper
1 teaspoon finely chopped
   lemon zest
1½ teaspoons dark soy sauce
   (page 23)
1½ tablespoons finely
   chopped fresh chives
1 tablespoon finely chopped
   fresh chervil
2 tablespoons finely
   chopped shallots,
   squeezed dry
1 tablespoon finely chopped
   fresh coriander
1 tablespoon finely chopped
   spring onions
250 g (9 oz) wonton skins
   (page 25)
Salt and freshly ground black
   pepper
1½ tablespoons finely
   chopped chives, to garnish

Fusion chefs have discovered the convenience and silky texture of wonton skins. Any one of a wide range of tasty fillings may be used to create a special dish by simply wrapping them in these pastry sheets.

For an East–West cookery demonstration at the Regent Restaurant in Sydney, I wanted to offer something that featured these wontons. In collaboration with Serge Dansereau, a very talented Australian chef, I came up with this oxtail wonton soup recipe. Oxtail meat has a rich flavour and works very congenially with these zesty Asian and western spices and seasonings. Together, they make a splendid filling for wontons and the ensemble transforms a prosaic soup into an exceptional treat.

Cook the oxtail pieces in boiling water for 15 minutes. Remove and drain well. Bring 2.25 litres (4 pints) of the stock to a simmer in a very large pan, add the oxtail, cover and simmer for 3 hours or until the oxtail is very tender. Skim the surface from time to time, removing any impurities. Cool thoroughly and remove all surface fat. Keep the stock for the soup – you should have about 1.2 litres (2 pints) left.

To make the wonton filling, remove all the meat from the bones and discard the bones. Finely chop the meat and combine it with the sesame oil, capers, mustard, salt, pepper, lemon zest, soy sauce, chives, chervil, shallots, coriander and spring onions; mix well.

When you are ready to stuff the wontons, put 1 tablespoon of the filling in the centre of the first wonton skin. Dampen the edges with a little water and bring up the sides of the skin around the filling. Pinch the edges together at the top so that the wonton is sealed. It should look like a small, filled bag. Repeat the process until all the filling has been used.

Reheat the soup stock and add the remainder of the chicken stock. Season with salt and pepper to taste.

In another pan, bring salted water to the boil and poach the wontons for 1 minute, or until they float to the top (you may have to do this in batches). Remove them immediately and transfer them to individual flat soup plates. Ladle a small amount of the stock into each soup plate, garnish with chopped chives and serve at once.

Ⓥ Ginger Pea Soup ≈

Serves 4

2 tablespoons extra virgin olive oil

1 small onion, coarsely chopped

1½ tablespoons finely chopped fresh ginger (page 17)

1 teaspoon salt

¼ teaspoon freshly ground white pepper

350 g (12 oz) frozen peas or 550 g (1¼ lb) fresh peas, podded

1.2 litres (2 pints) Home-made Vegetable Stock (page 33)

100 g (4 oz) potatoes, peeled and cut in small cubes

Fresh, sweet peas in season are a real treat, with their earthy flavour and pleasant texture. As legumes, they are quite nutritious in terms of the protein, iron and B vitamins they provide.

Here, a touch of fresh ginger adds zesty spice to this luscious soup. I use potatoes rather than cream or butter to thicken the soup slightly. The bonus is that it reheats very well, making it ideal for easy serving at your convenience.

Heat a wok or large frying-pan over a high heat until it is hot. Add the olive oil and, when it is very hot and slightly smoking, add the onion and ginger and stir-fry for 1 minute. Sprinkle on the salt and pepper to taste. Continue to stir-fry for 3 minutes or until the onion is soft and translucent.

Now add the peas and stir-fry for 1 minute. Pour in the stock and bring the mixture to a simmer. Add the potatoes, cover and simmer for 20 minutes.

Remove from the heat and allow to cool slightly. When it is cool enough, blend the entire soup mixture in a food processor or blender. Reheat the soup, ladle it into a soup tureen and serve at once.

ⓥEAST–WEST MUSHROOM SOUP ≈

MUSHROOMS – FROM THE EAST AND WEST – UNITE HERE IN A DELECTABLE SOUP. SIMPLE TO MAKE, THIS SOUP CAN ALSO BE MADE UP TO THE PURÉEING STAGE THE DAY BEFORE AS IT REHEATS NICELY. IT MAKES A LOVELY STARTER OR, SERVED WITH BREAD AND A LIGHT SALAD, A MEAL IN ITSELF. I USE HOME-MADE VEGETABLE STOCK, WHICH MAKES THIS SOUP IDEAL FOR VEGETARIANS.

Soak the Chinese mushrooms in warm water for 20 minutes. Drain them and squeeze out the excess liquid. Remove and discard the stems and finely shred the caps into thin strips. Wash and slice the button mushrooms.

Heat a wok or large frying-pan, with the butter and olive oil, over a high heat, until it is hot. Add the garlic and spring onions, onion and shallots and stir-fry for 3 minutes. Then add all the mushrooms and stir-fry for 5 minutes, mixing them well. Add the sugar, salt, pepper and stock. Turn the heat down and cook for 5 minutes, stirring continuously. Remove the soup from the heat and allow to cool enough to handle. Purée the mixture in a blender and return to the wok or pan. Reheat to a simmer and stir in the crème fraîche, mixing well. Garnish with chives and serve at once.

SERVES 4–6

50 g (2 oz) dried Chinese black mushrooms (page 18)

450 g (1 lb) button mushrooms

2 tablespoons (25 g/1 oz) unsalted butter

1 tablespoon extra virgin olive oil

1 tablespoon coarsely chopped garlic

3 tablespoons finely chopped spring onions

1 small onion, finely chopped

3 tablespoons finely chopped shallots

2 teaspoons sugar

2 teaspoons salt

½ teaspoon freshly ground five-pepper mixture (page 21) or black pepper

1.2 litres (2 pints) Home-made Vegetable Stock (page 33)

3 tablespoons crème fraîche

2 tablespoons finely chopped fresh chives, to garnish

ⓥ Spicy Lemon Grass, Coconut and Tomato Soup ≈

Serves 4–6

3 tablespoons extra virgin olive oil

100 g (4 oz) lemon grass (page 18), coarsely chopped

100 g (4 oz) onions, coarsely chopped

100 g (4 oz) spring onions, coarsely chopped

2 tablespoons finely chopped fresh ginger (page 17)

1 tablespoon coarsely chopped garlic

1 fresh red or green chilli (page 16), seeded and coarsely chopped

1.2 litres (2 pints) Home-made Vegetable (page 33) or Chicken (page 32) Stock

450 g (1 lb) tomatoes, peeled and seeded if fresh or drained if tinned, chopped

1 tablespoon sugar

1½ teaspoons salt

1 teaspoon freshly ground five-pepper mixture (page 21) or black pepper

3 tablespoons tinned coconut milk (page 16)

2 tablespoons single cream

To Garnish:

2 tablespoons finely chopped fresh chives

1 tablespoon finely chopped fresh coriander

Basil-flavoured Olive Oil (page 36) and Curry-flavoured Oil (page 38), (optional)

In this recipe, I have modified the traditional tomato soup by adding hints of Thailand – lemon grass and coconut – to make a subtle and fragrant alternative to this popular soup. It can be made ahead of time and, once made, it reheats extremely well.

Heat a large, heavy pan until it is hot and add the olive oil. When the oil is hot, add the lemon grass, onions, spring onions, ginger, garlic and chilli. Stir-fry the mixture for 5 minutes or until the onions are cooked through. Now add the stock, tomatoes, sugar, salt and pepper. Bring the mixture to the boil, turn the heat down and simmer for 20 minutes.

Remove from the heat and, when it is cool enough, purée the soup in a blender. Strain the soup through a fine sieve.

When you are ready to serve the soup, re-heat it and add the coconut milk and cream. Finally, garnish it with chives and coriander, and a drizzle of the basil and curry oils if you wish.

ⓥLIGHT AND SAVOURY TOMATO AND GINGER SOUP ≈

THIS IS SIMPLY A LOVELY SOUP THAT COMBINES EASTERN AND WESTERN INGREDIENTS FOR A UNIQUE AND TASTY FIRST COURSE.

Heat the olive oil in a wok or large frying-pan. Stir-fry the spring onions, ginger and shallots gently, without browning, for about 8 minutes. Transfer the mixture to a large pan and add the tomatoes, ground coriander, sugar, stock, salt and pepper. Mix well, bring the mixture to a simmer and cook for 10 minutes. Remove from the heat and allow to cool.

Stir in the cream, fresh coriander and chives. Ladle the soup into a blender in small batches and process until completely smooth. Slowly re-heat the soup, adding the butter, and stir well. Ladle the mixture into a soup tureen or individual bowls, garnish with coriander leaves and serve at once.

SERVES 4–6

3 tablespoons extra virgin olive oil

6 tablespoons finely chopped spring onions

2 tablespoons finely chopped fresh ginger (page 17)

100 g (4 oz) shallots, finely chopped

225 g (8 oz) tomatoes, peeled and seeded if fresh or drained if tinned, chopped

2 teaspoons ground coriander

1 tablespoon sugar

1.2 litres (2 pints) Home-made Vegetable (page 33) or Chicken (page 32) Stock

2 teaspoons salt

Freshly ground five-pepper mixture (page 21) or black pepper

125 ml (4 fl oz) double cream

6 tablespoons finely chopped fresh coriander

4 tablespoons finely chopped fresh chives

2 tablespoons (25 g/1 oz) unsalted butter, cut in small pieces

Fresh coriander leaves, to garnish

ⓥVEGETARIAN BEAN-THREAD SOUP ≈

SERVES 4

50 g (2 oz) dried bean
 thread (transparent)
 noodles (page 19)
1.2 litres (2 pints)
 Home-made Vegetable
 (page 33) or Chicken
 (page 32) Stock
1 tablespoon light soy sauce
 (page 23)
2 teaspoons dark soy sauce
 (page 23)
1 tablespoon Shaoxing rice
 wine (page 22) or dry
 sherry
2 teaspoons sugar
1 teaspoon salt
¼ teaspoon freshly ground
 five-pepper mixture (page
 21) or black pepper
2 teaspoons cornflour, mixed
 with 1 tablespoon water
2 teaspoons sesame oil

FOR CENTURIES, CHINESE VEGETARIANS HAVE CLEVERLY USED TEXTURES SIMILAR TO MEATS OR FISH IN THEIR VEGETARIAN DISHES. BUDDHISTS ARE ESPECIALLY TALENTED IN SUCH CULINARY MASQUERADES, WORKING ON THE THEORY THAT ONE MAY HAVE ONE'S CAKE AND EAT IT TOO. THAT IS, IF THE ARTIFICE IS WELL AND DELICIOUSLY DONE.

SHARK'S FIN HAS ALWAYS BEEN PRIZED IN CHINA BUT IT IS AN EXPENSIVE TREAT AND, BESIDES, IT IS OF ANIMAL ORIGIN. SO, THIS DISH WAS CREATED TO PLEASE VEGETARIANS WHO WISH TO SWIM WITH THE EATERS OF SHARK'S FIN WITHOUT GUILT. BEAN-THREAD NOODLES, WHICH HAVE A TOOTHSOME BITE AND ARE RATHER LONG AND CHEWY, PROVIDE THE ILLUSION OF THE SIMILARLY CHEWY AND, ON ITS OWN, RATHER TASTELESS, SHARK'S FIN. THIS SOUP IS A REAL TREAT, AND MUCH BETTER FOR EVERYONE, INCLUDING THE SHARK.

Soak the noodles in warm water for 15 minutes. Drain well.

Heat the stock in a medium-sized pan, turn the heat down to a simmer, add the bean thread noodles, soy sauces, rice wine or sherry, sugar, salt and pepper. Gently simmer for about 4 minutes. Add the cornflour mixture and continue to cook for another 3 minutes or until the soup has slightly thickened. Now add the sesame oil and give the soup several good stirs. Pour the soup into a tureen and serve at once.

ⓋCREAM OF BEANCURD SPINACH SOUP ≈

SERVING FOOD ON AIRLINES IS PERHAPS ONE OF THE MOST CHALLENGING TASKS IN THE FOOD SERVICE BUSINESS. THIS IS ESPECIALLY THE CASE ON LONG-HAUL FLIGHTS, IN WHICH SEVERAL MEALS ARE SERVED. RESEARCH SHOWS THAT THE PASSENGER IS BETTER OFF WITH LIGHT FOODS AS HEAVIER MEALS ARE DIFFICULT TO DIGEST AT HIGHER ALTITUDES. ASIAN AIRLINES ARE ESPECIALLY GOOD AT MEETING THIS CHALLENGE, BY OFFERING SATISFYING SOUPS. HERE IS A BRILLIANTLY CONCEIVED SOUP THAT I ENJOYED ON A SINGAPORE AIRLINES FLIGHT; IT IS A TRUE FUSION OF EAST AND WEST. A SAVOURY MIX OF SILKY-SOFT BEANCURD AND SPINACH IS PURÉED WITH GOOD STOCK SO THAT IT IS CREAMY BUT WITHOUT ANY OF THE FAT THAT COMES WITH REAL CREAM, AND SEEMINGLY HEAVY BUT WITHOUT REAL BULK. BITS OF CHOPPED BEANCURD AND FRESH SPINACH LEAVES ADD A TEXTURED GARNISH TO THIS MOST SATISFYING SOUP.

Remove the stems of the spinach and wash the leaves well. Gently cut the beancurd into 2.5 cm (1 in) cubes. Drain well.

Put the stock into a pan and bring it to a simmer. Add the spinach, beancurd, soy sauce, sugar, salt and pepper and simmer for 4 minutes. Remove from the heat and allow to cool.

When it is cool enough, purée the entire mixture in a blender. Reheat the puréed soup in a clean pan, add the garnish of chopped beancurd and spinach leaves and continue to simmer the soup until they are heated through. Serve at once.

SERVES 4

750 g (1½ lb) fresh spinach
8 oz (225 g) silky Japanese beancurd (page 13)
1.2 litres (2 pints) Home-made Vegetable (page 33) or Chicken (page 32) Stock
1 tablespoon light soy sauce (page 23)
2 teaspoons sugar
1 teaspoon salt
½ teaspoon freshly ground white pepper

To Garnish:

2 oz (50 g) silky Japanese beancurd (page 13) chopped
Small spinach leaves

FISH AND SHELLFISH

蝦蟹

Prawns in Tea Butter Sauce ≈

This recipe was inspired by a classic Chinese dish, in which green tea is paired with prawns. The stringent, tart taste of the tea is a good foil for the rich prawns. In this fusion recipe, I have transformed the dish by adding western elements. You can serve this dish with Steamed Rice (page 35).

Peel the prawns and discard the shells. Using a small, sharp knife, remove the fine digestive cords. Wash the prawns in cold water with a tablespoon of salt. Drain and repeat. Rinse well and pat dry with kitchen paper.

Put the tea leaves in a heatproof measuring jug or bowl and pour in the boiling water. Let the tea steep for 15 minutes.

Heat a wok or large frying-pan until it is hot and add the olive oil. Now add the prawns and stir-fry for 30 seconds. Strain the tea and pour in the liquid. Add half the leaves, discarding the rest. Cook for another minute. Remove the prawns with a slotted spoon. Add the rice wine or sherry, shallots, ginger and fish stock and, over high heat, reduce the liquid in the wok or pan by three-quarters. Season the remaining sauce with the salt and pepper. Whisk in the butter, a few pieces at a time. Return the prawns to the wok or pan and warm briefly. Garnish with spring onions and serve at once.

Serves 2–4

450 g (1 lb) raw prawns
2 tablespoons salt

For the Sauce:
1 tablespoon Chinese green tea leaves
250 ml (8 fl oz) boiling water
1½ tablespoons extra virgin olive oil
1 tablespoon Shaoxing rice wine (page 22) or dry sherry
2 tablespoons finely chopped shallots
1 teaspoon finely chopped fresh ginger (page 17)
150 ml (5 fl oz) Home-made Fish Stock (page 34)
1 teaspoon salt
½ teaspoon freshly ground five-pepper mixture (page 21) or black pepper
2 tablespoons (25 g/1 oz) cold unsalted butter, cut in very small pieces
2 tablespoons finely chopped spring onions, to garnish

GRILLED PRAWNS WITH JAPANESE VINAIGRETTE ≈

SERVES 2–4

450 g (1 lb) raw prawns
2 tablespoons salt

For the Marinade:

1 tablespoon light soy sauce
(page 23)
1 teaspoon Shaoxing rice
wine (page 22) or dry
sherry
½ teaspoon salt
¼ teaspoon freshly ground
five-pepper mixture
(page 21) or black pepper
2 teaspoons sesame oil

For the Sauce:

1 tablespoon light soy sauce
(page 23)
2 tablespoons Chinese white
rice vinegar (page 24)
1 teaspoon mirin (Japanese
sweet rice wine) (page 18)
or dry sherry
2 tablespoons finely
chopped fresh coriander
1 tablespoon finely chopped
fresh chives
1 teaspoon finely chopped
fresh ginger (page 17)

GRILLING PRAWNS IS ONE OF THE FASTEST WAYS TO GIVE A SPECIAL TOUCH TO A QUICK MENU. THEY COOK QUICKLY AND ARE ALWAYS IMPRESSIVE AS A FIRST COURSE IN A MULTICOURSE MEAL OR AS A MAIN COURSE. GRILLING GIVES THE PRAWNS A SMOKY FRAGRANCE AND THIS JAPANESE-INSPIRED SAUCE PROVIDES THE RIGHT BALANCE OF FLAVOURS.

Soak bamboo skewers in cold water for 15 minutes or more. Peel the prawns and discard the shells. Using a small, sharp knife, remove the fine digestive cords. Wash the prawns in cold water with a tablespoon of salt. Drain and repeat. Rinse well and pat dry with kitchen paper. Combine the marinade ingredients and mix with the prawns. Allow to marinate for 30 minutes. Skewer the prawns.

Pre-heat the oven grill to high or make a charcoal fire in the barbecue. When the grill is very hot or the charcoal is ash-white, grill the prawns for 3 minutes on each side or until they are cooked. Put the cooked prawns on a warm platter.

In a small bowl, combine the soy sauce, vinegar and rice wine or sherry. Then add the coriander, chives and ginger. Pour into a serving bowl. Drizzle some of the sauce over the prawns and serve at once with the remaining sauce.

MUSSELS IN LEMON GRASS AND COCONUT BUTTER SAUCE ≈

THE HIGH DEMAND FOR SEAFOOD HAS SEEN A SEVERAL-FOLD INCREASE IN THE PRICE. FORTUNATELY, MUSSELS REMAIN ECONOMICAL AND ARE AN IDEAL FUSION FOOD. THEY COOK RAPIDLY AND MARRY WELL WITH ALMOST ANY FLAVOUR. THEIR BRINY TASTE IS AN IDEAL FOIL FOR THE CITRUS ZEST OF LEMON GRASS AND THE RICHNESS OF COCONUT MILK. THE ONLY HARD WORK IS THE SCRUBBING; ONCE THAT IS DONE, THE REST TAKES LITERALLY MINUTES. THIS RECIPE ALSO MAKES AN ELEGANT STARTER FOR ANY MEAL.
DRIZZLE WITH ORANGE-FLAVOURED OIL FOR AN EXTRA SPECIAL TOUCH.

Peel the lemon grass stalks to the tender, whitish centres and crush them with the flat of a knife. Then cut them into 7.5 cm (3 in) pieces.

In a large wok or pan, combine the mussels with the rice wine or sherry and stock. Bring to the boil and cook for 3–4 minutes or until the mussels are barely opened. Remove them immediately with a slotted spoon and allow to cool. Discard any that do not open. Add the lemon grass, shallots, ginger, turmeric, saffron threads, salt and pepper to the stock and simmer for 5 minutes. Then remove the lemon grass stalks and discard them.

Meanwhile, remove the mussels from their shells and discard the shells. Set aside.

Now add the coconut milk to the stock, stir, then add the butter a piece at a time. Stir in the coriander, spring onions and chives and, finally, return the mussels to the sauce. Give the mixture a final stir, drizzle with the orange-flavoured oil, if using, and serve at once.

Serves 2–4

3 lemon grass stalks (page 18)

1.5 kg (3 lb) fresh mussels, well scrubbed

2 tablespoons mirin (Japanese sweet rice wine) (page 18) or Shaoxing rice wine (page 22) or dry sherry

250 ml (8 fl oz) Home-made Fish (page 34) or Chicken (page 32) Stock

3 tablespoons finely chopped shallots

1 tablespoon finely chopped fresh ginger (page 17)

1 teaspoon ground turmeric

A pinch of saffron threads

Salt and freshly ground five-pepper mixture (page 21) or white pepper

150 ml (5 fl oz) tinned coconut milk (page 16)

2 tablespoons (25 g/1 oz) cold unsalted butter, cut in small pieces

1 tablespoon finely chopped fresh coriander

2 tablespoons finely chopped spring onions

1 tablespoon finely chopped fresh chives

Orange-flavoured Oil (page 38), to serve (optional)

Scallop Pancakes with Chinese Greens ≈

Serves 4
(makes 8 pancakes)

For the Pancakes:
450 g (1 lb) scallops,
    including corals, coarsely
    chopped
2 tablespoons rice flour
2 tablespoons finely
    chopped shallots
2 tablespoons finely
    chopped chives
1 teaspoon salt
½ teaspoon freshly ground
    five-pepper mixture
    (page 21) or black pepper
2 tablespoons extra virgin
    olive oil plus extra if
    needed

For the Greens:
450 g (1 lb) Chinese greens,
    such as Chinese flowering
    cabbage or bok choy
    (page 14)
2 tablespoons extra virgin
    olive oil
3 tablespoons finely sliced
    garlic
1 teaspoon salt
1 teaspoon light soy sauce
    (page 23)
2 teaspoons lemon juice
1 tablespoon finely chopped
    fresh coriander, to garnish

In this delectable recipe, sweet scallops are made into tasty pancakes and paired with fresh, slightly bitter Chinese greens. It is a classic Chinese combination which I have altered slightly to create a fusion recipe that serves as a starter for eight or a main course for four.

Combine the scallops with the rice flour, shallots, chives, salt and pepper. Set aside.

Cut the Chinese greens into 7.5 cm (3 in) pieces.

Heat the 2 tablespoons of olive oil in a non-stick frying-pan. Form the scallop mixture into eight pancakes in the pan (you may have to do this in batches) and brown lightly on both sides. Add more olive oil, if necessary. Remove and keep warm on a baking tray in a low oven.

To prepare the Chinese greens, heat a wok or large frying-pan over a high heat until it is hot. Add the olive oil and, when it is hot, add the garlic and stir-fry for 20 seconds, until the garlic has browned. Then quickly add the Chinese greens and stir-fry for 3 minutes, or until the greens have wilted a little. Now add the salt, soy sauce and lemon juice and continue to stir-fry for 1 minute.

Arrange the greens and scallop pancakes on a platter, garnish with chopped coriander and serve at once.

CRISPY-FRIED PRAWNS WITH CURRY SPICES ≈

SERVES 4 AS A MAIN
COURSE

450 g (1 lb) raw prawns
2 tablespoons plus
  1 teaspoon salt
½ teaspoon freshly ground
  five-pepper mixture
  (page 21) or black pepper
1 tablespoon Madras curry
  powder (page 17)
Plain flour, for dusting
2 eggs, beaten
100 g (4 oz) dried
  breadcrumbs
600 ml (1 pint) groundnut
  or vegetable oil, for
  deep-frying
Lemon juice, to serve

THE AVAILABILITY OF CURRY SPICES IN CONVENIENT CURRY POWDER MIXTURES HAS BEEN A BOON TO BOTH CHEFS AND HOME COOKS. A DASH CAN TRANSFORM ORDINARY DISHES INTO A SPECIAL TREAT. HERE, I HAVE USED THEM TO ENHANCE AN EASY CRISPY PRAWN DISH, WHICH IS ENCHANTINGLY SPICY AS EITHER A MAIN COURSE, SERVED WITH STEAMED RICE (PAGE 35), OR A STARTER.

Peel the prawns and discard the shells. Using a small, sharp knife, remove the fine digestive cords. Wash the prawns in cold water with a tablespoon of salt. Drain and repeat. Rinse well and pat dry with kitchen paper.

In a bowl, combine the prawns with the remaining salt and the pepper and curry powder and mix well.

Flour the prawns, shaking off any excess flour. Then dip them in the beaten egg and, finally, in the breadcrumbs.

Heat a wok or large frying-pan over a high heat, until it is hot. Add the oil and, when it is very hot and slightly smoking, add a handful of prawns and deep-fry for 3 minutes, until golden and crisp. If the oil gets too hot, turn the heat down slightly. Drain them well on kitchen paper. Continue to fry the prawns until you have finished all of them. Serve immediately, with fresh lemon juice for a dipping sauce.

Stir-fried Prawns with Mustard Herb Sauce ≈

There are very few foods easier to prepare than prawns. They cook quickly and are also succulent and colourful and always popular. In this quick recipe, prawns are stir-fried with Chinese flavours and then rapidly finished off with a touch of western mustard and herbs for an unusually sumptuous, fast dish. For an even spicier dish, drizzle with Sesame and Chilli Oil. Serve with pasta, noodles or rice.

Peel the prawns and discard the shells. Using a small, sharp knife, remove the fine digestive cords. Wash the prawns in cold water with a tablespoon of salt. Drain and repeat. Rinse well and pat dry with kitchen paper.

Heat a wok or large frying-pan until it is very hot and then add the olive oil. Immediately add the prawns and garlic and stir-fry for 1 minute. Then add the rice wine or sherry, salt, pepper, sugar, stock and mustard. Cook for 2 minutes; then add the butter, a piece at a time, and stir for 1 minute. Add the spring onions and the fresh herbs. Give the mixture several good stirs and drizzle over the sesame and chilli oil, if using.

Turn onto a platter and serve at once.

Serves 4

450 g (1 lb) raw prawns

2 tablespoons salt

1 tablespoon extra virgin olive oil

1 tablespoon coarsely chopped garlic

1 tablespoon Shaoxing rice wine (page 22) or dry sherry

1 teaspoon salt

½ teaspoon freshly ground five-pepper mixture (page 21) or black pepper

½ teaspoon sugar

3 tablespoons Home-made Fish Stock (page 34)

2 tablespoons Dijon mustard

2 tablespoons (25 g/1 oz) cold unsalted butter, cut in small pieces

1 tablespoon finely chopped spring onions

1 tablespoon finely chopped fresh coriander

1 tablespoon finely chopped fresh flatleaf or curly parsley

1 tablespoon finely chopped fresh chives

Sesame and Chilli Oil (page 39), to serve (optional)

CRISP COCONUT PRAWNS FROM THE JERSEY POTTERY RESTAURANT ≈

SERVES 4 AS A SIDE DISH

450 g (1 lb) raw prawns
2 tablespoons salt
50 g (2 oz) desiccated
  coconut
100 g (4 oz) dried
  breadcrumbs
2 tablespoons finely
  chopped fresh flatleaf
  parsley
2 tablespoons finely
  chopped fresh coriander
1 tablespoon finely chopped
  chervil
Plain flour, for dusting
2 eggs, beaten
600 ml (1 pint) groundnut
  or vegetable oil, for
  deep-frying

For the Sweet and Spicy Dipping Sauce:

150 ml (5 fl oz) water
3 tablespoons sugar
3 tablespoons Chinese white
  rice vinegar (page 24) or
  cider vinegar
3 tablespoons tomato purée
  or ketchup
2 teaspoons chilli-bean sauce
  (page 22)
1 teaspoon salt
½ teaspoon freshly ground
  white pepper
1 teaspoon cornflour, mixed
  with 2 teaspoons water

DURING A VISIT TO JERSEY IN THE CHANNEL ISLANDS, I VISITED A CHARMING RESTAURANT CALLED THE JERSEY POTTERY RESTAURANT, WHICH WAS A CERAMIC FACTORY, STUDIO AND SHOWROOM AS WELL AS A RESTAURANT WITH CHARMING GARDENS – ALL IN ONE COMPLEX. AMONG THE TOOTHSOME DISHES WAS AN OUTSTANDING PRAWN ENTRÉE, SERVED WITH A SWEET AND SPICY SAUCE, WHICH I SAW IMMEDIATELY AS A FUSION-INFLUENCED DISH. THE HEAD CHEF, TONY DORRIS, GAVE ME THE RECIPE, WHICH I HAVE ADAPTED. IT'S EASY TO MAKE AND JUST AS EASY TO EAT.

Peel the prawns and discard the shells. Using a small, sharp knife, remove the fine digestive cords. Wash the prawns in cold water with a tablespoon of salt. Drain and repeat. Rinse well and pat dry with kitchen paper.

In a small pan, combine all the ingredients for the sweet and spicy dipping sauce, except the cornflour mixture. Bring them to the boil, stir in the cornflour mixture and cook for 1 minute. Set aside and allow to cool.

In a bowl, combine the coconut, breadcrumbs and herbs together, mixing well.

Flour the prawns, shaking off any excess flour. Then dip them in the beaten egg and finally in the breadcrumb mixture.

Heat a wok or large frying-pan over a high heat until it is hot. Add the oil and, when it is very hot and slightly smoking, add a handful of prawns and deep-fry for 3 minutes, until golden and crisp. If the oil gets too hot, turn the heat down slightly. Drain the prawns well on kitchen paper. Continue to fry the prawns until you have finished all of them. Serve immediately with the sweet and spicy dipping sauce.

STIR-FRIED PRAWNS AND SCALLOPS IN BLACK BEAN AND TOMATO BUTTER SAUCE ≈

SERVES 4

450 g (1 lb) raw prawns

2 tablespoons salt

450 g (1 lb) fresh scallops, including the corals

1½ tablespoons olive oil

1½ tablespoons coarsely chopped garlic

1 tablespoon finely chopped fresh ginger (page 17)

2 tablespoons finely chopped shallots

1 tablespoon coarsely chopped black beans (page 14)

1 tablespoon Shaoxing rice wine (page 22) or dry sherry

1 tablespoon light soy sauce (page 23)

120 ml (4 fl oz) Home-made Fish (page 34) or Chicken (page 32) Stock

175 g (6 oz) tomatoes, peeled and seeded if fresh, drained if tinned, coarsely chopped

2 tablespoons (25 g/1 oz) cold unsalted butter, cut in small pieces

Chive-flavoured Olive Oil (page 37), to serve (optional)

A small handful of fresh basil leaves, cut in strips, to garnish

IT IS NOT SURPRISING FOR ME TO SEE FUSION COOKS AND CHEFS ALL OVER THE WORLD USING CHINESE BLACK BEANS. THESE ARE SMALL BLACK SOYA BEANS THAT ARE PRESERVED WITH SALT AND SPICES. THEIR DISTINCTIVE, SALTY, PUNGENT AROMA IMPARTS A RICH FLAVOUR TO FOODS THEY ARE COOKED WITH. NOW WIDELY AVAILABLE, THESE BLACK BEANS TRANSFORM ORDINARY DISHES INTO A SPECIAL TREAT. IN THIS RECIPE, I HAVE STIR-FRIED PRAWNS AND SCALLOPS WITH THE BLACK BEANS AND FINISHED THEM OFF WITH A EUROPEAN TOUCH. THIS DISH MAKES AN ELEGANT DINNER-PARTY MAIN COURSE, SERVED WITH VEGETABLES. DRIZZLE WITH CHIVE-FLAVOURED OLIVE OIL FOR A SPECIAL TOUCH.

Peel the prawns and discard the shells. Using a small, sharp knife, remove the fine digestive cords. Wash the prawns in cold water with a tablespoon of salt. Drain and repeat. Rinse well and pat dry with kitchen paper. Clean the scallops and pull off the tough muscles.

Heat a wok or large frying-pan over a high heat, until it is hot. Add the olive oil, then prawns and scallops and stir-fry for 2 minutes. Remove them with a slotted spoon and set aside. Now add the garlic, ginger and shallots and stir-fry for 30 seconds. Then add the black beans and continue to stir-fry for another 30 seconds. Add the rice wine or sherry, light soy sauce and stock. Cook over a high heat for 1 minute. Return the scallops and prawns to the wok or pan and continue to cook for another 3 minutes, until just done and tender.

Finally, add the chopped tomatoes and, when the mixture is hot, slowly whisk in the butter a piece at a time. Turn onto a warm serving platter, drizzle with chive-flavoured olive oil, if using, garnish with basil and serve at once.

Stir-fried *Persillade* Prawns ≈

Persillade is a French culinary term, which implies a mixture of chopped parsley and garlic that is usually added to dishes at the end of the cooking process. This robust seasoning gives any dish a distinctly assertive flavour. In this recipe, I have added to the *persillade* an eastern touch of fresh coriander to give a refreshing new dimension to a classic seasoning. *Persillade* goes particularly well with a dish such as prawns. Drizzle with Garlic, Ginger and Spring Onion Oil and serve with Steamed Rice (page 35).

Peel the prawns and discard the shells. Using a small, sharp knife, remove the fine digestive cords. Wash the prawns in cold water with a tablespoon of salt. Drain and repeat. Rinse well and pat dry with kitchen paper. Combine the prawns with the egg white, cornflour, 1 teaspoon salt, sesame oil and pepper. Mix well and leave to sit in the refrigerator for 20 minutes.

Combine all the *persillade* ingredients together in a food processor or blender and process until finely chopped. If you are using a blender, be careful not to overblend the mixture to a purée.

If you are using the groundnut oil, heat a wok or large frying-pan over a high heat, until it is very hot, then add the oil. When the oil is very hot, remove the wok or pan from the heat and immediately add the prawns, stirring vigorously to keep them from sticking. When the prawns turn white, after about 2 minutes, quickly drain them in a stainless steel colander set in a bowl. Discard the oil.

If you choose to use water instead of oil, bring it to the boil in a pan. Remove the pan from the heat and immediately add the prawns, stirring vigorously to keep them from sticking. When the prawns turn white, after about 2 minutes, quickly drain them in a colander set in a bowl. Discard the water.

Clean and reheat the wok or frying-pan over a high heat until it is hot. Add the olive oil and, when it is hot, return the prawns to the wok and stir-fry for 20 seconds.

Quickly stir in the *persillade* mixture and mix well.

Turn onto a platter, drizzle with the garlic, ginger and spring onion oil and serve at once.

Serves 4

450 g (1 lb) raw prawns
2 tablespoons plus
   1 teaspoon salt
1 egg white
2 teaspoons cornflour
1 teaspoon sesame oil
½ teaspoon freshly ground
   white pepper
400 ml (15 fl oz) groundnut
   oil or water
1 tablespoon extra virgin
   olive oil
Garlic, Ginger and Spring
   Onion Oil (page 39), to
   serve (optional)

For the *Persillade*:

2 tablespoons extra virgin
   olive oil
1½ teaspoons finely chopped
   fresh ginger (page 17)
2 tablespoons finely
   chopped garlic
1 teaspoon salt
½ teaspoon freshly ground
   five-pepper mixture
   (page 21) or black pepper
½ teaspoon sugar
1 tablespoon finely chopped
   spring onions
1 tablespoon finely chopped
   fresh coriander
3 tablespoons finely
   chopped fresh flatleaf or
   curly parsley

CRISP-FRIED SQUID WITH BLACK BEAN AïOLI ≈

Serves 4

750 g (1½ lb) squid, fresh or
    frozen
50 g (2 oz) rice flour
50 g (2 oz) potato flour
2 teaspoons salt
1 teaspoon freshly ground
    five-pepper mixture
    (page 21) or black pepper
600 ml (1 pint) groundnut
    or vegetable oil, for
    deep-frying

For the Black Bean Aïoli:

2 egg yolks
1 tablespoon finely chopped
    garlic
2 tablespoons lemon juice
1 teaspoon salt
½ teaspoon freshly ground
    five-pepper mixture (page
    21) or black pepper
120 ml (4 fl oz) extra virgin
    olive oil
120 ml (4 fl oz) groundnut or
    vegetable oil
1 tablespoon black beans
    (page 14), rinsed and
    finely chopped
2 tablespoons finely
    chopped spring onions
About 2 tablespoons water

FRIED SQUID SEEMS TO BE ON EVERY FUSION MENU THROUGHOUT THE WORLD, AND NO WONDER AS IT IS DELICIOUSLY ADDICTIVE. CHEFS CAN FRY SQUID QUICKLY SO THAT IT IS TENDER AND TASTY – INSTANT SATISFACTION FOR HUNGRY DINERS, ESPECIALLY WHEN SERVED WITH CHIPS. I MATCHED THIS POPULAR SQUID DISH WITH A TRADITIONAL FRENCH MAYONNAISE GARLIC SAUCE, TO WHICH I ADDED AN ASIAN TOUCH OF BLACK BEANS. THIS DISH ALSO MAKES A WONDERFUL STARTER FOR SIX TO EIGHT.

Make the black bean aïoli by combining the egg yolks, garlic, lemon juice, salt and pepper in a bowl, food processor or blender. Slowly drizzle in the olive oil and the groundnut or vegetable oil, until the oil is fully incorporated and emulsified. If you are using a food processor or blender, transfer the aïoli to a bowl. Fold in the black beans and spring onions. Refrigerate until you are ready to use the aïoli. If it is too thick, add some or all of the water.

The edible parts of the squid are the tentacles and the body. If it has not been cleaned by your fishmonger, you can do it yourself. Pull the head and tentacles away from the body. Using a small, sharp knife, split the body in half. Remove the transparent, bony section. Wash the halves thoroughly under cold running water and then pull off and discard the skin. Cut the tentacles from the head, cutting just above the eye. (You may also have to remove the polyp, or beak, from the base of the ring of tentacles.) If you are using frozen squid, make sure it is properly thawed before cooking it.

Cut the squid meat into 3.5 cm (1½ in) strips. Blot them dry with kitchen paper. In a bowl, combine the rice and potato flours with the salt and pepper.

Heat a wok or large pan over high heat. Add the oil and, when it is moderately hot, quickly dredge the squid pieces in the flour mixture, shaking off any excess. Deep-fry immediately in batches. When the squid hits the hot oil it will splatter, so be careful. Remove with a slotted spoon and drain well on kitchen paper. Keep warm on a platter until all the squid is fried, then serve at once with the aïoli.

POACHED OYSTERS WITH CHAMPAGNE AND LEMON GRASS BUTTER SAUCE ≈

SERVES 4

1 kg (2 lb) oysters, shelled
(about 24)
4 lemon grass stalks
(page 18)
6 tablespoons finely
chopped shallots
1 tablespoon finely chopped
fresh ginger (page 17)
300 ml (10 fl oz)
champagne
300 ml (10 fl oz) Home-
made Fish (page 34) or
Chicken (page 32) Stock
6 tablespoons (75 g/3 oz)
cold unsalted butter, cut in
small pieces
Salt and freshly ground white
pepper
Tomato-flavoured Olive Oil
(page 40)
1 tablespoon finely chopped
fresh chives

OYSTERS ARE, RIGHTLY, ASSOCIATED WITH ELEGANCE AND STYLE. THEY ARE DELICATE AND I LOVE THEIR BRINY SEA FLAVOURS. HERE I HAVE COMBINED THEM WITH THE REFRESHING BITE OF LEMON GRASS IN A CHAMPAGNE BUTTER SAUCE. THESE OYSTERS ARE LOVELY SERVED WITH STEAMED RICE (PAGE 35). THIS DISH ALSO MAKES AN EXQUISITE STARTER FOR ANY DINNER PARTY. DRIZZLE WITH TOMATO-FLAVOURED OLIVE OIL FOR COLOUR AND TASTE.

Drain the oysters in a colander, saving the liquid. Rinse the oysters.

Peel the lemon grass stalks to the tender, whitish centres and finely chop them. Combine the chopped lemon grass with the shallots, ginger, champagne, stock and any oyster liquid in a pan and simmer for 15 minutes. Strain the liquid through a fine sieve.

Return the strained liquid to the pan and, over a high heat, reduce the liquid by half.

Turn the heat down to low, add the oysters and cook for 2 minutes. Remove the oysters with a slotted spoon to a warm dish. Quickly whisk the butter into the liquid; add salt and pepper to taste. Pour the sauce over the oysters and drizzle with tomato-flavoured olive oil. Sprinkle the chives, and serve at once.

CURED SALMON WITH SICHUAN PEPPERCORNS ≈

SERVES 15–20 AS A
PARTY DISH

3–3.5 kg (7–8 lb) whole
   fresh salmon
2 oranges
75 g (3 oz) coarse sea salt
1 tablespoon sugar
3 tablespoons Sichuan
   peppercorns (page 21),
   roasted and crushed
Lemon wedges, to garnish

THIS RECIPE WAS INSPIRED BY THE EXECUTIVE CHEF AT THE ORIENTAL HOTEL, BANGKOK. NORBERT KOSTNER IS ITALIAN AND HAS LIVED AND WORKED IN THAILAND FOR OVER 30 YEARS. TALENTED AND INSPIRED, HE INCORPORATES ASIAN SPICES AND INGREDIENTS INTO HIS WESTERN-STYLE COOKERY. I WAS MOST IMPRESSED BY HIS CURED SALMON, WHICH WAS AS DELICIOUS AS IT WAS EXCITING. INSTEAD OF SEASONING THE SALMON WITH DILL, THE TRADITIONAL HERB, HE USED WHOLE ROASTED, CRUSHED SICHUAN PEPPERCORNS AND ORANGE SLICES, WHICH PERMEATE THE RICH FISH, GIVING THE SALMON A WONDERFUL, DELICATE AROMA. THE SALMON IS SERVED RAW BUT HAS BEEN 'COOKED' OR CURED BY THE SALT AND SPICES FIRST. ALTHOUGH IT TAKES A WHOLE DAY TO MAKE, THE PROCESS IS FAIRLY STRAIGHTFORWARD AND SIMPLE. YOU WILL SEE IT IS WELL WORTH THE EFFORT, AS IT MAKES A PERFECT AND GRAND PARTY DISH. THE SALMON WILL KEEP FOR AT LEAST ONE WEEK IN THE REFRIGERATOR AND ANY LEFT-OVERS MAKE WONDERFUL SANDWICHES.

Have your fishmonger fillet the salmon and remove the head, as well as any small bones, so that you have two large fillets weighing about 1–1.25 kg (2–2½ lb) each, with the skin on. Make three shallow cuts in the skin of each fillet to allow the spices to penetrate. Keeping the skin on will help hold the shape of the fish during curing and when serving.

Cut the oranges into the thinnest possible slices and set aside.

Combine the salt, sugar and Sichuan peppercorns. Rub both sides of the fillets with the salt–sugar–peppercorn mixture.

Cut out a sheet of cling film on which a salmon fillet can fit comfortably. Lay one of the fillets on the cling film skin-side down and then place a layer of oranges over the top of the fillet so that it is entirely covered with orange slices. Place the other fillet on top skin-side up and cover well with cling film. Place on a tray and refrigerate for 24 hours.

After 24 hours, remove the cling film, slice thinly and arrange on a platter with lemon wedges.

Asian-flavoured Salmon Fishcakes ≈

Serves 4
(makes 6–8 fishcakes)

225 g (8 oz) boneless
  salmon fillets
2 tablespoons fresh ginger
  juice, squeezed from fresh
  ginger (page 17)
2 tablespoons mirin
  (Japanese sweet rice wine)
  (page 18)
2 teaspoons coarse sea salt
1 teaspoon freshly ground
  five-pepper mixture (page
  21) or black pepper
300 ml (10 fl oz) oil,
  preferably groundnut

For the Fishcakes:

3 tablespoons chopped
  fresh ginger (page 17)
4 tablespoons finely
  chopped spring onions
3 tablespoons finely
  chopped shallots
2 teaspoons salt
1 teaspoon freshly ground
  five-pepper mixture (page
  21) or black pepper
3 tablespoons finely
  chopped fresh coriander
2 tablespoons finely
  chopped garlic
3 tablespoons extra virgin
  olive oil
3 tablespoons Dijon mustard
175 g (7 oz) dried
  breadcrumbs
Plain flour, for coating
2 eggs, beaten

The Chinese prefer to purée their fish for fishcakes with egg white and seasoning and then either poach or fry them. The result is a bouncy and almost rubbery texture. I have always liked the English idea of fishcakes in which the texture is rather moist and flaky. I have added my own Asian touches of flavour: ginger (which is ideal for fish) and various herbs, such as fresh coriander, and spring onions. Here, I use rich salmon instead of the usual firm, white fish; I know you will find this a light, delectable dish. Serve with a salad, drizzled with Lemon-flavoured Oil (page 38).

Rub the salmon fillets with the ginger juice and mirin. Combine the salt and pepper and sprinkle evenly on both sides of the salmon. Marinate at room temperature for at least 30 minutes.

Next, set up a steamer or put a rack into a wok or deep pan and pour in 5 cm (2 in) of water. Bring the water to the boil over high heat. Put the salmon onto a heatproof plate and then carefully lower it into the steamer or onto the rack. Turn the heat to low and cover the wok or pan tightly. Steam the salmon gently for 5 minutes. Alternatively, you can microwave it at full power for 3 minutes, covered with microwave-safe film. Let the salmon cool.

Mash the cooked salmon in a large bowl, removing any bones. Then add the ginger, spring onions, shallots, salt, pepper, coriander and garlic. Drizzle in the olive oil, add the mustard and 100 g (4 oz) of the breadcrumbs and mix well.

Divide the salmon mixture into 6–8 pieces. On a floured surface, shape the pieces into round, flat patties with a butter knife. Dredge the cakes first in the flour, then the egg and finally the remaining breadcrumbs.

Heat a wok or large frying-pan over a high heat until it is hot. Add the oil and, when it is very hot and slightly smoking, turn the heat to low and add the salmon cakes. Fry for 3 minutes, then turn over and brown the other sides. Remove and drain on kitchen paper. Serve immediately.

East–West Salmon Sandwich ≈

Serves 2 as a snack

2 x 100 g (4 oz) boneless,
   skinless salmon fillets
2 tablespoons fresh ginger
   juice, squeezed from fresh
   ginger root (page 17)
4 tablespoons mirin
   (Japanese sweet rice wine)
   (page 18)
2 teaspoons salt
2 teaspoons freshly ground
   five-pepper mixture
   (page 21)

For the *Persillade*:

2 tablespoons finely
   chopped fresh ginger
   (page 17)
4 tablespoons finely
   chopped spring onions
½ teaspoon salt
Freshly ground black pepper
3 tablespoons extra virgin
   olive oil
3 tablespoons finely
   chopped fresh coriander
3 tablespoons finely chopped
   fresh curly parsley
3 tablespoons finely
   chopped fresh flatleaf
   parsley
2 teaspoons finely chopped
   garlic

For the Sandwich:

1 fresh, crisp baguette
6 fresh spinach leaves
10 basil leaves
1 ripe tomato, thinly sliced

In 1992 Mary Gostelow, a well-known restaurant- and hotel-industry consultant and writer, asked me to contribute to a special event for the 200th anniversary of the death of Lord Sandwich. I was thrilled to be in the company of some of the world's best chefs. Unfortunately, I was unable to attend the event, but Mary tells me that my sandwich was a big hit. I think you will also like it.

This recipe is for two, but can easily be increased for more if you wish.

Rub the salmon fillets with the ginger juice and mirin. Combine the salt and pepper and sprinkle evenly on both sides of the salmon. Marinate at room temperature for at least 30 minutes.

Prepare the *persillade*. Combine the ginger, spring onions, salt and pepper in a small, heatproof dish. Heat the olive oil until it is quite hot, but not smoking. Pour this hot oil over the ginger, spring onion, salt and pepper mixture. Scrape this mixture into a blender with the coriander, the two parsleys and the garlic and process until finely chopped and very well mixed. Add more olive oil, if necessary, as the mixture should be moist. Set the *persillade* aside.

Next, set up a steamer or put a rack into a wok or deep pan and pour in 5 cm (2 in) of water. Bring the water to the boil over a high heat. Put the salmon onto a heatproof plate and then carefully lower it into the steamer or onto the rack. Turn the heat to low and cover the wok or pan tightly. Steam gently for 5 minutes. Alternatively, you can microwave the salmon at full power for 3 minutes, covered with microwave-safe film. Let the salmon cool.

Pre-heat the oven to 180°C/350°F/gas mark 4 and warm the bread for 5 minutes. Divide the loaf in two, then split each half lengthways and scrape out the insides. Spread the *persillade* on the inside of the bread, and top with the salmon fillet, spinach leaves, basil leaves and tomato. Serve at once.

BLANQUETTE OF GINGERED SALMON AND PRAWNS ≈

BLANQUETTE IS A FRENCH CLASSICAL CULINARY TERM FOR A RAGOÛT OF WHITE MEAT (USUALLY VEAL OR POULTRY), OR OF FISH OR VEGETABLES, COOKED IN WHITE STOCK OR WATER WITH AROMATIC FLAVOURINGS. A SAUCE IS THEN MADE FROM A ROUX OF BUTTER AND FLOUR AND FINISHED WITH CREAM AND EGG YOLKS. BLANQUETTE BECAME A CLASSIC OF FRENCH BOURGEOIS COOKERY. THE SAUCE'S RICH, CREAMY, VELVETY TEXTURE ALSO HAS GREAT APPEAL TO MY PALATE. I HAVE USED THE SAME IDEA HERE BUT HAVE INCORPORATED SEASONING FROM MY CHINESE HERITAGE, WHICH ADDS TANG. GINGER HAS A GREAT AFFINITY TO FISH AND SHELLFISH IN THE SAME WAY THAT LEMON IS USED IN EUROPEAN COOKERY. THIS SIMPLE, BUT VERY ELEGANT, DISH, DRIZZLED PERHAPS WITH CHIVE-FLAVOURED OLIVE OIL, GOES EXTREMELY WELL WITH JUST PLAIN STEAMED RICE (PAGE 35).

SERVES 4–6

450 g (1 lb) raw prawns
2 tablespoons plus 1 teaspoon salt
450 g (1 lb) salmon fillet, skinned
½ teaspoon freshly ground five-pepper mixture (page 21) or white pepper
½ teaspoon cayenne pepper
450 g (1 lb) tomatoes, peeled and seeded if fresh, drained if tinned
350 g (12 oz) carrots
3 tablespoons (35 g/1½ oz) butter
1½ tablespoons finely chopped fresh ginger (page 17)
3 tablespoons finely chopped shallots
250 ml (8 fl oz) Home-made Fish (page 34) or Chicken (page 32) Stock
175 ml (6 fl oz) crème fraîche
Salt and freshly ground five-pepper mixture (page 21) or black pepper
225 g (8 oz) frozen petits pois
Chive-flavoured Olive Oil (page 37), to serve (optional)
2 tablespoons finely chopped fresh chives, to garnish

Peel the prawns and discard the shells. Using a small, sharp knife, remove the fine digestive cords. Wash the prawns in cold water with a tablespoon of salt. Drain and repeat. Rinse well and pat dry with kitchen paper. Cut the salmon into 2.5 cm (1 in) cubes. Sprinkle the salmon and prawns evenly with the rest of the salt plus the five-pepper mixture and cayenne pepper.

If you are using fresh tomatoes, cut them into 2.5 cm (1 in) cubes. If you are using tinned tomatoes, chop them into small chunks.

Peel and roll-cut the carrots by cutting a 5 cm (2 in) diagonal slice at one end and then rolling the carrot halfway before making the next diagonal slice. Blanch the carrots in salted, boiling water for 3 minutes. Remove and drain well.

Heat a wok or pan until it is hot, add the butter and quickly stir-fry the prawns and salmon cubes for 3 minutes. Remove and set aside.

Return the wok or pan to the heat, add the ginger and shallots and stir-fry over a high heat for 1 minute. Then add the stock and continue to cook over a high heat, stirring, until the stock has reduced by half. Now add the crème fraîche, season to taste, add the peas and carrots and cook for 2 minutes. Finally add the prawns, salmon and tomatoes and heat for 1 minute. Pour the mixture onto a warm platter, drizzle with chive-flavoured olive oil, if using, sprinkle with chives and serve at once.

GRILLED ASIAN CRÉPINETTES ≈

SERVES 4
(MAKES 20 CRÉPINETTES)

225 g (8 oz) caul fat
(*crépine*) (page 25)
450 g (1 lb) raw prawns
2 tablespoons plus
    1 teaspoon salt
225 g (8 oz) boneless,
    skinless firm white fish,
    such as halibut or cod,
    coarsely chopped
4 tablespoons finely
    chopped fresh basil
3 tablespoons finely
    chopped fresh coriander
1 tablespoon finely chopped
    fresh ginger (page 17)
2 teaspoons finely chopped
    garlic
2 teaspoons roasted and
    ground Sichuan
    peppercorns (page 21)
2 teaspoons seeded and
    coarsely chopped fresh red
    chillies (page 16)
1 tablespoon light soy sauce
    (page 23)
1 tablespoon dark soy sauce
    (page 23)
2 tablespoons Shaoxing rice
    wine (page 22) or dry
    sherry
1 tablespoon extra virgin
    olive oil

BOTH THE FRENCH AND CHINESE USE *CRÉPINE*, OR CAUL FAT FROM THE PIG, QUITE EXTENSIVELY. IT CAN BE ORDERED FROM YOUR BUTCHER. WRAPPING FOOD IN A LIGHT NET OF FAT KEEPS THE FILLING MOIST AND FLAVOURFUL, WHILE INFUSING IT WITH THE RICH TASTE OF THE CAUL FAT. THIS IS AN ADAPTATION OF THE CHINESE IDEA OF WRAPPING FISH, WHICH IS USUALLY POUNDED INTO A PASTE. IN THIS RECIPE I COARSELY CHOP THE SEAFOOD INSTEAD; THEN, AFTER WRAPPING IT IN THE CAUL FAT, I GRILL IT, WHICH GIVES IT A WONDERFUL, SMOKY AROMA. THE *CRÉPINETTES* ARE DELICIOUS WHEN SERVED WITH CHIPS.

Soak the caul fat in a bowl of cold water for 20 minutes. This will allow it to unravel easily.

Peel the prawns and discard the shells. Using a small, sharp knife, remove the fine digestive cords. Wash the prawns in cold water with a tablespoon of salt. Drain and repeat. Rinse well and pat dry with kitchen paper. Coarsely chop the prawns.

In a medium-sized bowl, mix the prawns, fish and all the other ingredients. Mix well.

Remove the caul fat from the water and pat dry with a tea-towel. Cut the caul fat into twenty 13 cm (5 in) squares. Lay out a square of caul fat and place 3 tablespoons of prawn–fish mixture in the middle. Fold in each side in turn to make a parcel. Repeat with the other squares until you have used up the entire mixture. Up to this point, the *crépinettes* can be made at least 3 hours ahead of time, refrigerated and wrapped with cling film until you are ready to cook them.

Pre-heat the oven grill to high or make a charcoal fire in the barbecue. When the grill is very hot or the charcoal is ash-white, grill the *crépinettes* on each side for 3 minutes, until golden brown and crisp. Serve at once.

Simple Grilled Fusion Fish ≈

Serves 4

4 x 150 g (5 oz) boneless, skinless halibut or sea bass fillets, or 1 whole fish, weighing 1 kg (2¼ lb)

For the Marinade:

6 tablespoons lime juice
3 tablespoons finely chopped fresh ginger (page 17)
6 tablespoons finely chopped spring onions
2 tablespoons fish sauce (page 23) or light soy sauce (page 23)
2 tablespoon mirin (Japanese sweet rice wine) (page 18)
1 tablespoon sesame oil
1 teaspoon salt
½ teaspoon freshly ground five-pepper mixture (page 21) or black pepper

To Garnish:

1½ tablespoons finely chopped fresh coriander
Orange-flavoured Oil (page 38), to serve
Lemon-flavoured Oil (page 38), to serve

Barbecue grilling is a favourite technique of many fusion chefs mainly because, besides being quick and easy, it is a way of adding new textures and flavours to foods, especially meats and seafood. Intense heat from the hot coals gives a nicely seasoned crust while imparting a lovely, smoky flavour. At the same time, the flesh below the crust remains moist. This style of cooking works especially well with fresh, firm white fish. Marinating it before grilling introduces even more subtle blends of flavour. This recipe is perfect for warm-weather al fresco dining, but the fish can of course be cooked under the grill. Serve with vegetables to make a complete, satisfying meal.

Blot the fish dry with kitchen paper. If you are using whole fish, make three slashes on each side of the fish.

Combine the marinade ingredients in a bowl. Add the fish and mix thoroughly. Marinate for 1 hour at room temperature, turning the fish from time to time.

Pre-heat the oven grill to high or make a charcoal fire in the barbecue. When the grill is very hot or the charcoal is ash-white, grill the fish fillets for 5–8 minutes (depending on their thickness) on each side, or the whole fish for 10–12 minutes on each side.

Garnish with chopped coriander and serve immediately, drizzled with either or both orange- and lemon-flavoured oils.

STEAMED FISH IN HERB BUTTER SAUCE ≈

FUSION COOKERY ENTAILS THE ADOPTION OF NEW TECHNIQUES AS WELL AS THE ACCEPTANCE OF NEW INGREDIENTS AND FOOD COMBINATIONS. I AM VERY HAPPY TO SEE THAT EUROPEAN CHEFS ARE DISCOVERING THE ADVANTAGES OF THE STEAMING TECHNIQUE, ESPECIALLY AS APPLIED TO FISH. MY SOUTHERN-CHINESE COOKING HERITAGE PRESCRIBES THIS METHOD AS THE BEST WAY TO PREPARE FRESH FISH. COOKED SO GENTLY, THE FISH RETAINS ITS SUCCULENCE, TENDERNESS AND FRESH TASTE.

HERE, I COMBINE FRESH FISH WITH DELICATE EUROPEAN AND ASIAN HERBS IN A LIGHT BUTTER SAUCE; TOGETHER, THEY HIGHLIGHT THE SUBTLE FLAVOUR OF THE FISH. STEAMED RICE (PAGE 35) COMPLEMENTS THE DISH PERFECTLY. ALWAYS ASK YOUR FISHMONGER FOR THE FRESHEST FISH POSSIBLE.

Pat the fish fillets dry with kitchen paper. Rub with the salt and pepper on both sides, and then set aside for 30 minutes at room temperature.

Next, set up a steamer or put a rack into a wok or deep pan and pour in 5 cm (2 in) of water. Bring the water to the boil over a high heat. Put the fish on a heatproof plate. Put the plate of fish into the steamer or onto the rack. Cover the pan tightly and gently steam the fish until it is just cooked. Flat fish such as sole or turbot will take about 5 minutes to cook. Thicker fish, such as sea bass and cod, or fillets of them, will take 12–14 minutes.

While the fish is steaming, heat a small pan and add the shallots. Cook in the dry pan for 2 minutes, until fairly dried but not browned. Add the rice wine or sherry and cook until all the liquid has evaporated; then add the stock and cook over a high heat until it has been reduced by half. Slowly whisk in the butter, a piece at a time.

Remove the plate of cooked fish and arrange on a warm platter. Add the fresh herbs to the sauce, pour this over the fish and serve at once.

SERVES 4

450 g (1 lb) firm white fish fillets, such as cod, sole or turbot
1 teaspoon salt
½ teaspoon freshly ground five-pepper mixture (page 21) or black pepper

For the Herb Butter Sauce:

3 tablespoons finely chopped shallots
3 tablespoons Shaoxing rice wine (page 22) or dry sherry
150 ml (5 fl oz) Home-made Fish (page 34) or Chicken (page 32) Stock
5 tablespoons (65 g/2½ oz) cold unsalted butter, cut in small pieces
1½ tablespoons finely chopped fresh chives
1 tablespoon finely chopped fresh coriander
1 tablespoon finely chopped fresh parsley
2 teaspoons finely chopped fresh chervil

WOK-ROASTED TUNA WITH SPICES ≈

SERVES 4

4 x 100 g (4 oz) thickly cut
tuna fillets
3 tablespoons olive oil

For the Marinade:

2 tablespoons light soy
  sauce (page 23)
2 tablespoons mirin
  (Japanese sweet rice wine)
  (page 18) or dry sherry
1 tablespoon sesame oil
½ teaspoon salt
¼ teaspoon freshly ground
  five-pepper mixture
  (page 21) or black pepper

For the Spice Mixture:

1 teaspoon roasted, ground
  Sichuan peppercorns
  (page 21)
1 teaspoon ground cumin
1 teaspoon freshly ground
  five-pepper mixture
  (page 21) or black pepper
1 teaspoon salt
½ teaspoon five-spice
  powder (page 17)
1 teaspoon sugar

To Garnish:

1 tablespoon finely chopped
  fresh coriander
2 tablespoons finely
  chopped spring onions

JAPANESE FOOD, ESPECIALLY *SUSHI* AND *SASHIMI*, USING FRESH AND HIGH-QUALITY TUNA, HAS BECOME POPULAR. FUSION COOKS HAVE USED THE IDEA OF RAW TUNA BUT WITH A TWIST: TUNA IS SEARED QUICKLY ON THE OUTSIDE, WITH THE INTERIOR REMAINING RARE. IT MAKES SENSE, AS TUNA CAN OVERCOOK QUICKLY AND DRY OUT. HOWEVER, THE TUNA NEEDS A MARINADE AND SPICES TO COMPENSATE FOR THE SHORT COOKING TIME. ASIAN SPICES ARE IDEAL FOR ADDING ZEST TO AN OTHERWISE BLAND DISH. AGAIN, IT IS IMPORTANT TO GET THE BEST-QUALITY TUNA YOU CAN AFFORD. STEAMED RICE (PAGE 35) GOES WELL WITH THIS DISH.

Lay the tuna fillets on a platter. In a small bowl, combine the marinade ingredients and drizzle the mixture evenly over the tuna. Allow to sit for 1 hour at room temperature.

In a bowl, combine the Sichuan peppercorns, cumin, pepper, salt, five-spice powder and sugar and mix well.

Remove the tuna from the marinade with a slotted spoon and dry with kitchen paper. Set the marinade aside; it will be used later. Sprinkle the spice mixture evenly on both sides of the tuna fillets.

Heat a frying-pan over a high heat and when it is hot, add the oil. When the oil is slightly smoking, add the tuna fillets and sear them on one side for 2 minutes; turn over and sear the other side for another 2 minutes. Remove them to a warm platter. The tuna should remain rare. Quickly pour off the excess oil, pour in the reserved marinade and deglaze the pan for 30 seconds. Pour this liquid over the tuna, garnish with coriander and spring onions and serve at once.

WOK-SMOKED FISH ≈

SERVES 4

2 teaspoons sugar
1 teaspoon plus ½ teaspoon
   salt
250 ml (8 fl oz) water
450 g (1 lb) fresh firm white
   fish fillets, such as sea bass
   or cod
1 teaspoon five-spice
   powder (page 17)
1 teaspoon dried thyme
¼ teaspoon ground five-
   pepper mixture (page 21)
   or black pepper
Vegetable oil, for greasing

For the Smoking Mixture:
50 g (2 oz) long-grain
   white rice
3 tablespoons brown sugar
25 g (1 oz) black tea leaves
   (page 24)

SMOKED FOODS HAVE A SUBTLE, HAUNTING AROMA AND TASTE. SMOKING IS A POPULAR TECHNIQUE USED BY FUSION COOKS BECAUSE IT IS EASY TO COMBINE ANY INGREDIENT AND TASTE.

MOST RESTAURANTS HAVE LARGE SMOKING OVENS; THE HOME COOK, HOWEVER, CAN EASILY REPLICATE THE METHOD BY USING A WOK OR A LARGE CASSEROLE. THE FISH IS BRIEFLY SOAKED AND THEN RUBBED WITH A COMBINATION OF EASTERN AND WESTERN SPICES AND SMOKED. SIMPLE AND QUICK, SMOKED FISH CAN BE MADE IN ADVANCE FOR CONVENIENCE. SERVE IT WITH VEGETABLES AS A MAIN COURSE OR WITH A SALAD AS A STARTER.

Mix the sugar, 1 teaspoon of salt and the water together and pour into a deep dish. Then add the fish, cover and put in the refrigerator for 30 minutes.

Combine the five-spice powder, thyme, the rest of the salt and the pepper in a small bowl. Remove the fish and blot dry with kitchen paper. Sprinkle the spice mixture evenly on both sides of the fish.

Line the inside of a wok with foil. Add the rice, sugar and tea leaves. Rub a rack with vegetable oil and place it over the smoking ingredients. Slowly heat the wok and, when the smoking mixture begins to smoke, put the fish on the rack and cover the wok tightly with foil. Turn the heat to moderate and smoke for 8–10 minutes, depending on the thickness of the fish. Remove from the heat and allow the fish to sit, covered, for another 2 minutes. When the fish is cool enough to handle, cut it into slices. Discard the smoking mixture and the foil, and serve the fish.

Steamed Fish with Lettuce and Chillies ≈

STEAMING IS A HEALTHY AND EASY TECHNIQUE FOR COOKING PERFECT FISH. THE HOT STEAM KEEPS THE FISH MOIST AND ALL THE NATURAL FLAVOURS ARE PRESERVED. IT IS A COMMON AND POPULAR METHOD, WIDELY USED IN ASIA AND NOW IN EUROPE TOO. IN THIS RECIPE, THE FISH IS STEAMED AND SERVED WITH BRAISED LETTUCE AND CHILLIES – AN UNUSUAL AND DELICIOUS ACCOMPANIMENT. DRIZZLE WITH ORANGE-FLAVOURED OIL.

Sprinkle the fish fillets evenly with salt, pepper and paprika. Put the fillets on a deep, heatproof plate and evenly scatter with the garlic and ginger.

Next, set up a steamer or put a rack into a wok or deep pan and pour in 5 cm (2 in) of water. Bring the water to the boil over a high heat. Carefully lower the fish and plate into the steamer or onto the rack. Turn the heat to low and cover the wok or pan tightly. Steam gently for 8–10 minutes, depending on the thickness of the fillets. Top up with boiling water from time to time.

While the fish is steaming, separate the lettuce leaves, trimming the tops. Then melt the butter in a large pan, add the chillies, water, salt, pepper, sugar and lettuce. Bring to a simmer, cover and simmer for 15 minutes.

When the fish is cooked, remove the plate from the steamer or wok. Drain the lettuce, reserving the liquid. Place the lettuce on a warm platter, arranging the fish on top. Reduce the liquid by half, stir in the crème fraîche, then pour this over the fish. Drizzle with the orange-flavoured oil and serve at once.

Serves 4

450 g (1 lb) fish fillets, such as cod or sea bass, divided into 4 equal parts
1 teaspoon salt
½ teaspoon freshly ground five-pepper mixture (page 21) or white pepper
1 teaspoon paprika
1 tablespoon coarsely chopped garlic
2 teaspoons finely chopped fresh ginger (page 17)
2 tablespoons crème fraîche
Orange-flavoured Oil (page 38), to serve

For the Lettuce:

450 g (1 lb) cos lettuce
2 tablespoons (25 g/1 oz) unsalted butter
2 fresh red or green chillies (page 16), seeded and finely shredded
4 tablespoons water
1 teaspoon salt
½ teaspoon freshly ground five-pepper mixture (page 21) or black pepper
1 teaspoon sugar

STEAMED FISH IN CHINESE LEAVES ≈

SERVES 4

450 g (1 lb) fresh, firm white
    fish fillets, such as cod or
    sea bass
1 head of Chinese leaves
    (page 14)
1 teaspoon sea salt
1 teaspoon roasted and
    ground Sichuan peppercorns
    (page 21)

For the Sauce:

3 tablespoons chopped shallots
1 tablespoon finely chopped
    fresh ginger (page 17)
3 tablespoons Shaoxing rice
    wine (page 22) or dry sherry
6 tablespoons Home-made Fish
    (page 34) or Chicken
    (page 32) Stock
2 teaspoons fine lemon zest
1 teaspoon fine orange zest
2 tablespoons (25 g/1 oz)
    cold unsalted butter, cut in
    small pieces
Salt and freshly ground white
    pepper
2 teaspoons finely chopped
    fresh coriander
2 teaspoons finely chopped
    fresh chives
1 teaspoon finely chopped
    spring onion
1 tablespoon finely chopped
    red pepper
Basil-flavoured (page 36) and
    Tomato-flavoured (page 40)
    Olive Oil, to serve (optional)

GROWING UP IN A CHINESE HOUSEHOLD, I HAVE ALWAYS KNOWN THAT STEAMING IS THE BEST WAY TO COOK THE FRESHEST FISH. DELICATE, HOT VAPOURS KEEP THE FISH MOIST AND SUCCULENT, WITHOUT COMPROMISING ITS BRINY FLAVOUR. HERE, I HAVE WRAPPED THE FISH IN CHINESE LEAVES (ALSO KNOWN AS CHINESE CABBAGE) FOR A SPECTACULAR PRESENTATION WHICH ALSO KEEPS THE FISH EVEN MOISTER. THEN I SERVE IT WITH A FUSION SAUCE, WHICH MAKES THE BEST OF EAST AND WEST. THIS IS A PERFECT DISH FOR A SPECIAL DINNER PARTY, ESPECIALLY WHEN DRIZZLED WITH FLAVOURED OLIVE OILS. SERVE IT WITH VEGETABLES OR RICE.

Divide the fillets into four equal portions. Remove four of the largest leaves from the Chinese leaves and blanch them in boiling water for 1 minute. Drain and allow to cool. Place each fillet on one end of a leaf. Sprinkle with sea salt and Sichuan peppercorns. Roll up each leaf, folding in the sides as you go.

Next, set up a steamer or put a rack into a wok or deep pan and pour in 5 cm (2 in) of water. Bring the water to the boil over a high heat. Put the wrapped fish onto a heatproof plate and then carefully lower it into the steamer or onto the rack. Turn the heat to low and cover the wok or pan tightly. Steam gently for 8 minutes, or until the fish is cooked. Remove the fish from the steamer, pour off any liquid on the plate into a small bowl and reserve.

While the fish is steaming, combine the shallots and ginger in a pan and cook for 1 minute until dry; then add the rice wine or sherry and cook over a high heat until all the wine has evaporated. Now add the stock and any reserved steaming liquid and reduce by half. Add the lemon and orange zest. Then slowly whisk in the butter and salt and pepper to taste. Toss in the coriander, chives, spring onion and pepper. Cook for 30 seconds. Pour the sauces over each leaf-wrapped fish. Drizzle with basil-flavoured and tomato-flavoured olive oils, if using, and serve.

MEAT

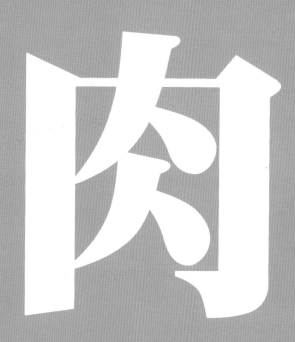

Fast-grilled Steak with Five Spices ≈

Serves 4

4 entrecôte (sirloin) or rump
   steaks, weighing about
   175–225 g (6–8 oz) each
1 tablespoon olive oil

For the Spice Mixture:

2 teaspoons salt
½ teaspoon freshly ground
   five-pepper mixture
   (page 21) or black pepper
1 teaspoon five-spice
   powder (page 17)
½ teaspoon roasted and
   ground Sichuan
   peppercorns (page 21)
2 teaspoons paprika
1 teaspoon Madras curry
   powder (page 17)

SPICES FROM ASIAN CUISINES ARE FREQUENTLY USED TO INCORPORATE EXOTIC TASTES AND FLAVOURS INTO FOOD. THEY ARE ABSORBED QUICKLY, MAKING THEM IDEAL FOR GRILLED FOODS. IN THIS RECIPE, I HAVE RELIED ON TRADITIONAL CHINESE FIVE-SPICE POWDER, COMBINED WITH OTHER SPICES TO INFUSE AN ORDINARY STEAK WITH SPECIAL AROMAS. SERVE THIS WITH SIMPLE BOILED OR SAUTÉD POTATOES.

Lay the steaks on a tray and rub with the olive oil.

In a small bowl, combine the spice mixture ingredients and mix well. Sprinkle the mixture evenly over the steaks on both sides and allow to sit in a cool place for 1 hour.

Pre-heat the oven grill to high or make a charcoal fire in the barbecue. When the oven grill is very hot or the charcoal is ash-white, grill the steaks on each side for about 5–6 minutes (if you like them rare) or longer if you want them well done.

Transfer to a warm platter and allow to rest for 10 minutes before serving.

Barbecued East–West Pork Satay ≈

A truly East-meets-West city is Singapore, where several different races and cultures merge harmoniously in a thriving, modern metropolis. I love eating in Singapore and always make a point of visiting the street food stalls that sell so many different styles of cooking, from Chinese regional cuisine and indigenous Malay foods to authentic Indian treats. The best of western food is also offered in restaurants and hotels. A personal favourite is satay: marinated meats, skewered and simply grilled. Here, I offer a version that combines the spices of two worlds. You can easily double the recipe for a larger crowd.

Cut the pork into 2.5 cm (1 in) cubes, trimming off any excess fat.

In a large bowl, combine the pork cubes with the marinade ingredients, mix well and allow to marinate for 2 hours in a cool place. Turn the meat from time to time.

Meanwhile, soak bamboo skewers in water for 30 minutes or so. Skewer the pork and set aside.

Pre-heat the oven grill to high or make a charcoal fire in the barbecue. When the grill is very hot or the charcoal is ash-white, cook the satay for 2 minutes on each side, until golden brown. Serve at once, drizzled with sesame and chilli oil, if you wish.

Serves 4

450 g (1 lb) tender, thick, boneless pork chops

For the Marinade:
1 tablespoon light soy sauce (page 23)
1 tablespoon pineapple juice
½ teaspoon salt
¼ teaspoon freshly ground five-pepper mixture (page 21) or black pepper
1 tablespoon mirin (Japanese sweet rice wine) (page 18) or dry sherry
½ teaspoon dried thyme
¼ teaspoon ground coriander
1 teaspoon sugar
1 tablespoon olive oil
2 teaspoons finely chopped lemon zest
Sesame and Chilli Oil (page 39), to serve (optional)

GRILLED PORK CHOPS WITH CHINESE SPICES ≈

SERVES 4

4 x 100 g (4 oz) boneless
    pork chops

For the Seasoning Mixture:

1 teaspoon five-spice
    powder (page 17)
1½ teaspoons salt
½ teaspoon freshly ground
    five-pepper mixture
    (page 21) or black pepper
½ teaspoon roasted and
    ground Sichuan
    peppercorns (page 21)
½ teaspoon Madras curry
    powder (page 17)
1 teaspoon dried thyme
½ teaspoon cumin powder
Orange-flavoured Oil
    (page 38), to serve

GRILLING PORK CHOPS IS AN EASY METHOD FOR PUTTING TOGETHER AN APPETIZING MEAL WITH LITTLE EFFORT. THE SMOKE FROM THE GRILL CONTRIBUTES RICH FLAVOURS OF ITS OWN. THIS RECIPE IS ESPECIALLY EASY, USING CHINESE SEASONING COMBINED WITH A WESTERN TOUCH. SERVE THE CHOPS WITH VEGETABLES OR WITH CORN CRÊPES (PAGE 194) AND A SALAD.

Lay the pork chops on a large platter or tray. Combine the seasoning mixture in a small bowl, mixing well. Sprinkle half the seasoning mixture evenly over the pork chops, turn them over and sprinkle the remaining seasoning on the other side. Let the chops sit in a cool place for an hour.

Pre-heat the oven grill to high or make a charcoal fire in the barbecue. When the grill is very hot or the charcoal is ash-white, grill the pork chops on each side for about 8 minutes. Remove to a platter and let sit for another 8 minutes before serving.

Serve with orange-flavoured oil drizzled on the side.

GRILLED PORK *CRÉPINETTES* ≈

SERVES 4
(MAKES 14–15
CRÉPINETTES)

225 g (8 oz) caul fat
  (*crépine*) (page 25)
450 g (1 lb) minced fatty
  pork
2 egg whites
1 teaspoon salt
½ teaspoon freshly ground
  five-pepper mixture
  (page 21) or black pepper
½ teaspoon roasted and
  ground Sichuan
  peppercorns (page 21)
2 teaspoons paprika
2 teaspoons cognac
3 tablespoons finely
  chopped spring onions
2 tablespoons finely
  chopped fresh chives
2 tablespoons finely
  chopped fresh coriander
2 tablespoons finely
  chopped fresh parsley
3 tablespoons finely
  chopped fresh basil
2 tablespoons finely
  chopped garlic
2 teaspoons finely chopped
  fresh ginger (page 17)
Plain flour, for dredging
2 eggs, beaten
25 g (1 oz) dried
  breadcrumbs

CRÉPINETTE IS THE FRENCH TERM FOR A SMALL, FLAT SAUSAGE, GENERALLY MADE OF MINCED MEAT WITH CHOPPED PARSLEY AND WRAPPED IN LACY CAUL FAT (*CRÉPINE*) FROM THE PIG. THE CAUL CAN BE OBTAINED FROM YOUR BUTCHER. THE LACY WRAPPING KEEPS THE MEAT MOIST AND JUICY. YOU CAN MAKE LITERALLY ANY MEAT AND SEASONING COMBINATION — AN IDEAL VEHICLE FOR FUSION CHEFS. IN THIS RECIPE, I HAVE CREATED A MARRIAGE OF EASTERN AND WESTERN SPICES AND HERBS FOR AN EASY AND SUCCULENT DISH. IT GOES ESPECIALLY WELL WITH POTATO AND CUCUMBER MASH (PAGE 186).

Soak the caul fat in a bowl of cold water for 20 minutes. This will allow it to unravel easily.

In a large bowl, combine the pork with the egg whites, salt, pepper, Sichuan pepper, paprika, cognac, spring onions, all the herbs, the garlic and ginger and mix well.

Remove the caul fat from the water and pat dry with a tea-towel. Cut the caul fat into twenty 13 cm (5 in) squares. Lay out a square of caul fat and place 3 tablespoons of pork mixture. Fold in each side in turn to make a parcel. Repeat until you have used up the entire mixture. Up to this point, the *crépinettes* can be made at least 3 hours ahead of time, wrapped with cling film and refrigerated until ready to cook.

When you are ready to cook the *crépinettes*, dust them with flour, shaking off any excess, then dip in the beaten egg and, finally, roll them in the breadcrumbs.

Pre-heat the oven grill to high or make a charcoal fire in the barbecue. When the oven grill is very hot or the charcoal is ash-white, grill the *crépinettes* on each side for 3 minutes, until golden brown and crisp. Serve at once.

BRAISED EAST-WEST OXTAIL STEW ≈

Here we have a delectable fusion of East and West flavours – soy sauce and rice wine from the East and tomatoes and orange zest from the West. Such flavours are assertive enough to stand up against the robust deliciousness of the oxtail. This is a hearty and satisfying autumn or winter dish that can easily be reheated. In fact, I think it tastes even better the next day. Serve with Steamed Rice (page 35) or pasta.

In a large pan, cook the oxtail pieces in boiling water for 20 minutes. Remove and drain well.

Heat a wok or large frying-pan until it is hot. Add the groundnut oil and slowly brown the oxtail on all sides. Remove the oxtail with a slotted spoon and pour off and discard the excess fat. Now add the olive oil, onions, shallots and garlic and stir-fry the mixture for about 3 minutes. Then add the tomatoes, stock, the two rice wines or sherry, orange zest, hoisin sauce, soy sauce, salt and pepper. Bring the mixture to the boil, reduce the heat to a simmer, cover tightly and cook for 3 hours, or until the oxtail pieces are tender.

Skim off any surface fat, garnish with coriander sprigs and serve at once.

SERVES 4–6

1.5 kg (3 lb) oxtail, jointed
2 tablespoons groundnut oil
2 tablespoons extra virgin olive oil
2 small onions, coarsely chopped
3 tablespoons finely sliced shallots
3 tablespoons coarsely chopped garlic
750 g (1½ lb) tinned tomatoes
250 ml (8 fl oz) Home-made Chicken Stock (page 32)
3 tablespoons Shaoxing rice wine (page 22) or dry sherry
2 tablespoons mirin (Japanese sweet rice wine) (page 18) or dry sherry
2 tablespoons finely chopped orange zest
3 tablespoons hoisin sauce (page 22)
2 tablespoons light soy sauce (page 23)
2 teaspoons salt
1 teaspoon freshly ground five-pepper mixture (page 21) or black pepper
Sprigs of fresh coriander, to garnish

KOREAN-STYLE GRILLED BEEF ≈

SERVES 4

450 g (1 lb) chuck steak,
  preferably on the fatty side
2 tablespoons light or
  Japanese soy sauce
  (page 23)
3 tablespoons pineapple juice
2 tablespoons mirin (Japanese
  sweet rice wine) (page 18)
  or dry sherry
1 tablespoon Shaoxing rice
  wine (page 22) or dry sherry
2 tablespoons finely chopped
  garlic
3 tablespoons finely chopped
  spring onions
1 tablespoon sesame oil
1 tablespoon sesame seeds,
  toasted (page 23)
1 teaspoon salt
1 teaspoon freshly ground five-
  pepper mixture (page 21)
  or black pepper
Gordon's Cranberry-ginger
  Relish (page 199), to serve

ONE OF THE TASTIEST BEEF DISHES I HAVE EVER EATEN WAS THIS DELECTABLE ONE FROM KOREA, POPULARLY KNOWN AS *KALBY*. IT RELIES ON A SIMPLE MARINADE AND QUICK GRILLING, WHICH GIVES THE BEEF A SMOKY FRAGRANCE. AND THE BONUS IS THAT YOU DON'T NEED AN EXPENSIVE CUT; ON THE CONTRARY, THE FAT FROM A CHEAPER CUT CONTRIBUTES ADDITIONAL FLAVOUR. THE PINEAPPLE JUICE BREAKS DOWN THE FIBRES OF THE BEEF AND MAKES IT QUITE TENDER AS WELL. RICE OR POTATOES GO WELL WITH THIS DISH.

Cut the chuck steak into 10 cm x 5 mm (4 x ¼ in) pieces. Combine the soy sauce, pineapple juice, mirin and rice wine or sherry, garlic, spring onions, sesame oil, sesame seeds and salt and pepper. Let the beef marinate for 1 hour at room temperature.

Pre-heat the oven grill to high or make a charcoal fire in the barbecue.

Meanwhile, soak long bamboo skewers in cold water. Remove from the water after 30 minutes.

Skewer the beef on the bamboo sticks and set aside. When the grill is very hot or the charcoal is ash-white, grill the beef for a few minutes on each side. Serve at once with Gordon's cranberry-ginger relish.

FAST-BARBECUED RIBS ≈

SERVES 4–6

1.5 kg (3½ lb) pork
    spare ribs
2 teaspoons salt
1 teaspoon freshly ground
    five-pepper mixture
    (page 21) or black pepper

For the Sauce:
5 tablespoons hoisin sauce
    (page 22)
3 tablespoons sesame oil
2 tablespoons light soy
    sauce (page 23)
2 tablespoons dark soy
    sauce (page 23)
2 tablespoons mirin
    (Japanese sweet rice wine)
    (page 18) or Shaoxing
    rice wine (page 22) or dry
    sherry
3 tablespoons coarsely
    chopped garlic
2 teaspoons finely chopped
    fresh ginger (page 17)
2 tablespoons chilli-bean
    sauce (page 22)
2 teaspoons sugar
3 tablespoons dried thyme
1 tablespoon Dijon mustard

THERE ARE VERY FEW FOODS WHICH ARE AS MUCH FUN TO EAT AS PORK SPARE RIBS. JUICY AND BURSTING WITH FLAVOURS – THEY ARE FAIRLY EASY TO PREPARE IF YOU TRY MY METHOD. THE SPARE RIBS ARE FIRST COOKED IN A LOW OVEN FOR 1 HOUR TO RENDER SOME OF THE FAT AND TO TENDERIZE THEM AT THE SAME TIME. THIS CAN BE DONE HOURS IN ADVANCE. THEN I MAKE A SIMPLE SAUCE USING CHINESE AND EUROPEAN INGREDIENTS. SINCE THE SPARE RIBS ARE ALREADY COOKED, IT TAKES BUT 20 MINUTES TO FINISH THEM OFF. THIS IS A WONDERFUL SUMMERTIME TREAT WHEN COOKED ON A CHARCOAL GRILL BUT CAN BE JUST AS EASILY COOKED UNDER THE OVEN GRILL. THESE RIBS GO EXTREMELY WELL WITH COLD KOREAN-STYLE NOODLES (PAGE 216).

Pre-heat the oven to 150°C/300°F/gas mark 2.

Put the spare ribs in a baking dish and sprinkle both sides evenly with salt and pepper. Put into the oven and cook for 1 hour. Remove from the oven. The spare ribs can be done at least four hours in advance up to this point.

Combine the sauce ingredients in a blender and mix well.

Pre-heat the oven grill to high or make a charcoal fire in the barbecue. When the oven grill is very hot or the charcoal is ash-white, baste the ribs on both sides with the sauce ingredients and grill for 10 minutes on each side. Serve at once.

Neil Perry's Red-cooked Pork Belly with Chinese Mushrooms ≈

Neil Perry is a talented chef, with a personal style that typifies fusion cookery. He uses his finely honed skills to create contemporary Australian cuisine, drawing from Europe and Asia. I especially love this recipe from his flagship restaurant, Rockpool. Neil's love of Asian food was such that he later opened another popular restaurant, Wokpool, which made only foods from Asia. Fortunately, this classic dish remains on the menu and is still one of my favourites from his repertoire. Neil uses pork hock, which I have changed to pork belly. The long braising infuses the pork with the types of flavours which fusion chefs are using throughout the world. Serve this with Green Rice (page 203).

Cut the unpeeled ginger into six fine slices. Put the ginger with the water and rice wine or sherry into a large pan or casserole. Bring the liquid to a simmer and then add the pork belly. Simmer slowly for 45 minutes, skimming all the while.

Then add the soy sauces, sugar, star anise, cinnamon, chillies, garlic, spring onions and salt. Cover the pan tightly and continue to simmer for 1½–2 hours or until the pork is very tender.

While the pork is simmering, soak the mushrooms in warm water for 20 minutes. Then drain them and squeeze out the excess liquid. Remove and discard the stems, leaving the mushrooms whole.

When the pork is cooked, add the mushrooms and simmer for an additional 15 minutes. Remove the pork from the pan and let it cool slightly. (The braising liquid can now be cooled and frozen for re-use. Remove any surface fat before transferring it to the freezer.) Slice the meat thinly and arrange on a warm platter with the mushrooms and sauce. Serve at once.

Serves 6–8

1.5 kg (3 lb) boneless pork belly, with rind
50g (2 oz) dried Chinese black mushrooms (page 18)

For the Braising Liquid:

2.5 cm (1 in) fresh ginger (page 17)
1.2 litres (2 pints) water
600 ml (1 pint) Shaoxing rice wine (page 22) or dry sherry
150 ml (5 fl oz) light soy sauce (page 23)
50 ml (2 fl oz) dark soy sauce (page 23)
150 g (5 oz) Chinese rock sugar (page 24) or plain sugar
4 star anise (page 23)
3 cinnamon sticks
3 dried red chillies (page 15)
6 garlic cloves, crushed
6 spring onions, whole
2 teaspoons salt

ROAST LAMB WITH ASIAN FLAVOURS ≈

SERVES 4–6

2 x 350–450 g
(12 oz–1 lb) best ends of
Welsh lamb
½ teaspoon salt
½ teaspoon freshly ground
five-pepper mixture
(page 21) or black pepper
1 tablespoon groundnut oil
3 tablespoons finely
chopped shallots,
squeezed dry
2 tablespoons finely
chopped fresh coriander
2 tablespoons finely chopped
fresh flatleaf parsley
2 teaspoons finely chopped
garlic
2 teaspoons finely chopped
fresh ginger (page 17)
25 g (1 oz) fresh
breadcrumbs
1 tablespoon sesame oil
3 tablespoons (35 g/1½ oz)
melted butter

There are few dishes as exquisite as roast lamb cutlets. Though expensive, they are worth every penny, particularly for a special occasion. The French method of roasting best end of lamb with a seasoned breadcrumb mixture is a popular and easy preparation which I love. However, I cannot resist altering the recipe to add my own fusion touches. Serve with either Ginger-leek Purée (page 191) or Gordon's Cranberry-ginger Relish (page 199).

Ask your butcher to trim the silvery-blue skin off the lamb and to dress the bones by removing the meat and fat between the bones. Season the lamb all over with salt and pepper.

Pre-heat the oven to 240°C/475°F/gas mark 9.

Heat the oil in a large frying-pan and, when it is hot and slightly smoking, brown the lamb until it is golden brown. Remove and arrange inside a roasting tin.

In a bowl, combine the shallots, coriander, parsley, garlic, ginger, breadcrumbs, sesame oil and butter, mixing with chopsticks. Cover the lamb on all sides with this mixture, pressing down with your hands so the mixture adheres to the meat.

Roast in the oven with the meaty side up for 15 minutes. Remove and keep warm for 15 minutes before serving. Carve and serve at once.

Asian Roast Beef with East–West Yorkshire Pudding ≈

Serves 6–8

2.75 kg (6 lb) beef joint on the bone

For the Seasoning:

1 teaspoon salt
1 teaspoon five-spice powder (page 17)
2 teaspoons freshly ground five-pepper mixture (page 21) or black pepper
1 teaspoon ground cumin
2 teaspoons roasted and ground Sichuan peppercorns (page 21)
2 tablespoons dried thyme
1 tablespoon dried oregano
2 teaspoons paprika
1 teaspoon chilli powder

For the East–West Yorkshire Pudding:

5 eggs, beaten
150 g (5 oz) plain flour
475 ml (16 fl oz) milk
1½ teaspoons salt
½ teaspoon freshly ground five-pepper mixture (page 21) or black pepper
3 tablespoons finely chopped spring onions
2 tablespoons finely chopped fresh chives
2 teaspoons finely chopped fresh ginger (page 17)
1 tablespoon finely chopped fresh coriander
150 ml (5 fl oz) reserved fat from the roasting tin

Although I rarely eat beef, when I do I always try to get the best that I can afford. I look for organic beef, where possible, with meat marbled throughout; the fat melts during cooking and gives the meat an intense flavour. Here, I have taken the English traditional roast beef and have added a dash of Asian-inspired spices, together with dried European herbs. I wholeheartedly agree with Delia Smith's advice to buy a joint *on the bone*. A good bit of advice is to have your butcher remove the beef from the bones and then retie it, with the bones. The bones act as good conductors of heat and help the beef to cook evenly with less loss of juices.

I like my roast beef rare throughout and the secret is to let the beef rest for an hour in a turned-off oven. It will continue to cook slowly, with all the juices intact. Of course, if you prefer beef well cooked, simply increase the cooking time by 15–30 minutes. Serve with your favourite vegetables.

Pre-heat the oven to 220°C/425°F/gas mark 7.

Combine all the ingredients for the seasoning in a small bowl. Rub this mixture all over the top and sides of the joint. Place the beef, bone-down, in a large roasting tin.

Put the beef in the oven for 25 minutes. Then reduce the heat to 190°C/375°F/gas mark 5 and cook for 1 hour.

Now turn off the heat and let the beef rest in the oven for 1 hour.

Remove the beef and pour off the fat (which can be saved for your favourite Yorkshire pudding recipe or the East–West recipe below); the juices can also be saved and served with the carved beef. Let the roast rest at room temperature for 20 minutes before carving.

Turn the oven back up to 220°C/425°F/gas mark 7 to cook the pudding. Combine the eggs and flour in a large bowl or food processor and beat until smooth. Then add the milk, salt, pepper and the herbs.

Put the reserved fat in a large roasting tin and place on the hob. Heat until the fat is very hot and sizzling. Pour the batter mixture into the roasting pan and put it immediately in the oven. Cook for 30 minutes or until the pudding is golden and crisp. Serve at once, with the roast beef.

MEAT

ROAST MUSTARD-SOY SAUCE LEG OF LAMB ≈

ROAST LEG OF LAMB IS A DISCOVERY I MADE WHILE LIVING IN FRANCE, DURING MY UNIVERSITY DAYS IN PROVENCE. MY ADOPTIVE FRENCH MOTHER WOULD ROAST LAMB SIMPLY, WITH GARLIC AND FRESH ROSEMARY. I COULD NOT RESIST ADDING MY ASIAN CULINARY HERITAGE TO THIS CLASSIC RECIPE – SOY SAUCE. I OBSERVED THAT IT WORKED WONDERS ON LAMB. THIS EAST–WEST ADAPTATION ADDS A SAVOURY TWIST TO THIS DELICIOUS DISH. IT GOES ESPECIALLY WELL WITH GORDON'S CRANBERRY-GINGER RELISH (PAGE 199); SERVE WITH POTATOES AND OTHER VEGETABLES.

Pre-heat the oven to 180°C/350°F/gas mark 4.

Slice the garlic into small slivers. With a small, sharp knife, make small slits throughout the leg of lamb and insert the slivers of garlic.

Mix the mustard, soy sauces, salt, pepper, sesame oil, rosemary and ginger in a blender. Rub this mixture all over the lamb.

Place the lamb in a roasting tin and cook for 1½ hours. If you like it well done, give it another 30 minutes. Remove the joint to a warm serving dish in a warm place and let it rest for at least 30 minutes before you begin to carve. Serve at once.

SERVES 4–6

5 garlic cloves
1 leg of lamb,
    about 1.75 kg (4 lb)
5 tablespoons Dijon mustard
3 tablespoons dark soy
    sauce (page 23)
2 tablespoons light soy
    sauce (page 23)
2 teaspoons salt
1 teaspoon freshly ground
    five-pepper mixture
    (page 21) or black pepper
2 tablespoons sesame oil
3 tablespoons crushed fresh
    rosemary leaves
2 teaspoons finely chopped
    fresh ginger (page 17)

Grilled Lamb with Sesame Sauce ≈

Serves 4

4 x 175 g (6 oz) lean
  lamb chops

For the Marinade:
1½ tablespoons sesame oil
2 teaspoons light soy sauce
  (page 23)
1 teaspoon salt
1 teaspoon roasted and
  ground Sichuan
  peppercorns (page 21)
½ teaspoon freshly ground
  five-pepper mixture
  (page 21) or black pepper
1 tablespoon dried thyme
2 teaspoons whole dried
  rosemary leaves

For the Sesame Sauce:
3 tablespoons highest quality
  Japanese sesame paste
  (page 23) or creamy
  peanut butter
2 tablespoons mirin
  (Japanese sweet rice wine)
  (page 18) or dry sherry
1 tablespoon Japanese white
  rice vinegar (page 24)
1 teaspoon salt
½ teaspoon freshly ground
  black pepper
6 tablespoons Home-made
  Chicken Stock (page 32)
2 tablespoons finely
  chopped spring onions

Lamb was not a meat I had known in my Chinese childhood. The first time I had lamb was in France; I was surprised by its assertive, but delectable, flavour. I quickly learned that lamb marries well with Asian spices. In this recipe, I serve the lamb with a Japanese-inspired sauce. Use the most expensive Japanese sesame paste you can afford; the higher the price, the better the quality. Serve this delicious lamb with potatoes done to your liking.

Mix the marinade ingredients together in a small bowl. Rub the lamb chops evenly with this mixture. Allow the meat to marinate for 1 hour at room temperature.

Pre-heat the oven grill to high or make a charcoal fire in the barbecue. When the grill is very hot or the charcoal is ash-white, grill the lamb chops for about 8 minutes on each side, until medium rare. Remove from the grill, reserving any cooking juices, and let the chops sit on a warm platter for at least 20 minutes.

In a pan, combine the sesame paste, mirin or sherry, vinegar, salt, pepper and stock. Mix vigorously. Bring to the boil and reduce slightly. Meanwhile, pour the reserved lamb juices and any that may have accumulated on the platter into the sauce, with the spring onions. Pour the sauce over the lamb chops and serve at once.

Braised Shoulder of Lamb with Chinese Flavours ≈

Serves 4–6

1.5 kg–1.75 kg (3½–4 lb)
  shoulder of lamb
2 teaspoons salt
1 teaspoon freshly ground
  five-pepper mixture
  (page 21) or black pepper
3 tablespoons groundnut oil
20 garlic cloves, unpeeled
1 tablespoon finely chopped
  fresh ginger (page 17)
3 tablespoons finely sliced
  shallots
3 tablespoons Shaoxing
  rice wine (page 22)
  or dry sherry
2 tablespoons light soy
  sauce (page 23)
1 tablespoon chilli-bean
  sauce (page 22)
475 ml (16 fl oz) Home-
  made Chicken Stock
  (page 32)
4 small fresh sprigs of
  rosemary
3 fresh sprigs of thyme
2 tablespoons finely
  chopped fresh coriander
2 tablespoons finely
  chopped fresh chives

Shoulder of lamb is not only economical but deliciously sweet, especially when rolled and braised. Although it is not a food that I have grown up with, I learned to appreciate it while living in France. I think it goes especially well with a hint of Chinese combined with a touch of European seasoning. You will also find this an excellent dinner-party dish, especially when served with Fragrant Fried Ginger and Spring Onion Rice (page 202). The bonus is that it also reheats well.

Ask your butcher to bone the shoulder of lamb. Be sure to ask for the bone.

Pre-heat the oven to 190°C/375°F/gas mark 5.

Sprinkle the salt and pepper evenly over the lamb. Heat a wok or large frying-pan over a high heat until it is hot. Add the oil and, when it is very hot and slightly smoking, turn the heat to low. Add the lamb and slowly brown on all sides for about 15 minutes. Transfer the lamb to a large, heavy casserole.

Drain off all excess fat from the wok or frying-pan, leaving just enough for stir-frying, then add the garlic, ginger and shallots and stir-fry for 2 minutes. Transfer this mixture to the casserole, add the rice wine or sherry, soy sauce, chilli-bean sauce and chicken stock. Bring the mixture to a simmer and add the rosemary and thyme. Cover tightly and cook in the oven for 1½ hours, or until the meat is very tender. Let the meat rest at room temperature for 20 minutes before carving.

Slice the lamb and place the slices on a warm platter; remove the garlic with a slotted spoon and arrange the cloves around the lamb. Remove all surface fat from the liquid and reduce by one-third. Pour this over the lamb, sprinkle with coriander and chives and serve at once.

SPICY GRILLED SATAY LAMB ≈

One of the joys of visiting Singapore is to roam its famous food centres where you can literally eat your way through an array of open food stalls. The variety is amazing – ranging from noodles to seafood, or my favourite, satay. Thin strips of lamb, beef, pork or chicken are grilled on skewers and served with a peanut sauce. Here, I have used that inspiration to make my version of lamb satay. The marinade is briefly simmered and makes a nice dipping sauce. Serve these lamb satays drizzled with Curry-flavoured Oil (page 38) for a savoury starter and with rice for a main course.

Soak bamboo skewers in water for 30 minutes or so, to prevent them from burning.

Cut the lamb into slices 7.5 cm (3 in) long x 4 cm (1½ in) wide x 3 mm (⅛ in) thick. Thread the slices on the bamboo skewers and place on a long platter.

Combine the marinade ingredients in a medium-sized bowl. Pour this over the lamb and leave to marinate for 1 hour at room temperature. Turn the lamb skewers once or twice. Remove them from the marinade. Put the marinade in a pan and simmer for 3 minutes to thicken it slightly. Set aside.

Pre-heat the oven grill to high or make a charcoal fire in the barbecue.

When the grill is very hot or the charcoal is ash-white, grill the lamb satays on each side for 1 minute. Place on a warm platter and let them rest for 5 minutes before serving with the reserved marinade.

Serves 4–6

750 g (1½ lb) best end lamb loin

For the Marinade:
250 ml (8 fl oz) pineapple juice
2 tablespoons best quality Japanese sesame paste (page 23) or peanut butter
2 tablespoons light soy sauce (page 23)
2 teaspoons chilli-bean sauce (page 22)
1 teaspoon freshly ground five-pepper mixture (page 21) or black pepper
2 tablespoons chopped spring onions
1 tablespoon finely chopped garlic
2 tablespoons crushed dried sage

STIR-FRIED BEEF WITH FIVE PEPPERCORNS ≈

SERVES 4

450 g (1 lb) lean beef steak
1 tablespoon light soy sauce
  (page 23)
1 tablespoon Shaoxing rice
  wine (page 22) or dry
  sherry
2 teaspoons cornflour
2 teaspoons sesame oil
3 tablespoons oil, preferably
  groundnut
2 tablespoons cognac
100 g (4 oz) shallots, finely
  chopped
2 tablespoons five-pepper
  mixture (page 21), crushed
½ teaspoon salt
250 ml (8 fl oz) Home-made
  Chicken Stock (page 32)
2 tablespoons (25 g/1 oz)
  butter, cut in small pieces

STEAK *AU POIVRE* IS A POPULAR FRENCH BISTRO DISH THAT HAS FALLEN OUT OF FASHION; HOWEVER, IT IS A SAVOURY DISH THAT I HAVE ALWAYS ENJOYED. IN MY VERSION I LIKE THE MIXTURE OF FIVE PEPPERCORNS, WHICH IS MUCH MORE FRAGRANT THAN USING JUST ONE TYPE. THE CHINESE OFTEN FIND LARGE PIECES OF BEEF INTIMIDATING, PREFERRING TO CUT MEAT INTO SLICES AND STIR-FRYING IT QUICKLY, AS IN THIS RECIPE. THE RESULT IS A FAST DISH THAT COMBINES FUSION ELEMENTS OF EAST AND WEST, FOR A UNIQUE SLANT ON A CLASSIC. SERVE WITH NOODLES, AS ILLUSTRATED OPPOSITE.

Cut the beef into thick slices 5 cm x 5 mm (2 x ¼ in), cutting against the grain. Put the beef in a bowl with the soy sauce, rice wine or sherry, cornflour and sesame oil. Mix well and then let the mixture marinate for about 20 minutes.

Heat a wok or large frying-pan over a high heat until it is very hot. Add the oil and, when it is very hot and slightly smoking, remove the beef from the marinade with a slotted spoon. Add it to the pan and stir-fry it for 2 minutes, until it is barely cooked. Remove and leave to drain in a colander or sieve. Pour out all the oil, reheat the wok or pan over a high heat, then add the cognac to deglaze. Quickly add the shallots, peppercorns, salt and stock and reduce by half over a high heat. Finally, add the butter, piece by piece. Then return the beef to the wok or pan and stir-fry for 30 seconds to warm it through. Serve at once.

MEAT

FUSION STEAMED MEATLOAF ≈

SERVES 4

50 g (2 oz) fresh
  breadcrumbs
450 g (1 lb) minced beef
225 g (8 oz) minced pork
1 small onion, finely
  chopped
1 egg, beaten
1 tablespoon finely chopped
  fresh ginger (page 17)
2 tablespoons finely
  chopped spring onions
1 tablespoon finely chopped
  fresh coriander
2 teaspoons finely chopped
  fresh thyme or 1 teaspoon
  dried thyme
2 teaspoons finely chopped
  fresh marjoram or
  1 teaspoon dried
  marjoram
1 tablespoon finely chopped
  fresh chives
2 tablespoons light soy
  sauce (page 23)
1 teaspoon salt
½ teaspoon freshly ground
  five-pepper mixture
  (page 21) or black pepper
175 ml (6 fl oz) milk

MEATLOAF IS A BAKED AMERICAN DISH OF CHOPPED MEAT, USUALLY BEEF, PORK, LAMB OR ANY COMBINATION THEREOF, WITH BREADCRUMBS. THIS HEARTY MAIN DISH WAS QUITE POPULAR IN 1950S' AMERICA. USING BREADCRUMBS WAS AN ACCEPTABLE METHOD FOR STRETCHING WHAT WAS THEN EXPENSIVE MEAT. MEATLOAF FELL OUT OF FASHION IN THE 1970S. HOWEVER, SINCE THE LATE 1980S IT HAS MADE A DRAMATIC COMEBACK IN MANY UP-MARKET AMERICAN BISTRO-TYPE RESTAURANTS. THIS HUMBLE DISH CAN BE MADE QUITE DELECTABLE BY VARYING, OR ADDING TO, ITS USUAL FLAVOURINGS. HERE I USE SOME TRADITIONAL CHINESE SEASONINGS MIXED WITH DISTINCTIVE WESTERN HERBS. RATHER THAN BAKING IT, I STEAM IT – A FAVOURITE ASIAN METHOD OF KEEPING FOOD MOIST AND JUICY. THE FIRM TEXTURE OF THE FILLING ENSURES THE LOAF REMAINS INTACT. MAKE THIS DISH AHEAD OF TIME: IT REHEATS WELL AND MAKES LOVELY SANDWICHES BESIDES. IT GOES EXTREMELY WELL WITH POTATO AND CUCUMBER MASH (PAGE 186) AS ILLUSTRATED OPPOSITE.

Combine all the ingredients in a large bowl and mix well.

Lightly brush a 1.2 litre (2 pint) heatproof dish or non-stick loaf tin with a film of oil and spoon the mixture into it.

Next, set up a steamer or put a rack into a wok or deep pan and pour in 5 cm (2 in) of water. Bring the water to the boil over a high heat, then carefully lower the dish or pan into the steamer or onto the rack. Turn the heat to low and cover the wok or pan tightly. Steam gently for 1 hour, or until the meat is cooked. Check the water level from time to time, adding more if necessary. Pour off any fat which may have accumulated.

Invert onto a warm platter and serve at once.

Asian-flavoured Grilled Steak ≈

Serves 4

4 entrecôte (sirloin) or rump
   steaks, about 175–225 g
   (6–8 oz) each

For the Marinade:
1 tablespoon dark soy sauce
   (page 23)
3 tablespoons light soy
   sauce (page 23)
2 tablespoons oyster sauce
   (page 23)
1 tablespoon sugar
3 tablespoons mirin
   (Japanese sweet rice wine)
   (page 18)
2 tablespoons sesame oil

THIS IS ONE OF THE EASIEST AND TASTIEST METHODS OF COOKING STEAKS.
SOY SAUCE IS AN ANCIENT CHINESE SEASONING THAT WORKS
WONDERFULLY ON MEATS. THE GRILLED STEAK GOES PERFECTLY WITH
POTATOES AND SALAD.

Lay the steaks on a tray.

In a medium-sized bowl, mix all the marinade ingredients together
and spread the mixture evenly over each side of the steaks. Allow the
steaks to sit and marinate at room temperature for at least 1 hour.

Pre-heat the oven grill to high or make a charcoal fire in the
barbecue. When the oven grill is very hot or the charcoal is ash-
white, grill the steaks on each side for about 5–6 minutes (if you like
them rare) or more if you want them well cooked.

Transfer to a warm platter and allow to rest for 10 minutes
before serving.

MEAT

WOLFGANG PUCK'S SICHUAN-STYLE BEEF ≈

WOLFGANG PUCK IS UNDOUBTEDLY ONE OF THE MOST SUCCESSFUL CHEFS IN AMERICA TODAY. AN AUSTRIAN, HE TRAINED IN FRANCE AND HONED HIS ART IN LOS ANGELES. HIS WELL-DESERVED SUCCESS COMES FROM HIS ABILITY TO BLEND THE BEST OF AMERICA INTO A CUISINE OF HIS OWN. IN FACT, HE IS AMONG THE WORLD'S PIONEERS IN THE ART OF FUSION COOKING. THIS RECIPE IS AN ADAPTATION OF PUCK'S VERSION OF SICHUAN BEEF: INSTEAD OF THE TRADITIONAL STIR-FRYING, HE RELIES ON THE GRILL TO COOK THE BEEF. SLICED AND PAIRED WITH A LIGHT SALAD, THIS DISH IS PERFECT FOR WARM-WEATHER ENTERTAINING.

FOR THOSE WHO HAVE A SPICIER PALATE, DRIZZLE SESAME AND CHILLI OIL ON THE COOKED DISH.

SERVE WITH SPRING SALAD WITH SESAME OIL AND SHALLOT DRESSING (PAGE 54) OR A SIMPLE GREEN SALAD.

Lay the steaks on a tray. Rub them with sesame oil and sprinkle the Sichuan peppercorns evenly over each side of the steaks. Allow to marinate in the refrigerator overnight or for at least several hours.

In a small pan, bring the rice wine and shallots to the boil and continue to cook until reduced by two-thirds. Then add the stock, garlic, ginger and chilli flakes and continue to boil until the liquid is again reduced by two-thirds. It should be slightly thick by now. Slowly whisk in the butter, a piece at a time. Finally, add the soy sauce and coriander. Remove from the heat and set aside.

Pre-heat the oven grill to high or make a charcoal fire in the barbecue. When the oven grill is very hot or the charcoal is ash-white, grill the steaks on each side for about 5–6 minutes (if you like them rare) or more if you want them well cooked.

Transfer to a warm platter and allow to rest for 10 minutes. Reheat the sauce. Cut the steak into thin slices, pour the sauce over them, then drizzle over the sesame and chilli oil, if using, and serve at once.

SERVES 4

4 entrecôte (sirloin) or rump steaks, about 175–225 g (6–8 oz) each
2 tablespoons sesame oil
1 tablespoon roasted ground Sichuan peppercorns (page 21)
Sesame and Chilli Oil (page 39), to serve (optional)

For the Sauce:

120 ml (4 fl oz) mirin (Japanese sweet rice wine) (page 18)
3 tablespoons finely chopped shallots
250 ml (8 fl oz) Home-made Chicken Stock (page 32)
2 tablespoons coarsely chopped garlic
2 teaspoons finely chopped fresh ginger (page 17)
1 teaspoon dried chilli flakes
3 tablespoons (35 g/1½ oz) cold unsalted butter, cut in small pieces
1 tablespoon dark soy sauce (page 23)
2 tablespoons finely chopped fresh coriander

Neil Perry's Braised Oxtail in Coconut Milk Paste ≈

1.5 kg (3 lb) oxtail, jointed

2.25 litres (4 pints) Home-
made Chicken Stock
(page 32)

**For the Coconut Milk
Paste:**

8 garlic cloves

225 g (8 oz) shallots,
coarsely chopped and
squeezed dry

15 white peppercorns

3 tablespoons groundnut or
vegetable oil

50 ml (2 fl oz) fish sauce
(page 22) or light soy
sauce (page 23)

75 g (3 oz) palm, rock or
ordinary sugar (page 24)

2 teaspoons salt

1 teaspoon freshly ground
five-pepper mixture
(page 21) or black pepper

900 ml (1½ pints) tinned
coconut milk (page 16)

To Garnish:

2 teaspoons groundnut or
vegetable oil for
microwaving or 300 ml
(10 fl oz) vegetable oil
for frying

225 g (8 oz) shallots, thinly
sliced

A large handful of fresh basil
leaves

A large handful of fresh mint
leaves

Neil Perry, one of the best chefs in Sydney, has ingeniously combined the flavours of Asia in his ground-breaking cuisine. This dish is typical of his mouthwatering cooking – oxtail is braised and then stir-fried in a flavourful coconut milk paste. Much of the work can be done ahead of time and the bonus is that the dish reheats well. Add the fresh herbs at the last moment, in any case. Steamed Rice (page 35) is ideal for this juicy dish.

Cook the oxtail pieces in boiling water for 15 minutes. Remove and drain well. Bring the stock to a simmer in a very large pan, add the blanched oxtails, cover and simmer for 3 hours or until the oxtail is very tender. Skim the surface from time to time, removing any impurities. Remove the oxtail pieces with a slotted spoon and set aside. The liquid can then be skimmed of fat and impurities, strained through a fine sieve and saved for soup. Or alternatively, it can be frozen and used for Oxtail Wonton Soup (page 70).

To make the coconut milk paste, first finely chop the garlic, shallots and peppercorns in a food processor. Then heat a wok or large pan until it is hot, add the oil then add the garlic mixture and stir-fry for 1 minute or until it turns golden. Now add the fish sauce or light soy sauce, sugar, salt, pepper and coconut milk. Add the cooked oxtail and cook until most of the coconut milk has evaporated. Turn the heat down to low and keep warm.

For the garnish, mix the shallots with the oil. Then scatter the sliced shallots so that they are in one layer on two plates. Microwave one plate of shallots on full power for 8–9 minutes (microwave oven temperatures vary). Check from time to time, making sure the shallots do not burn. They should be dry and slightly crisp. Do the same to the second batch. This can be done hours ahead of time. If you don't have a microwave, fry the shallots in 300 ml (10 fl oz) oil until slightly crisp.

Stir the basil and mint leaves into the oxtail and turn the mixture onto a warm platter. Garnish with the crisp sliced shallots and serve at once.

Braised Fusion Pork Stew ≈

Serves 4

225 g (8 oz) carrots
225 g (8 oz) potatoes
4 thick spare rib chops,
   about 750 g (1½ lb)
3 teaspoons salt
1½ teaspoons freshly ground
   five-pepper mixture
   (page 21) or black pepper
2 tablespoons plain flour
2 tablespoons groundnut oil
1 small onion, sliced
8 garlic cloves
2 tablespoons finely
   chopped lemon zest
3 tablespoons finely
   chopped sun-dried
   tomatoes
3 tablespoons mirin
   (Japanese sweet rice wine)
   (page 18) or Shaoxing
   rice wine (page 22) or dry
   sherry
2 tablespoons light soy
   sauce (page 23)
1 tablespoon dark soy sauce
   (page 23)
1 tablespoon hoisin sauce
   (page 22)
3 star anise (page 24)
2 tablespoons rock sugar
   (page 24), crushed, or
   granulated sugar
475 ml (16 fl oz)
   Home-made Chicken Stock
   (page 32)
225 g (8 oz) button
   mushrooms

This is a hearty, cold-weather dish that is mouthwatering and satisfying. Long, slow cooking infuses flavours from East and West. I like to use meaty spare rib chops, as they are rich and are perfect for simmered dishes like this one. An additional bonus is that the stew reheats well.

Serve this lovely dish with Herbal Vegetarian Fried Rice (page 206).

Peel the carrots and cut at a slight diagonal in 5 cm (2 in) pieces. Peel the potatoes and cut into chunks.

Blot the chops dry with kitchen paper. Combine 2 teaspoons of the salt, 1 teaspoon of the pepper and the flour. Sprinkle this mixture evenly on both sides of the chops, shaking off any excess flour.

Heat a wok or frying-pan until it is hot, add the oil and when it is very hot, turn the heat to low and brown the chops on each side. Remove and set aside.

Add the onion and garlic and stir-fry for 3 minutes or until they are slightly soft. Then add the lemon zest, sun-dried tomatoes, rice wine or sherry, soy sauces, hoisin sauce, star anise, the rest of the salt and pepper and the sugar. Pour the mixture into a heavy casserole and add the chicken stock. Bring the mixture to a simmer, add the mushrooms and chops to the casserole. Cover tightly and simmer gently for 45 minutes. Then add the carrots and potatoes and continue to cook for another 20 minutes, or until the meat and vegetables are tender. Skim off any surface fat and serve at once.

POULTRY

STIR-FRIED CHICKEN WITH CHINESE AND BUTTON MUSHROOMS ≈

SERVES 4

450 g (1 lb) boneless, skinless chicken thighs or 900 g (2 lb) chicken thighs on the bone

For the Marinade:
2 teaspoons light soy sauce (page 23)
2 teaspoons Shaoxing rice wine (page 22) or dry sherry
1 teaspoon sesame oil
2 teaspoons cornflour

For the Stir-fry:
25 g (1 oz) dried Chinese mushrooms (page 18)
350 g (12 oz) button mushrooms
1½ tablespoons groundnut oil
1 onion, thinly sliced
2 tablespoons coarsely chopped garlic
2 teaspoons salt
½ teaspoon freshly ground five-pepper mixture (page 21) or black pepper
2 teaspoons finely chopped orange zest
2 tablespoons Shaoxing rice wine (page 22) or dry sherry
3 tablespoons oyster sauce (page 22)
2 teaspoons sugar
A large handful of fresh basil leaves

CHICKEN STIR-FRY IS SUCH AN EASY AND APPETIZING DISH TO SERVE. HERE, I HAVE COMBINED IT WITH TWO KINDS OF MUSHROOMS, THE DRIED BLACK ONES SO POPULAR IN CHINESE COOKING AND PLAIN BUTTON MUSHROOMS. THE TEXTURES OF THE MUSHROOMS ARE WONDERFULLY CHEWY, WHICH ADDS RICHNESS TO THIS UNUSUALLY TASTY DISH. FOR A SIMPLE MEAL, SERVE THIS DISH WITH VEGETABLE SALAD WITH CURRY-SOY VINAIGRETTE (PAGE 195).

Remove the skin and bones from the unboned chicken thighs, or have your butcher do it for you. Cut the chicken into 2.5 cm (1 in) chunks and combine them in a bowl with the soy sauce, rice wine or sherry, sesame oil and cornflour. Allow to marinate for 20 minutes at room temperature.

Meanwhile, soak the Chinese mushrooms in warm water for 20 minutes. Then drain them, squeeze out the excess liquid and discard all the water. Remove and discard the stems and cut the caps into thick strips. Slice the button mushrooms.

Heat a wok or large frying-pan until it is very hot, add the oil and then the chicken. Stir-fry for 5 minutes, until the chicken is brown. Remove the chicken and drain off most of the oil, leaving just 2 teaspoons. Reheat the wok or pan until it is hot, quickly add the onion and garlic and stir-fry for 2 minutes. Then add the salt, pepper, the Chinese mushrooms and the button mushrooms and stir-fry for 1 minute. Now, return the chicken and add the orange zest and rice wine or sherry and continue to stir-fry for 4 minutes, or until the liquid has been absorbed by the mushrooms or has evaporated. Finally, add the oyster sauce, sugar and basil leaves, give the mixture a good stir and cook for another minute. Serve at once.

Marinated Chicken with Rice-herb Stuffing ≈

Serves 4–6

1 teaspoon salt

½ teaspoon freshly ground
five-pepper mixture
(page 21) or black pepper

1.5 kg (3–3½ lb) corn-fed or
free-range chicken

1 tablespoon sesame oil

2 tablespoons lemon juice

Chicken is such a versatile food and is so adaptable to any flavouring that it is easy to see why fusion cooks love using it. In this recipe, the chicken is first marinated overnight with sesame oil and lemon juice and then stuffed with glutinous rice and an explosion of fresh herbs. The glutinous rice, which is also known as sweet or sticky rice and which can be found in Chinese supermarkets, must be soaked first and then stir-fried with seasonings. It is short, round and pearl-like and has a higher gluten content than other rices. This special rice does not disintegrate with long cooking, making it ideal for stuffings. It absorbs flavours like a sponge and is well worth the search. Much of the work can be done the day before, making it ideal for a dinner party or a special evening. The result is an elegant dish that is a profusion of tastes, especially if served with Stir-fried Cauliflower with Fresh Coriander (page 193). Any left-over chicken makes a delicious light lunch or terrific sandwiches.

Combine the salt and pepper. Sprinkle this mixture evenly over the skin and the interior cavity of the chicken. Now rub the chicken, inside and out, with the sesame oil and lemon juice. Cover with cling film and put in the refrigerator overnight.

Cover the glutinous rice for the stuffing with water and let it sit overnight at room temperature.

The next day, drain the glutinous rice. Heat a wok or large frying-pan over a high heat until it is hot. Add the oil, garlic and shallots and stir-fry for 20 seconds. Then add the pork and continue to stir-fry for 3 minutes. Now add the drained rice, soy sauce, rice wine or sherry, salt, pepper and chicken stock. Turn the heat to low, cover and cook for 20 minutes or until the rice has absorbed all the liquid. Remove from the heat and stir in the spring onions and all the fresh herbs. Allow the mixture to cool thoroughly.

Pre-heat the oven to 240°C/475°/gas mark 9.

Fill the chicken with the rice stuffing; any extra can be served separately. Close the body cavity with a bamboo skewer.

Place the chicken on a roasting rack in a roasting tin, breast-side up. Now put the chicken inside the oven and roast it for 15 minutes. Then turn the heat down to 180°C/350°F/gas mark 4 and continue to roast for 40 minutes. Turn the chicken over and continue to roast for 10 minutes.

Remove the chicken from the oven and let it sit for at least 15 minutes before you carve it. Carefully remove the skewer and drain any liquid that may have accumulated. Using a sharp knife, cut the chicken into serving portions, arrange them on a warm serving platter and serve at once.

For the Rice Stuffing:

200 g (7 oz) sweet glutinous rice

1½ tablespoons extra virgin olive oil

1 tablespoon coarsely chopped garlic

3 tablespoons finely chopped shallots

100 g (4 oz) minced pork

1 tablespoon light soy sauce (page 23)

1 tablespoon Shaoxing rice wine (page 22) or dry sherry

1 teaspoon salt

½ teaspoon freshly ground five-pepper mixture (page 21) or black pepper

475 ml (16 fl oz) Home-made Chicken Stock (page 32)

2 tablespoons finely chopped spring onions

1 tablespoon finely chopped fresh coriander

1 tablespoon finely chopped fresh chives

1 tablespoon finely chopped fresh chervil

1 tablespoon finely chopped fresh thyme or 2 teaspoons dried thyme

1 tablespoon finely chopped fresh tarragon

HONEY-SOY-GLAZED POUSSINS ≈

SERVES 4

4 x 350 g (12 oz) poussins

For the Marinade:
2 teaspoons salt
1½ teaspoons freshly ground
   five-pepper mixture
   (page 21) or black pepper
2 tablespoons light soy
   sauce (page 23)
2 tablespoons mirin
   (Japanese sweet rice wine)
   (page 18) or dry sherry
2 tablespoons Dijon mustard
3 tablespoons honey

POUSSINS ARE BABY CHICKENS AND ARE PERFECT FOR TODAY'S BUSY LIFESTYLE. THEY ARE NOT ONLY TASTY BUT COOK QUICKLY. HERE, I OFFER A SIMPLE MARINADE THAT FUSES FRENCH AND ASIAN FLAVOURS AND RESULTS IN THE SWEET AND SAVOURY GLAZE THAT MAKES THESE POUSSINS SO APPEALING. THEY CAN ALSO BE COOKED ON THE GRILL. SERVE THE POUSSINS WITH LIGHT RICE NOODLES WITH FRESH HERBS (PAGE 207).

Using a sharp knife, cut through the backbone of a poussin, lengthways. Cut off the backbone and tail. Crack the breast bone, so that the poussin lies flat. Now make two small holes through the skin *below* and on either side of the breast. Tuck the legs through these holes. This will help hold the shape of the poussin during cooking. Repeat the procedure with the other three poussins.

In a small bowl, mix the marinade ingredients very well. Rub the mixture both inside and outside each poussin. Place the poussins, skin-side up, in a heavy roasting tin. Let the poussins marinate in the refrigerator for 1 hour.

Pre-heat the oven to 240°C/475°F/gas mark 9 and roast the poussins for about 10–15 minutes, or until they are brown. Reduce the temperature to 180°C/350°F/gas mark 4, and continue to roast for another 20 minutes. Remove the poussins from the oven and allow them to sit for at least 15 minutes before serving.

Barbecued Spicy Chicken Wings ≈

SERVES 4

1.5 kg (3 lb) chicken wings

For the Marinade:

3 tablespoons dark soy
sauce (page 23)
1 tablespoon light soy sauce
(page 23)
3 tablespoons mirin
(Japanese sweet rice wine)
(page 18) or dry sherry
2 tablespoons sugar
2 tablespoons chilli-bean
sauce (page 22)
1 tablespoon finely chopped
orange zest
1½ tablespoons Madras
curry powder (page 17)
1 teaspoon chilli oil
(page 15)

CHICKEN WINGS SEEM TO ME TO BE THE MOST UNAPPRECIATED FOOD IN EUROPEAN COOKING. IN MY CHINESE HOUSEHOLD, WE FREQUENTLY ENJOYED CHICKEN WINGS BECAUSE THEY WERE INEXPENSIVE AND WE REGARDED THEM AS TASTY MORSELS. IN THIS RECIPE, I COMBINE SPICY EASTERN FLAVOURS WITH WESTERN TASTES FOR A QUICK, EASY MARINADE THAT IS SO SAVOURY WHEN BARBECUED. THE RECIPE CAN BE EASILY DOUBLED OR TRIPLED FOR A LARGER CROWD. SERVE THE WINGS WITH RICE OR EVEN COLD FOR A PICNIC TREAT.

Pierce the skins of the chicken wings with a fork; this will allow the marinade to penetrate. In a small bowl, mix the marinade ingredients. Pour the mixture over the chicken wings and mix well. Let them marinate in the refrigerator for 1 hour.

Pre-heat the oven grill to high or make a charcoal fire in the barbecue.

When the grill is very hot or the charcoal is ash-white, grill the chicken wings for about 10 minutes, turning from time to time to avoid burning.

Serve at once or allow to cool and serve at room temperature.

Grilled Soy Sauce-mustard Chicken Thighs ≈

Soy sauce and mustard are two ingredients that fuse beautifully, even though they are from two completely different food cultures. Chicken thighs can withstand the strong flavours of this easy-to-make sauce. Serve it with a salad for a light meal.

Remove the skin and bone from unboned chicken thighs. Lay the chicken thighs on a baking tray.

In a blender or food processor, mix the soy sauce, mustard, pepper, garlic, ginger, orange zest, coriander, parsley, sesame oil and olive oil until smooth. With a spatula, smear each side of the thighs evenly with this mixture.

Pre-heat the oven grill to high or make a charcoal fire in the barbecue.

When the grill is very hot or the charcoal is ash-white, grill the chicken thighs on each side for 10–15 minutes, until they are brown and slightly firm to the touch. Remove the thighs from the grill and set aside to rest in a warm place for 10–15 minutes before serving.

Serves 4

450 g (1 lb) boneless, skinless chicken thighs or 900 g (2 lb) chicken thighs on the bone

3 tablespoons light soy sauce (page 23)

2 tablespoons Dijon mustard

1 teaspoon freshly ground five-pepper mixture (page 21) or black pepper

1½ tablespoons finely chopped garlic

2 teaspoons finely chopped fresh ginger (page 17)

1 tablespoon finely chopped orange zest

1 tablespoon finely chopped fresh coriander

1 tablespoon chopped fresh flatleaf parsley

1 tablespoon sesame oil

1 tablespoon extra virgin olive oil

Stir-fried Chicken with Grilled Peppers ≈

4 peppers, red, yellow and green

2 tablespoons extra virgin olive oil

450 g (1 lb) boneless chicken breasts, skinned and cut into 2.5 cm (1 in) cubes

1 egg white

1 teaspoon salt

2 teaspoons cornflour plus 1 teaspoon cornflour blended with 1 tablespoon water

300 ml (10 fl oz) groundnut oil or water, plus 1 tablespoon groundnut oil

2 tablespoons finely sliced garlic

150 ml (5 fl oz) Home-made Chicken Stock (page 32)

2 teaspoons chilli-bean sauce (page 22)

2 teaspoons sugar

1½ tablespoons Shaoxing rice wine (page 22) or dry sherry

1 tablespoon light soy sauce (page 23)

As a student living in southern France, I discovered the taste of grilled or roasted peppers. Cooked over an open flame on a hob or barbecue, the peppers acquire a sweet, smoky flavour that is simply exquisite. In this recipe, I have combined this very western cooking technique with the Chinese method of stir-frying. The result, I think you will agree, is fusion bliss. Serve it simply with rice.

Using tongs, hold each pepper directly over the flames of a gas hob and grill all over until the skin has blackened. If you don't have a gas hob, put them under a hot grill, turning occasionally. Place in a plastic bag and close it tightly. When the peppers have cooled, remove from the bag and peel off the charred skin. Clean the insides and discard the seeds. Cut into long strips, drizzle them with the olive oil and set aside.

Mix the chicken with the egg white, salt and 2 teaspoons of cornflour in a small bowl; refrigerate for about 20 minutes.

If using oil, heat a wok or large frying-pan over a high heat until hot; then add the oil. When the oil is very hot, remove the wok or pan from the heat and immediately add the chicken pieces, stirring vigorously to keep them from sticking. When they turn white, about 2 minutes, quickly drain the chicken in a stainless steel colander set in a bowl. Discard the oil.

If you choose to use water instead of oil, bring it to the boil in a pan. Remove the pan from the heat and immediately add the chicken pieces, stirring vigorously to keep them from sticking. When the chicken pieces turn white, about 2 minutes, quickly drain them in a colander set in a bowl. Discard the water.

Wipe the wok or pan clean and reheat until it is very hot. Then add the tablespoon of oil. When very hot, add the garlic slices and stir-fry them for 2 minutes or until golden brown. Then add the stock, chilli-bean sauce, sugar, rice wine or sherry and soy sauce. Cook for another 2 minutes. Add the cornflour and water mixture and cook for 20 seconds; add the chicken and pepper strips and stir-fry for another 2 minutes, coating the chicken thoroughly with the sauce. Serve at once.

ROAST GINGER CHICKEN ≈

Chinese home cooks tend either to steam, braise or fry a whole chicken. It is rarely roasted, as most Chinese homes lack ovens. Roast chicken is therefore a great discovery for the Chinese who emigrate to European countries.

A simple procedure results here in a delicious dish with very little work. A mixture of East–West flavourings is sprinkled on the inside of the chicken to enhance it further. Serve this dish with Potato and Cucumber Mash (page 186) for a complete hearty meal.

Combine the five-spice powder, Sichuan peppercorns, pepper and salt. Sprinkle this mixture evenly throughout the interior cavity of the chicken. Now mix the sage, marjoram, ginger and garlic in another bowl. Put the mixture loosely inside the cavity of the chicken. Close the body cavity with a bamboo skewer.

Pre-heat the oven to 240°C/475°F/gas mark 9.

Meanwhile, place the chicken on a roasting rack in a roasting tin, breast-side up. Now put the chicken inside the oven and roast it for 15 minutes. Then turn the heat down to 180°C/350°F/gas mark 4 and continue to roast for 40 minutes. Now turn the chicken over and continue to roast for 10 minutes.

Remove the chicken from the oven, turn it the right way up and let it sit for at least 15 minutes before you carve it. Carefully remove the skewer and drain any liquid that may have accumulated. Using a sharp knife, cut the chicken into serving portions, arrange them on a warm serving platter and serve at once.

SERVES 4–6

2 teaspoons five-spice powder (page 17)

2 teaspoons roasted and ground Sichuan peppercorns (page 21)

1 teaspoon freshly ground five-pepper mixture (page 21) or black pepper

2 teaspoons salt

1.5 kg (3–3½ lb) corn-fed or free-range chicken

3 sprigs of fresh sage or 2 teaspoons dried sage

2 sprigs of fresh marjoram or 1 teaspoon dried marjoram

20 slices of unpeeled fresh ginger (page 17) (size unimportant)

10 unpeeled garlic cloves, lightly crushed

Vietnamese-style Barbecued Five-spice Chicken ≈

Serves 4

900 g (2 lb) chicken thighs
on the bone

For the Marinade:
3 tablespoons coarsely
chopped shallots
3 tablespoons coarsely
chopped garlic
2 tablespoons dark or
ordinary sugar
2 teaspoons five-spice
powder (page 17)
2 tablespoons mirin
(Japanese sweet rice wine)
(page 18) or dry sherry
1 tablespoon Shaoxing rice
wine (page 22) or dry
sherry
2 tablespoons fish sauce
(page 22) or light soy
sauce (page 23)
1 teaspoon sesame oil
½ teaspoon freshly ground
five-pepper mixture
(page 21) or black pepper

I grew up in a Chinese household, totally oblivious to other Asian cuisines. Only when I lived in California did I discover the richness of Vietnamese, as well as Thai, cuisine. Young Australian chefs have made the same discovery with the influx of the Vietnamese to Sydney. The result is an adaptation of spices to modern Australian cooking.

A particular dish which captured my culinary fancy in my student days was this five-spice chicken. The secret, I learned, was that the chicken should be marinated overnight to capture the essential deep flavours. Then it is simply grilled, a perfect party dish that is mouthwateringly delicious, especially when it is served with Malaysian Curry Mee (page 218).

Blot the chicken thighs dry with kitchen paper.

In a food processor, combine the marinade ingredients and purée them.

In a large bowl, combine the chicken with the marinade and mix well. Cover with cling film and refrigerate overnight.

When you are ready to barbecue the chicken, remove the chicken from the refrigerator and leave at room temperature for 40 minutes.

Pre-heat the oven grill to high or make a charcoal fire in the barbecue. When the grill is very hot or the charcoal is ash-white, grill the chicken thighs for 10 minutes on each side or until they are cooked.

Place on a warm platter and serve immediately.

POULTRY

WOK-SMOKED CHICKEN ≈

CHICKEN IS A WONDERFULLY VERSATILE FOOD AND A FAVOURITE WITH FUSION COOKS AND CHEFS AROUND THE WORLD. AN ECONOMICAL MEAT, THE BREAST COOKS QUICKLY, PERFECT FOR TODAY'S BUSY RESTAURANT OR HOME KITCHEN. IN THIS RECIPE, CHICKEN BREASTS ARE RUBBED WITH A COMBINATION OF EASTERN AND WESTERN SPICES AND SMOKED IN A WOK OR A DEEP CASSEROLE. YOU CAN SERVE THEM WITH A SALAD AS A STARTER OR LIGHT LUNCH. THEY ALSO MAKE DELECTABLE SANDWICHES.

Combine the sugar, salt, Sichuan peppercorns, pepper and thyme in a small bowl. Sprinkle this mixture on all sides of the chicken breasts. Place the chicken on a plate, cover with cling film and put in the refrigerator overnight.

The next day, line the inside of a wok and its lid with foil. Place the rice, sugar and tea leaves in the bottom of the wok. Rub a rack with vegetable oil and place it over the smoking ingredients. Slowly heat the wok and, when the mixture begins to smoke, put the chicken breasts on the rack, covering tightly. Turn the heat to very low and slowly smoke for 30 minutes. Remove from the heat and allow the chicken to sit, covered, for another 5 minutes. When the chicken breasts are cool enough to handle, cut them into slices. Discard the smoking mixture and the foil. Serve at room temperature or cold.

SERVES 4

2 teaspoons brown sugar
1½ teaspoons salt
1 teaspoon roasted and ground Sichuan peppercorns (page 21)
½ teaspoon freshly ground five-pepper mixture (page 21) or black pepper
2 teaspoons dried thyme
4 x 100 g (4 oz) skinless, boneless chicken breasts
Vegetable oil, for greasing

For the Smoking Mixture:
50 g (2 oz) long-grain white rice
3 tablespoons brown sugar
50 g (2 oz) black tea leaves (page 24)

FUSION CHICKEN STEW ≈

1.5 kg (3-3½ lb) corn-fed or
free-range chicken

2 teaspoons salt plus salt
and freshly ground five-
pepper mixture (page 21)
or black pepper to taste

6 slices unpeeled fresh
ginger (page 17)
(size unimportant)

9 spring onions

2 tablespoons whole Sichuan
peppercorns roasted
(page 21)

1 tablespoon whole five-
peppercorn mixture
(page 21) or black
peppercorns

4 sprigs of fresh thyme or
2 teaspoons dried thyme

4 unpeeled garlic cloves,
crushed

225 g (8 oz) carrots

225 g (8 oz) asparagus

225 g (8 oz) red or yellow
peppers (1 large or about
2 small)

225 g (8 oz) mangetout

3 tablespoons crème fraîche

To Garnish:

1 tablespoon finely chopped
fresh coriander

1 tablespoon finely chopped
fresh chives

2 tablespoons finely
chopped spring onions

THE CHINESE ARE MASTERS OF COOKING FOOD EFFICIENTLY AT LOW HEAT. BECAUSE OF THE COST AND SCARCITY OF FUEL, THEY DEVISED STEWING AND BRAISING TECHNIQUES THAT ALLOWED THEM TO PRODUCE DELICIOUS FOODS DONE TO PERFECTION. THIS IS PARTICULARLY TRUE WHEN IT COMES TO CHICKEN. OFTEN CHICKEN THAT IS IMPROPERLY STEWED IS STRINGY AND TASTELESS. THE CHINESE TECHNIQUE OF STEEPING PRODUCES MOIST CHICKEN WITH A SILKY, VELVETY TEXTURE. IN THIS QUICK RECIPE, THE STEEPING STOCK IS REDUCED, SEASONED AND ENRICHED WITH A TOUCH OF CRÈME FRAÎCHE. THE STEW MAKES A COMPLETE MEAL SERVED WITH STEAMED RICE (PAGE 35).

Rub the chicken evenly with 2 teaspoons of salt. Place the chicken in a large pan, cover with water and bring to the boil. Skim off any impurities; then add the ginger, 6 spring onions, Sichuan peppercorns, five-peppercorn mixture or black peppercorns, thyme and garlic. Reduce the heat to a simmer, cover tightly and cook for 20 minutes. Turn off the heat and leave tightly covered for 1 hour.

Meanwhile, prepare the vegetables. Peel the carrots and cut diagonally into 5 mm (¼ in) dice. Cut the asparagus diagonally into 5 cm (2 in) pieces, discarding any tough ends. Cut the peppers into 2.5 cm (1 in) pieces. Cut the rest of the spring onions diagonally into 5 cm (2 in) pieces. Trim the mangetout.

When the chicken has been steeped for 1 hour, drain and allow it to cool enough to handle. Cut the chicken into serving pieces.

Strain the steeping liquid through a fine sieve and skim off all surface fat. It is now a light broth. Return the broth to the pan and reduce by half over a high heat. Add the carrots to the broth for 2 minutes; then add the asparagus and peppers and cook for another minute. Finally, add the spring onions and mangetout and cook for another minute. Remove the vegetables with a slotted spoon, and continue to reduce the liquid until you have about 300 ml (10 fl oz) left. Stir in the crème fraîche and salt and pepper to taste. Return the chicken and vegetables to the pan and reheat for 2 minutes, or until warm throughout.

Arrange the chicken and vegetables on a warm platter, pour the sauce over, sprinkle coriander, chives and spring onions on top and serve.

Five-spice Roast Poussins with Rice-wine Butter Sauce ≈

SERVES 4

4 x 350 g (12 oz) poussins
1 tablespoon sesame oil

For the Marinade:

1 tablespoon five-spice
   powder (page 17)
2 teaspoons salt
1 teaspoon freshly ground
   five-pepper mixture
   (page 21) or black pepper
2 tablespoons finely
   chopped orange zest

For the Sauce:

3 tablespoons finely
   chopped shallots
150 ml (5 fl oz) Shaoxing
   rice wine (page 22)
   or dry sherry
150 ml (5 fl oz) Home-made
   Chicken Stock (page 32)
2 tablespoons (25 g/1 oz)
   cold unsalted butter, cut in
   small pieces
2 tablespoons finely
   chopped spring onions

IN THIS RECIPE, I HAVE USED POUSSINS, WHICH ARE BABY CHICKENS, FOR AN ELEGANT DINNER-PARTY DISH THAT IS EASY ENOUGH FOR TODAY'S BUSY COOK. THEY TAKE LITTLE TIME TO COOK AND LOOK SO SPECTACULAR. SERVE THIS WITH CURRY COUSCOUS WITH FRESH CHIVES AND APPLE (PAGE 198), FOR A COMPLETE MEAL.

Using a sharp knife, cut through the backbone of a poussin, lengthways. Cut off the backbone and tail. Crack the breast bone so that the poussin lies flat. Now make two small holes through the skin *below* and on each side of the breast. Tuck the legs through these holes. This will help hold the shape of the poussin during cooking. Rub sesame oil on both sides of the poussin. Repeat the procedure with the other three poussins.

In a small bowl, mix the marinade ingredients very well. Rub the mixture inside and outside each poussin. Place the poussins, skin-side up, in a heavy roasting tin. Let the poussins marinate at room temperature for 1 hour.

Pre-heat the oven to 240°C/475°F/gas mark 9 and roast the poussins for about 10–15 minutes or until they are brown. Reduce the temperature to 180°C/350°F/gas mark 4 and continue to roast for another 20 minutes. Remove the poussins from the oven, place them on a platter and allow them to sit for at least 15 minutes before serving.

While the poussins are resting, place the roasting tin on a hob, add the shallots and cook for a minute; then add the rice wine or sherry and continue to cook, over a high heat, until the wine has evaporated. Now add the stock and bring to the boil, scraping the bottom of the tin as you stir. Remove the tin from the heat and whisk in the butter, a piece at a time. Once the butter is thoroughly incorporated into the sauce, sprinkle in the spring onions. Spoon a few tablespoons of sauce on individual plates, place the poussins on top and serve at once.

GRILLED COCONUT CHICKEN CURRY ≈

Here is fusion cooking with an enticing combination: coconut, curry and lemon grass, blended to make a delicious marinade. The familiar grilled chicken is enhanced by these exotic touches. The secret is to allow enough time for the marinade to permeate the chicken. Then the marinade itself is briefly cooked and used for a sauce. Grilling the chicken adds a smoky deliciousness that transforms this ordinary dish into something special indeed. Serve with Ginger-leek Purée (page 191) and Steamed Rice (page 35).

Sprinkle the chicken thighs with the salt and pepper. Peel the lemon grass stalk to reveal the tender, whitish centre and finely chop the centre. Mix the lemon grass with the other marinade ingredients in a large bowl. Add the chicken thighs and mix well. Leave in the refrigerator overnight, covered with cling film.

Remove the chicken thighs from the refrigerator about 1 hour before you are ready to cook them. With a slotted spoon, remove the chicken thighs from the marinade and reserve the marinade. Pre-heat the oven grill to high or make a charcoal fire in the barbecue. When the grill is very hot or the charcoal is ash-white, grill the chicken thighs for about 15 minutes on each side. They are cooked when they are slightly firm to the touch or can be easily pierced in the thickest part with a wooden skewer and the juices run clear. Remove the thighs from the grill and set aside for 5 minutes before serving.

While the chicken is grilling, put the reserved marinade in a small pan and bring to the boil. Turn down the heat and simmer for 5 minutes. Then strain the sauce through a fine sieve and put in a bowl. Serve with the grilled chicken thighs.

Serves 4

900 g (2 lb) chicken thighs
  on the bone
2 teaspoons salt
1 teaspoon freshly ground
  five-pepper mixture
  (page 21) or black pepper

For the Marinade:
1 lemon grass stalk
  (page 18)
400 ml (14 fl oz) tin of
  coconut milk (page 16)
2 tablespoons fish sauce
  (page 22) or light soy
  sauce (page 23)
3 tablespoons lime juice
2 teaspoons lime zest
3 tablespoons Madras curry
  powder (page 17)

Stir-fried Thai Green Curry Chicken with Aubergines ≈

Serves 4

450 g (1 lb) skinless, boneless chicken thighs or 900 g (2 lb) chicken thighs on the bone

1 kg (2 lb) Chinese or ordinary aubergines (page 13)

2 teaspoons light soy sauce (page 23)

2 teaspoons Shaoxing rice wine (page 22) or dry sherry

1 teaspoon sesame oil

2 teaspoons cornflour

1½ tablespoons oil, preferably groundnut

3 tablespoons chopped garlic

1 tablespoon finely chopped fresh ginger (page 17)

3 tablespoons finely chopped spring onions

2–3 tablespoons Thai green curry paste (page 23)

1 tablespoon fish sauce (page 22) or light soy sauce (page 23)

2 teaspoons sugar

A large handful of fresh basil leaves

Thai dishes have become very popular in the West, especially with many chefs who are practising fusion cuisine. No wonder; Thai cooking is full of many fragrant aromas that are so enticing. Thai curry pastes are time-consuming and laborious to make but, fortunately, there are now high-quality Thai pastes available that can be bought at the supermarket. I find them perfectly acceptable and many have the authentic Thai flavours.

This recipe is very popular and is found often in restaurants in Sydney.

To cut down the fat, I first roast the aubergines in the oven, instead of frying them the traditional Thai way. In this manner, they don't absorb any oil. This step can be done hours ahead and the rest is a quick and easy stir-fry. Serve this with plain Steamed Rice (page 35).

Remove the skin and bones from unboned chicken thighs or have your butcher do it for you.

Pre-heat the oven to 200°C/400°F/gas mark 6. If you are using Chinese aubergines, roast them for 20 minutes; if you are using large aubergines, roast them for about 30–40 minutes or until they are soft and cooked through. Allow the aubergines to cool and then peel them. Put them in a colander and let them drain for 30 minutes or more. Chop the aubergine flesh. This procedure can be done hours in advance.

Cut the chicken into 2.5 cm (1 in) chunks and combine them in a bowl with the soy sauce, rice wine or sherry, sesame oil and cornflour.

Heat a wok or large frying-pan until it is very hot; then add the oil, then the chicken. Stir-fry for 5 minutes, then remove the chicken and drain off most of the fat and oil, leaving 2 teaspoons. Return the drained chicken to the wok or pan and add the garlic, ginger and spring onions and stir-fry for 5 minutes. Then add the chopped aubergine flesh and all the remaining ingredients except the basil leaves. Continue to cook for another 3 minutes, stirring from time to time. When the chicken is cooked, add the basil leaves and give the mixture a good stir. Transfer to a platter and serve at once.

Soy-braised Duck ≈

1.6–1.8 kg (3½–4 lb) fresh or
    frozen duck (preferably a
    white Peking duck)
450 g (1 lb) Chinese leaves
    (page 14), cut in
    5 cm (2 in) pieces
Sprigs of fresh coriander
    (optional), to garnish

For the Sauce:

1.7 litres (3 pints) Home-made
    Chicken Stock (page 32)
    or water
600 ml (1 pint) dark soy
    sauce (page 23)
300 ml (10 fl oz) light soy
    sauce (page 23)
400 ml (14 fl oz) Shaoxing
    rice wine (page 22) or dry
    sherry, or 200 ml (7 fl oz)
    dry sherry mixed with 200 ml
    (7 fl oz) Home-made
    Chicken Stock (page 32)
100 g (4 oz) rock sugar
    (page 24) or granulated
    sugar
5 star anise (page 23)
3 pieces of Chinese
    cinnamon bark (page 16) or
    3 cinnamon sticks
6 spring onions
3 slices of fresh ginger
    (page 17)
5 garlic cloves, crushed
3 tablespoons coarsely
    chopped sun-dried tomatoes
2 tablespoons dried thyme

The rich flavour and easy availability of soy sauce has inspired fusion chefs and home cooks everywhere. Here is a fine example of a soy-braised duck, which I sampled at the Mandarin Duck Bistro in Adelaide, Australia, which, alas, is no longer in business. At one time, this excellent restaurant was widely known as a pioneer in East–West fusion cookery. This dish can be made ahead of time and reheats well. Serve it with Green Rice (page 203). Left-overs make great sandwiches or you can use them in salads. The sauce can be frozen and re-used to braise duck or chicken.

Blanch the duck in a large pan of boiling water for 20 minutes. Remove and drain well.

Rinse the pan well, combine all the sauce ingredients in it and bring the mixture to the boil. Add the duck and turn the heat down to a simmer. Cover the pot and slowly braise the duck for 1 hour or until it is tender. Skim the surface fat from time to time; this procedure will prevent the duck from becoming greasy. Remove the duck. Skim off any remaining fat from the sauce. Then add the Chinese leaves and cook for 20 minutes.

Remove the Chinese leaves and place on a warm platter. Carve the duck into four or six serving pieces. Lay the duck on top of the leaves, add a ladle or two of sauce, garnish with coriander, if using, and serve at once.

Alternatively, you can let the duck cool thoroughly and serve it at room temperature. Once the sauce has cooled, remove any lingering surface fat.

Neil Perry's Wok-smoked Quail ≈

Another palate-enticing recipe from one of Australia's top chefs, Neil Perry. Smoking is one of his favourite techniques and provides a taste he loves. This delicate bird makes a smashing opener for a meal. The jasmine tea gives the quails a haunting aroma. Neil serves them with an aubergine salad; I highly recommend Asian-flavoured Aubergine Crostini (page 60), which I think go very well with this delicious dish.

Set up a steamer or put a rack into a wok or deep pan and pour in 5 cm (2 in) of water. Bring the water to the boil over a high heat. Put the quail onto a heatproof plate and then carefully lower it into the steamer or onto the rack. Turn the heat to low and cover the wok or pan tightly. Steam gently for 8 minutes. Remove the quail and allow them to cool. Then rub the sesame oil all over them.

Next, line the inside of a wok and a wok lid with foil. Place the rice, sugar and tea leaves in the bottom of the wok. Rub a rack with vegetable oil and place it over the smoking ingredients. Slowly heat the wok and, when the mixture begins to smoke, put the quail on the rack, covering tightly. Turn the heat to very low and slowly smoke for 5 minutes. Remove from the heat and allow the quail to sit, covered, for another 5 minutes. When the quail are cool enough to handle, place on a platter and serve. Discard the smoking mixture and the foil.

Serve with the salt and pepper mixture and lemon wedges.

Serves 4

4 x 100 g (4 oz) quail
1 tablespoon sesame oil
1 tablespoon roasted and ground Sichuan peppercorns (page 21), mixed with 1½ tablespoons salt, to serve
Lemon wedges, to serve

For the Smoking Mixture:

50 g (2 oz) long-grain white rice
3 tablespoons brown sugar
50 g (2 oz) jasmine tea leaves

Peking Lemon Duck ≈

Serves 4

1.75–2 kg (4–4½ lb) duck,
fresh or frozen, preferably
Cherry Valley

1 teaspoon coarsely ground
five-pepper mixture
(page 21) or black pepper

2 teaspoons salt

2 teaspoons five-spice
powder (page 17)

2 lemons, quartered

6 slices of unpeeled fresh
ginger (page 17) (size
unimportant)

I have never considered myself chauvinistic but I firmly believe that no one cooks duck as well as the Chinese. What can be more wondrous than to bite into a crackling skin of a tempting, deep-mahogany colour and moist, rich duck meat? The secret is two-fold: first, the skin is separated from the fat when air is forced into it through the neck by blowing through a straw or with a bicycle pump. Later, when the duck is roasting, the fat melts away while the skin crisps separately.

The duck is given a bath of very hot water and vinegar and allowed to air-dry for a few hours. Later, it is doused in a bath of honey and dark soy sauce, which gives the skin a lovely glazed, lacquered look. In fact, the French call Chinese roast duck 'lacquered duck', which I think describes it rather aptly.

In this recipe, I have again mined my Chinese culinary heritage, which I have merged with my interest in western tastes and flavours to produce a duck dish that takes the best from both worlds.

Don't worry if you are unable to pump air into the duck to separate the skin from the fat; it is a step that can be skipped. You can usually find whole ducks with necks, etc. in Chinese supermarkets. However, what is more important is the drying of the duck, which helps to produce the crisp skin that is the hallmark of this dish. In order to save time, I have also skipped the hot water and vinegar stage in this recipe.

I have flavoured the duck with a mixture of five-spice powder, as well as five-pepper mixture and lemons. The result is an uncommonly elegant dish that will bring compliments from your family and friends. Serve the duck with potatoes and vegetables.

If the duck is frozen, thaw it thoroughly. Rinse the duck well and blot it completely dry with kitchen paper.

If you have a whole duck with the neck on, hold the cavity shut with a tea-towel and, with a clean bicycle pump, force air in to separate the skin from the fat. This is an optional step for whole ducks. Pull off any excess fat from the cavity.

In a small bowl, combine the pepper, salt and five-spice powder and mix well. Sprinkle inside the cavity of the duck with this mixture. Then stuff the cavity with the lemon quarters and ginger slices. Seal the flap of the cavity with a bamboo or metal skewer and secure the cavity with string.

Insert a meat hook near the neck.

Using a sharp knife, cut the lemons for the syrup mixture into 5 mm (¼ in) slices, leaving the rinds on. Combine the lemon slices with the rest of the syrup ingredients in a large pan and bring the mixture to the boil. Turn the heat to low and simmer for about 20 minutes.

Holding the hook, place the duck over the pan and then, using a large ladle or spoon, pour the syrup mixture over the duck several times, as if to bathe it, until all the skin of the duck is completely coated with the mixture. Hang the duck in a cool, well-ventilated place to dry; or, alternatively, hang it in front of a cold fan for about 4–5 hours, longer if possible. (Be sure to put a tray or roasting tin underneath to catch any drips.) Once the duck has dried, the surface of the skin will feel like parchment.

Pre-heat the oven to 160°C/ 325°F/gas mark 3. Meanwhile, place the duck on a roasting rack in a roasting tin, breast-side up. Put 150 ml (5 fl oz) of water into the roasting tin. (This will prevent the fat from splattering.) Now put the duck into the oven and roast it for 1¼ hours. Then turn the heat up to 220°C/450°F/gas mark 8 and continue to roast for 15 minutes, or until the skin is a rich, dark brown and very crisp.

Remove the duck from the oven and let it sit for at least 20 minutes before you carve it. Using a cleaver or a sharp knife, cut the duck into pieces and arrange them on a warm platter. Serve at once.

For the Honey and Lemon Syrup Mixture:
2 lemons
1.2 litres (2 pints) water
3 tablespoons honey
3 tablespoons dark soy sauce (page 23)

CHICKEN ESCALOPES WITH FRIED GINGER ≈

SERVES 4

250 ml (8 fl oz) plus
  2 tablespoons ground-
  nut oil
3 tablespoons finely
  shredded fresh ginger
  (page 17)
4 x 100 g (4 oz) boneless,
  skinless, chicken breasts
1½ teaspoons salt
½ teaspoon freshly ground
  five-pepper mixture
  (page 21) or black pepper
Plain flour, for dusting
2 eggs, beaten
25 g (2 oz) dried
  breadcrumbs
2 tablespoons (25 g/1 oz)
  unsalted butter
Lemon wedges, to garnish

THIS RECIPE IS INSPIRED BY MY LOVE FOR THE FAMOUS MILANESE-STYLE BREADED VEAL. I SUBSTITUTE MORE READILY AVAILABLE CHICKEN FOR THE VEAL. THIS EFFORTLESS DISH IS THEN PAIRED WITH CRISPY-FRIED GINGER FOR AN UNCOMMONLY ELEGANT PRESENTATION THAT IS QUITE DELECTABLE. SERVE IT WITH FIRECRACKER CORN (PAGE 182).

Heat a wok or large frying-pan over a high heat until it is hot. Add the 250 ml (8 fl oz) of oil and, when it is very hot and slightly smoking, turn the heat to low and deep-fry the ginger until it is crisp and slightly browned. Remove with a slotted spoon and drain well on kitchen paper. The oil, now flavoured with ginger, can be saved and used for stir-frying once cooled.

Place each chicken breast between two pieces of cling film. With a large wooden mallet or empty bottle, pound the breasts until they are flat and about 5 mm (¼ in) thick. Sprinkle them evenly with the salt and pepper then dust with the flour, shaking off any excess. Now dip the chicken breasts in the beaten egg and, finally, in the breadcrumbs.

Heat a large frying-pan with the butter and the rest of the oil. Turn the heat to moderate and slowly pan-fry the breasts for 5 minutes on each side, until they are golden brown. Remove to a warm platter, scatter with the fried ginger, garnish with the lemon wedges and serve at once.

Japanese-style Marinated Grilled Quail ≈

Quail is a wonderful delicacy that is becoming more and more available. This small bird is quite delicious and easy to prepare. I especially like the Japanese method, which is a marinade that seeps into the quail meat, making it a savoury treat. Once marinated, they cook quickly on a smoky grill. This dish is perfect with a salad in summer and also makes an ideal starter.

Dry the quail inside and out with kitchen paper.

In a medium-sized bowl, mix all the marinade ingredients together and pour into a large, thick plastic bag. Put the quail inside, seal and leave to marinate at room temperature for at least 1 hour. Remove the quail from the plastic bag and keep the marinade.

Pre-heat the oven grill to high or make a charcoal fire in the barbecue. When the charcoal is ash-white or the oven grill is very hot, grill the quail, turning them frequently, for about 6 minutes so that they are cooked but slightly pink inside. Baste the quail with the remaining marinade.

Transfer to a warm platter and allow to rest for 10 minutes before serving.

Serves 6

6 x 100 g (4 oz) quail

For the Marinade:
1 tablespoon dark soy sauce (page 23)
1½ tablespoons light soy sauce (page 23)
2 teaspoons sugar
3 tablespoons mirin (Japanese sweet rice wine) (page 18)
1 tablespoon extra virgin oil

ASIAN DUCK CONFIT ≈

SERVES 6

6 fresh or frozen and thawed
  duck thighs and legs,
  about 1.5 kg (3 lb) in total
100 g (4 oz) coarse sea salt
6 x 350 g (12 oz) tins of
  duck or goose fat
8 unpeeled garlic cloves,
  lightly crushed
8 fresh ginger slices
  (page 17)
6 star anise (page 23)
3 cinnamon sticks (page 16)
2 tablespoons Sichuan
  peppercorns, roasted
  (page 21)

I SPEND A FEW MONTHS EACH YEAR IN SOUTH-WEST FRANCE, A REGION OF
EXCELLENT BUT RELATIVELY UNKNOWN CUISINE. I HAVE GAINED A DEEP
APPRECIATION FOR THE UNIQUELY DELICIOUS FOOD OF THAT AREA. MY GOOD
FRIENDS, MONIQUE AND JACQUES PÉBEYRE, TAUGHT ME HOW TO MAKE
SOME OF THEIR WONDERFUL REGIONAL SPECIALITIES.

   ONE OF MY FAVOURITES IS DUCK CONFIT, THAT IS, DUCK COOKED IN ITS
OWN FAT AND STORED IN A JAR, COVERED IN THE SAME FAT TO PRESERVE IT. IT
IS ONE OF THE OLDEST FORMS OF PRESERVING FOOD. CONFIT IS SURPRISINGLY
EASY TO MAKE AND, SINCE IT KEEPS SO WELL, I THINK IT WORTHWHILE TO
MAKE A LARGE BATCH. IN THIS RECIPE, I HAVE INCLUDED ASIAN SPICES TO
GIVE THE CONFIT AN EVEN MORE AROMATIC TASTE AND FLAVOUR. THE CONFIT
GOES BEAUTIFULLY WITH LENTILS OR OTHER PULSES, OR POTATOES.

Lay the duck pieces on a tray and evenly sprinkle the salt on both
sides. Cover the duck with a tea-towel and keep in a cool place or
the refrigerator overnight.

   The next day, wipe off the salt, heat the duck or goose fat in a
large pan and add the garlic, ginger, star anise, cinnamon and
peppercorns. Now add the duck pieces and cook slowly over a low
heat for 1 hour. The duck should be cooked and tender.

   Let the duck pieces cool in the fat, then transfer to an airtight
container with the fat covering them until ready to use. The confit will
keep for months if stored in this way in the refrigerator.

   When you are ready to cook the duck confit, pre-heat the oven to
180°C/350°F/gas mark 4.

   Scoop the duck pieces from the fat and cook in a shallow roasting
tin for 40 minutes, or until they are crisp. Remove them from the hot fat
which will have collected in the tin and drain on kitchen paper. Strain
the hot fat and keep for future use. (You can use it to sauté potatoes.)
Serve the duck at once.

BRINED DUCK WITH CHINESE LEAVES ≈

SERVES 4

3 tablespoons roasted and
  crushed Sichuan
  peppercorns (page 21)
50 g (2 oz) coarse sea salt
1.6 –1.8 kg (3½– 4 lb) fresh
  or frozen duck (preferably
  a white Peking duck)

For the Stock:

2 tablespoons cumin seeds
1.2 litres (2 pints) water
100 g (4 oz) sugar
6 star anise (page 23)
3 cinnamon sticks (page 16)
2 tablespoons Sichuan
  peppercorns, roasted
  (page 21)
8 unpeeled garlic cloves,
  lightly crushed
8 slices of unpeeled fresh
  ginger (page 17)
  (size unimportant)
Peel from 1 fresh orange
2 spring onions

ADELAIDE, AUSTRALIA, HAS BEEN A CENTRE OF FUSION-STYLE COOKERY FOR YEARS NOW. I HAVE BEEN INVITED THERE A NUMBER OF TIMES TO COOK MY VERSION OF FUSION OR EAST–WEST COOKING. IT WAS THERE THAT I MET THE EXTREMELY TALENTED URS INAUEN. HE IS A EUROPEAN CHEF, GROUNDED IN THE CLASSICS, BUT HE IS NEVERTHELESS OPEN TO ASIAN INFLUENCES AND IDEAS. TOGETHER, WE MADE A NUMBER OF SPECIAL DINNERS FOR AUSTRALIAN WINERIES.

I WAS IMPRESSED BY URS'S CULINARY SKILL, WHICH IS PARTICULARLY APPARENT IN THIS DELICIOUS DUCK RECIPE. IT IS OF CHINESE INSPIRATION AND PRESENTED ON A BED OF BRAISED CHINESE LEAVES. IT IS ABSOLUTELY DELICIOUS AND A WONDERFUL ALTERNATIVE METHOD FOR COOKING DUCK.

THIS IS NOT A FAST-FOOD DISH BUT MUCH OF THE WORK IS EASY, INCLUDING THE SALTING AND THE COOKING, AND THE NECESSARY PREPARATIONS MUST BE DONE BEFOREHAND. THE RESULT IS A VERY IMPRESSIVE MAIN COURSE THAT IS WELL WORTH THE EFFORT.

Heat a wok or large frying-pan over a high heat until it is hot. Add the cumin seeds and dry-roast for 2 minutes. Set aside. Add the Sichuan peppercorns and salt and stir-fry for 1 minute. Lay the duck on a tray and rub the warm salt and pepper mixture over the duck. Cover the duck with a tea-towel and keep in a cool place or the refrigerator overnight.

The next day, soak the duck in cold water for 1 hour. Then blanch the duck in a large pan of boiling water for 5 minutes. Rinse in cold water and set aside.

Heat the water for the stock in a pan that is just large enough to hold the duck. Add the sugar, star anise, cinnamon, peppercorns, cumin, garlic, ginger, orange peel and spring onions. Simmer the stock for 45 minutes. Strain the stock, discarding the spices, and return the stock to the pan. Add the duck, then cover and simmer for 45 minutes. Turn off the heat and when the liquid is cool, refrigerate. Allow the duck to steep in the liquid overnight.

The next day, remove the duck and all traces of fat from the liquid. Bring the duck liquid to a simmer in a heavy casserole.

Cut the Chinese leaves into 5 cm (2 in) thick strips. Add these to the simmering duck liquid. Whisk in the butter, a piece at a time. Season with the salt and pepper and cook for 10 minutes or until the leaves are very tender. These braised leaves can be made ahead of time and reheated.

Remove the duck skin and cut it into thick strips. Heat the oil in a small pan and deep-fry the strips; turn the heat to low and fry until the strips are crisp. Drain well on kitchen paper.

Warm the duck meat briefly in the liquid in which the leaves were braised. Carve the duck into slices. To present the duck, place a portion of Chinese leaves on each plate. Then put the duck meat on top, pour on some of the braising liquid to moisten the duck, garnish with the crisp skin strips and serve at once.

To Finish:

750 g (1½ lb) Chinese leaves (page 14)

2 tablespoons (25 g/1 oz) cold unsalted butter, cut in pieces

1 teaspoon salt

1 teaspoon freshly ground five-pepper mixture (page 21) or black pepper

150 ml (5 fl oz) groundnut oil

WOLFGANG PUCK'S STIR-FRIED CHICKEN WITH GARLIC AND FRESH CORIANDER ≈

SERVES 4–6

450 g (1 lb) boneless, skinless
  chicken thighs
1 tablespoon Shaoxing rice
  wine (page 22) or dry sherry
1 tablespoon light soy sauce
  (page 23)
1 teaspoon freshly ground five-
  pepper mixture (page 21)
  or black pepper
2 teaspoons sesame oil
2 teaspoons cornflour

For the Vinaigrette:
3 tablespoons white rice vinegar
  (page 24) or cider vinegar
2 tablespoons light soy sauce
  (page 23)
2 tablespoons groundnut oil
1 tablespoon sesame oil
1 tablespoon lemon juice
½ teaspoon salt
¼ teaspoon freshly ground
  black pepper

For the Stir-fry:
225 g (8 oz) red or green
  peppers
2½ tablespoons groundnut oil
3 tablespoons thinly sliced garlic
6 tablespoons finely shredded
  spring onions
3 tablespoons mirin (Japanese
  sweet rice wine) (page 18)
  or dry sherry
2 teaspoons sesame oil
3 tablespoons finely chopped
  fresh coriander
225 g (8 oz) iceberg lettuce

ONE OF THE BEST PRACTITIONERS OF FUSION COOKING IS UNDOUBTEDLY WOLFGANG PUCK, WHO MADE HIS REPUTATION AS CHEF TO THE STARS OF HOLLYWOOD. WOLFGANG, A TALENTED CLASSICAL EUROPEAN-TRAINED CHEF WORKING IN LOS ANGELES, WAS THE FIRST TO MIX ASIAN INFLUENCES IN HIS WESTERN COOKING. HIS LANDMARK RESTAURANT, CHINOIS, BROKE NEW GROUND BY SERVING FOOD THAT WAS A TRUE MIXTURE OF EAST AND WEST. HIS SUBSEQUENT SUCCESS PROVED THAT THE PUBLIC LOVED THE MIXTURE, ESPECIALLY WHEN COOKED BY THE SKILFUL HANDS OF WOLFGANG PUCK. A DISH THAT I PARTICULARLY ENJOY, AND WAS INSPIRED BY, WAS THIS CHICKEN, EATEN WITH LETTUCE LEAVES. IT IS FUN TO SERVE AND DELICIOUS.

Cut the chicken into 2.5 cm (1 in) chunks and combine them in a bowl with the rice wine or sherry, soy sauce, pepper, sesame oil and cornflour. Leave to marinate for 20 minutes.

Make the vinaigrette by combining the vinegar, soy sauce, groundnut and sesame oils, lemon juice, salt and pepper in a small bowl. Mix well and set aside.

Meanwhile, cut the peppers into small dice.

Heat a wok or large frying-pan over a high heat until it is hot. Add 1½ tablespoons of the oil and, when it is very hot and slightly smoking, stir-fry the chicken for about 5 minutes. Remove the chicken, drain in a colander and put into a bowl. Wipe the wok or pan clean. Reheat the wok or pan over a high heat and, when it is hot, add the remaining tablespoon of groundnut oil. When it is smoking slightly, add the garlic and stir-fry for 30 seconds. Then add the peppers and spring onions and stir-fry for another minute. Now add the rice wine or sherry and sesame oil and stir-fry for 1 minute; return the chicken to the mixture and continue to stir-fry for 1 minute, mixing well. Add the coriander and mix well. Turn onto a platter. Gently separate the lettuce leaves and arrange around the platter. Pour the vinaigrette into a small bowl and serve at once.

Each diner puts some chicken mixture on lettuce leaves, adds the vinaigrette and eats with his or her hands.

MULTI-SPICED GRILLED PIGEON ≈

As a child growing up in a Chinese community, I attended many banquets celebrating weddings and birthdays. A popular dish which everyone looked forward to was the crispy fried pigeon. Since then, I have had an abiding passion for pigeon. I love its rich and slightly gamey flavour and taste. Its assertive nature makes an ideal marriage with East–West spices. This easy-to-make but nevertheless impressive recipe is perfect for any special dinner party. Look for squab pigeons which are young, tender birds; you can, however, substitute quail or other small game birds. Serve with Penang Rice Noodles (page 217).

Serves 4

4 x 350–450 g
(12 oz–1 lb) squab
pigeons
2 tablespoons extra virgin
olive oil

For the Marinade:

1 tablespoon salt
1 teaspoon cayenne pepper
1 teaspoon paprika
2 teaspoons five-spice
powder (page 17)
1 teaspoon roasted and
ground Sichuan
peppercorns (page 21)
1 teaspoon freshly ground
five-pepper mixture (page
21) or black pepper
½ teaspoon ground cumin
powder
1 teaspoon Madras curry
powder (page 17)

First butterfly the squabs by slitting them open through the back. Cut out the backbone and flatten the squabs with the palm of your hand. With a small, sharp knife, make a small hole beneath either side of the breast bone and tuck the legs through each of the holes. This will help hold the shape of the squabs while they grill.

In a small bowl, mix the marinade ingredients together and rub this mixture evenly on each side of the squabs. Allow to marinate for 1 hour.

Pre-heat the oven grill to high or make a charcoal fire in the barbecue. When the oven grill is very hot or the charcoal is ash-white, drizzle the olive oil over the squabs and grill them for 8 minutes on each side or until they are cooked. Serve at once.

Steamed *Foie Gras* in Chinese Leaves ≈

I discovered the joys of *foie gras*, or fattened duck livers, in France. It was there that I had an opportunity to cook this highly prized delicacy for French friends. I could not resist applying flavours from my culinary heritage. Here, then, is a good example of how ancient spices can add a new twist to a traditional European food. Steaming preserves the delicate and subtle flavours of the *foie gras*. This is worth making, particularly for a special occasion, as a spectacular opener.

Remove four of the largest leaves from the Chinese leaves or spinach and blanch them in boiling water for 1 minute. Drain and allow to cool. Place a slice of *foie gras* on one end of a cabbage or spinach leaf. Sprinkle with sea salt and Sichuan peppercorns. Roll up the leaf, folding in the sides as you go. Repeat until you have four rolls.

Next, set up a steamer or put a rack into a wok or deep pan containing 5 cm (2 in) of water. Bring the water to the boil over a high heat. Put the wrapped *foie gras* onto a heatproof plate and then carefully lower it into the steamer or onto the rack. Turn the heat to low and cover the wok or pan tightly. Steam gently for 5 minutes. Remove the *foie gras* from the steamer and discard any liquid on the plate.

While the *foie gras* is steaming, put the ginger in a pan and cook for 1 minute until it is dry; then add the rice wine or sherry and cook over a high heat until all the wine has evaporated. Now add the chicken stock and slowly whisk in the butter, a piece at a time, with salt and pepper to taste. Toss in the coriander, stir and serve over each wrapped *foie gras*.

Serves 4

1 head of Chinese leaves (page 14) or spinach

4 pieces of raw *foie gras*, about 75 g (3 oz) each

1 teaspoon sea salt

1 teaspoon roasted and ground Sichuan peppercorns (page 21)

1 tablespoon finely chopped fresh ginger (page 17)

2 tablespoons Shaoxing rice wine (page 22) or dry sherry

3 tablespoons Home-made Chicken Stock (page 32)

2 tablespoons (25 g/1 oz) cold unsalted butter, cut in small pieces

Salt and freshly ground five-pepper mixture (page 21) or white pepper

2 teaspoons finely chopped fresh coriander

Fast, Fusion Barbecued Chicken ≈

Serves 4–6

1.5 kg (3 lb) chicken thighs
 on the bone
2 teaspoons salt
1 teaspoon freshly ground
 five-pepper mixture
 (page 21) or black pepper

For the Barbecue Sauce:
3 tablespoons hoisin sauce
 (page 22)
1 tablespoon light soy sauce
 (page 23)
2 tablespoons oyster sauce
 (page 22)
2 tablespoons dark soy
 sauce (page 23)
2 tablespoons Shaoxing rice
 wine (page 22) or dry
 sherry
2 tablespoons mirin
 (Japanese sweet rice wine)
 (page 18) or dry sherry
2 teaspoons white rice
 vinegar (page 24)
1½ tablespoons dried thyme
1 tablespoon chilli-bean
 sauce (page 22)

GRILLING CONTINUES TO BE A POPULAR COOKING TECHNIQUE FOR FUSION CHEFS. NO WONDER: IT IS FAST, EASY AND IT HELPS TO RETAIN FLAVOURS. HERE IS A QUICK RECIPE THAT USES THE BEST OF EAST–WEST SEASONINGS TO CREATE A TASTY DISH. IT GOES EXTREMELY WELL WITH THAI-STYLE VEGETARIAN CURRY RICE (PAGE 201).

Lay the chicken thighs on a tray and evenly sprinkle on the salt and pepper.

In a bowl, mix the sauce ingredients.

Pre-heat the oven grill to high or make a charcoal fire in the barbecue. When the grill is very hot or the charcoal is ash-white, grill the chicken thighs on each side for 10 minutes; then baste the thighs on both sides with the sauce and continue to grill for 10 minutes on each side or until they are cooked through. Serve at once.

VEGETABLES

蔬菜

ⓋBeancurd with Fragrant Lemon Grass ≈

SERVES **4** AS A MAIN
COURSE

4 lemon grass stalks
(page 18)
900 g (2 lb) firm, fresh
beancurd (page 13)
3 tablespoons oil, preferably
groundnut
6 tablespoons finely
shredded spring onions
3 tablespoons finely
shredded fresh ginger
(page 17)
2 tablespoons coarsely
chopped garlic
4 teaspoons Madras curry
powder (page 17)
2 teaspoons chilli powder or
flakes (page 15)
3 tablespoons Shaoxing
rice wine (page 22)
or dry sherry
4 tablespoons dark soy
sauce (page 23)
½ teaspoon freshly ground
black pepper
2 teaspoons sugar
4 teaspoons sesame oil
4 tablespoons ready-bought
roasted peanuts, coarsely
chopped

I FIRST TASTED THIS DELIGHTFUL DISH AT LE CHEVAL, A POPULAR VIETNAMESE RESTAURANT IN OAKLAND, CALIFORNIA. LEMON GRASS IS A HERB MOST IDENTIFIED WITH THAI AND VIETNAMESE COOKING; BUT THE CHINESE, LIKE ME, ARE EAGER TO ADOPT WHATEVER NEW FOODS AND INGREDIENTS WILL ENHANCE THEIR OWN CUISINE; IT IS A MATTER OF EAST MEETING EAST.

LEMON GRASS HAS A MILD BUT DISTINCTIVE FLAVOUR WHICH GOES VERY NICELY WITH THE CONGENIAL BEANCURD, IMPARTING A REFRESHING TASTE TO THIS VEGETARIAN MAIN-COURSE DISH. AND, FORTUNATELY, LEMON GRASS HAS BECOME MORE AND MORE EASILY AVAILABLE. SERVE THIS DISH WITH RICE.

Peel the lemon grass stalks to the tender, whitish centres and crush them with the flat of a knife. Cut them into 7.5 cm (3 in) pieces.

Cut the beancurd into 2.5 cm (1 in) cubes. Drain on kitchen paper for 20 minutes.

Heat a wok or large frying-pan over a high heat until it is hot. Add the oil and, when it is very hot and slightly smoking, add the lemon grass, spring onions, ginger and garlic and stir-fry for 20 seconds. Push the aromatics to the side of the wok, turn the temperature down, add the beancurd cubes and brown slowly on all sides. When the cubes are golden brown on all sides, sprinkle on the curry powder and chilli powder or flakes, mixing well. Now add the rice wine or sherry, soy sauce, pepper and sugar. Stir-fry this mixture for 1 minute. Add the sesame oil and turn the mixture gently several times to mix well. Top with the peanuts and serve at once, or allow to cool and reheat when ready to serve.

ⓋBeancurd in Aromatic Coconut Milk ≈

Soft beancurd is like custard, very tender and silky. It thus makes for a light, refreshing style of vegetarian dish. (In most supermarkets, this kind is labelled 'Japanese beancurd'.) Braised in coconut milk, it absorbs all the rich flavours of that exotic fruit.

In this recipe, again generously provided by master chefs at the Vietnamese restaurant, Le Cheval, in Oakland, California, the beancurd and coconut milk are combined with aromatic spices in a delectable ensemble for a meat-free main course. Rice complements this dish well.

Gently cut the beancurd into 2.5 cm (1 in) cubes. Drain on kitchen paper for at least 30 minutes.

In a medium-sized pan, combine the coconut milk, curry paste, spring onions, ginger, rice wine or sherry, soy sauce, salt, pepper and sugar. Bring the mixture to a simmer. Gently add the beancurd and simmer for 15 minutes.

Turn the mixture onto a platter, garnish with coriander and serve at once.

Serves 4 as a main course

900 g (2 lb) fresh silky Japanese beancurd (page 13)

2 x 400 ml (14 fl oz) tins of coconut milk (page 16)

4 tablespoons red Thai curry paste (page 23)

6 tablespoons finely shredded spring onions

3 tablespoons finely shredded fresh ginger (page 17)

3 tablespoons Shaoxing rice wine (page 22) or dry sherry

2 tablespoons light soy sauce (page 23)

2 teaspoons salt

1 teaspoon freshly ground black pepper

2 teaspoons sugar

Sprigs of fresh coriander, to garnish

ⓥCRACKLING RICE-PAPER ASPARAGUS ROLLS ≈

SERVES 4 AS A MAIN
COURSE (MAKES
ABOUT 15 ROLLS)

For the Filling:
450 g (1 lb) asparagus
1 teaspoon salt
½ teaspoon freshly ground
    five-pepper mixture
    (page 21) or black pepper
1½ tablespoons extra virgin
    olive oil
3 tablespoons finely chopped
    fresh chives
2 tablespoons finely chopped
    spring onions
1 tablespoon finely chopped
    fresh coriander
3 tablespoons drained and
    finely chopped sun-dried
    tomatoes in oil

For the Sealing Mixture:
3 tablespoons plain flour
3 tablespoons water

For the Rolls:
One packet dried rice paper
    rounds (page 22) in 22 cm
    (8½in) rounds
150 ml (5 fl oz) olive oil

ASPARAGUS, NATIVE TO THE MEDITERRANEAN, HAS BEEN CULTIVATED IN THE WEST SINCE ANTIQUITY. NOW WIDELY GROWN THROUGHOUT THE WORLD, IT IS A POPULAR VEGETABLE, PRIZED FOR ITS DELICATE FLAVOUR. IN THIS RECIPE, I USE RICE PAPER, WHICH IS MADE FROM RICE FLOUR, WATER AND SALT. I LOVE ITS ABILITY TO ENVELOP FOOD WITH A CRISP, CRACKLING SKIN, WHILE KEEPING THE FOOD MOIST. THE ROLLS ALSO MAKE EXCELLENT STARTERS.

Trim the asparagus to leave 10 cm (4 in) spears and discard the tough ends.

Blanch the asparagus spears in a large pan of boiling, salted water for 3 minutes. Drain immediately and plunge into cold water to stop the asparagus from cooking. Drain well.

Combine the asparagus with the salt, pepper, olive oil, chives, spring onions, coriander and sun-dried tomatoes.

Make the flour paste by mixing the flour and water together.

When you are ready to make the rolls, fill a large bowl with warm water. Dip a round of rice paper in the water and let it soften for a few seconds. Remove and drain on a tea-towel.

Place three asparagus spears and a little of the tomato–herb mixture in the middle of the rice paper and roll the top and the bottom edges over the asparagus at once. Fold up one side of the rice paper, and continue to roll to the end. Seal the end with a little of the flour-paste mixture. The roll should be compact and tight, rather like a short, thick cigar, about 10 cm (4 in) long. Set the roll on a clean plate and continue the process until you have used up all the asparagus. (The rolls can be made ahead to this point; cover loosely with a clean, dry tea-towel and refrigerate for up to 4 hours.)

Heat a wok or large frying-pan over a high heat until it is hot. Add the oil and, when it is hot and smoking, turn the heat down to medium and pan-fry the rolls, a few at a time, until they are golden brown. Should they stick together, do not attempt to break them apart until they have been removed from the oil. Continue frying until you have cooked all the rolls. Drain them on kitchen paper, slice them in half if you wish, and serve at once.

ⓥ FRITTO MISTO OF ASIAN VEGETABLES ≈

SERVES 4–6

225 g (8 oz) lotus root
    (page 18)
225 g (8 oz) taro root
    (page 24)
225 g (8 oz) potatoes
1.2 litres (2 pints) groundnut
    oil
A handful of fresh Italian
    flatleaf parsley
A handful of fresh basil
    leaves
Salt and freshly ground black
    pepper

THE RISE OF FUSION COOKING AROUND THE WORLD HAS LED TO A SURGE IN THE AVAILABILITY OF ASIAN VEGETABLES IN SUPERMARKETS. HERE, I OFFER A CRISP VEGETARIAN SIDE DISH THAT IS ADDICTIVE. *FRITTO MISTO* IS AN ITALIAN CULINARY TERM THAT LITERALLY MEANS 'FRIED MIXTURE' OF ANY FOODS. I COMBINE LOTUS ROOT, A LACY AQUATIC PLANT THAT HAS A CRISP, FIBROUS TEXTURE AND A MILD, DISTINCTIVE FLAVOUR SOMEWHAT AKIN TO ARTICHOKES, WITH TARO ROOT, A STARCH THAT WAS USED IN CHINA AND SOUTH-EAST ASIA LONG BEFORE RICE AND POTATOES. TARO ROOT TUBERS VARY IN SHAPE, BUT THEY ARE ROUGHLY SPHERICAL, ANYTHING FROM TENNIS-BALL SIZE TO ABOUT 23 CM (9 IN) DIAMETER, AND OFTEN COVERED WITH A ROUGH SKIN AND BROWNISH HAIRS. THEY ARE STARCHY, WITH A SWEET FLAVOUR, DOUGHY TEXTURE AND A WHITISH FLESH, OFTEN WITH PURPLE STREAKS. BOTH LOTUS AND TARO ROOTS CAN BE FOUND AT CHINESE SUPERMARKETS OR GROCERS. THIS IS A PERFECT VEGETARIAN DISH.

Peel the lotus root and cut it crossways into 3 mm (⅛ in) slices. Do the same with the taro root and potatoes.

Heat a wok or deep frying-pan over a high heat until it is hot. Add the oil and, when it is very hot and slightly smoking, lower the temperature to moderate. Fry half of the vegetables for 5–6 minutes or until they are crisp. Remove them with a slotted spoon and drain on kitchen paper. Prepare the second batch in the same way.

Quickly fry the parsley and basil leaves; drain on kitchen paper. Transfer the fried vegetables and herbs to a warm platter, toss with salt and pepper to taste and serve at once.

ⓥ STIR-FRIED CURRIED CELERY ≈

CELERY IS AN UNDERVALUED VEGETABLE AND DESERVES MORE RESPECT. IT IS DELICIOUS IN ITS OWN CRUNCHY, MILD AND UNASSUMING WAY AND ITS DISTINCTIVE TASTE MAKES IT AN IDEAL FOIL FOR SPICY FLAVOURS.

HERE, IT IS COMBINED WITH CURRY IN A SIMPLE, EASY-TO-MAKE DISH. YOU WILL SEE THAT THIS HUMBLE VEGETABLE HAS A REAL ROLE TO PLAY.

Trim the base of the celery and all the top leaves. Separate the sticks. With a small, sharp knife, string any tough sticks. Chop the sticks into 2.5 cm (1 in) sections.

Heat a wok or large frying-pan over a high heat until it is hot. Add the oil and, when it is very hot and slightly smoking, add the garlic and ginger and stir-fry for 10 seconds. Then add the celery and continue to stir-fry for 1 minute. Add the rice wine or sherry, curry powder, soy sauce, sugar and salt and continue to stir-fry for another minute. Then add the water and continue to cook over a high heat for 3–4 minutes, until the celery is just tender. Sprinkle the mixture with the spring onions and coriander, mix well, transfer to a warm platter and serve at once.

SERVES 4 AS AN ACCOMPANIMENT

450 g (1 lb) celery
1 tablespoon groundnut oil
2 tablespoons coarsely chopped garlic
2 teaspoons finely chopped fresh ginger (page 17)
1 tablespoon Shaoxing rice wine (page 22) or dry sherry
2 teaspoons Madras curry powder (page 17)
1 teaspoon light soy sauce (page 23)
2 teaspoons sugar
½ teaspoon salt
3 tablespoons water

To Garnish:
2 tablespoons finely chopped spring onions
1 tablespoon finely chopped fresh coriander

ⓥBEANCURD SATAYS ≈

SERVES 2–4 AS A MAIN COURSE

450 g (1 lb) firm, fresh beancurd (page 13)

For the Marinade:
3 tablespoons light soy sauce (page 23)
1 tablespoon Shaoxing rice wine (page 22) or dry sherry
1 tablespoon mirin (Japanese sweet rice wine) (page 18) or dry sherry
2 teaspoons sesame oil

For the Peanut Sauce:
3 tablespoons smooth peanut butter or sesame paste (page 22)
1 tablespoon chilli-bean sauce (page 22)
1 tablespoon chopped garlic
2 teaspoons chilli oil (page 15)
2 tablespoons Chinese white rice vinegar (page 24) or cider vinegar
2 tablespoons light soy sauce (page 23)
½ teaspoon salt
¼ teaspoon freshly ground five-pepper mixture (page 21) or black pepper
2 teaspoons sugar
2 tablespoons hot water

To Garnish:
100 g (4 oz) onions, sliced
225 g (8 oz) cucumbers, thinly sliced

IN THIS RECIPE, FIRM BEANCURD CUBES ARE MARINATED AND GRILLED, THEN SERVED WITH A SAVOURY PEANUT SAUCE AND A GARNISH OF RAW ONION SLICES AND CUCUMBER. ROLL THOSE FLAVOURS OVER YOUR TONGUE FOR A MOMENT: THEY SOUND DELICIOUS AND THEY ARE.

THIS PARTICULAR RECIPE IS REALLY AN EAST–WEST COMBINATION, INSPIRED BY A WONDERFUL VEGETARIAN RESTAURANT CALLED GREENS IN SAN FRANCISCO. AS PREPARED BY ITS MASTER CHEFS, IT NICELY ILLUSTRATES BEANCURD'S VERSATILITY AND ITS ABILITY TO ABSORB FLAVOURS, THUS TRANSFORMING ITSELF FROM BLAND MEEKNESS INTO AN ASSERTIVE, TASTY FOOD. BEANCURD READILY ACCEPTS THE ATTRIBUTES OF THE MARINADE AND STANDS UP BEAUTIFULLY TO THE GRILLING PROCESS. EXPERIMENT WITH YOUR OWN MARINADES: BEANCURD WELCOMES YOUR EFFORTS.

ALWAYS BUY THE FRESHEST BEANCURD; FOR THIS RECIPE YOU WILL NEED THE FIRM VARIETY, AS SOFT BEANCURD IS NOT SUITABLE FOR SKEWERING. YOU CAN ADD OTHER VEGETABLES, SUCH AS SMALL TOMATOES, PEPPERS AND ONIONS, TO MAKE 'SHISH KEBABS'. THIS IS AN EXCELLENT SIDE DISH, OR A STARTER WITH DRINKS FOR MORE PEOPLE, AS WELL AS A MAIN COURSE.

Place the beancurd between several layers of kitchen paper with a weight such as a heavy lid on top. Leave for 1 hour.

Mix all the marinade ingredients in a small bowl. Cut the beancurd into 5 cm (2 in) cubes and add to the marinade. Let the mixture soak into the cubes for 45 minutes.

Put all the ingredients for the peanut sauce in a blender and mix well. Transfer to a serving bowl.

Meanwhile, soak some wooden skewers in water for 30 minutes.

Pre-heat the oven grill or prepare the barbecue. Thread the beancurd cubes on the skewers, taking care to put no more than three or four on each. When the grill is very hot or the charcoal is ash-white, cook the beancurd cubes, basting once with the marinade. When one side is brown, turn them over, baste again and cook until they are hot all through and quite firm.

Arrange the beancurd skewers on a platter. Garnish with onion and cucumber slices and serve at once with the peanut sauce.

ⓥ Asparagus and Coconut Quiche ≈

Serves 4–6 as a main course

For the Pastry:
150 g (5 oz) plain flour
4 tablespoons (50 g/2 oz) butter
½ teaspoon salt
2 tablespoons cold water
2 tablespoons single cream

For the Filling:
350 ml (12 fl oz) single cream
6 tablespoons tinned coconut milk (page 16)
1 tablespoon finely chopped fresh ginger (page 17)
250 g (6 oz) fresh asparagus, trimmed
3 eggs, beaten
1 teaspoon salt
¼ teaspoon freshly ground five-pepper mixture (page 21) or black pepper
A pinch of sugar
2 tablespoons finely chopped spring onions
2 tablespoons finely chopped fresh chives
3 tablespoons desiccated coconut

This vegetarian quiche, a western dish, is enhanced with eastern seasoning and spices. A light tasty dish, it makes a perfect luncheon main course, served with a salad, or can easily be a lovely starter for an elegant meal.

Combine all the pastry ingredients in a mixing bowl or a food processor in the usual way. Roll the dough into a ball on a lightly floured board. Cover with cling film and refrigerate for 30 minutes.

Pre-heat the oven to 180°C/350°F/gas mark 4.

Roll out the pastry to 3 mm (⅛ in) thick and press the pastry into a greased 20 cm (8 in) tart tin. Place a sheet of foil over the surface of the pastry and put about 350 g (12 oz) of dried beans on the foil, to weigh it down. Bake the pastry for 12 minutes. Remove the beans and foil. Lightly mark tiny holes in the pastry surface with a fork. Return the pastry to the oven and bake for 10 minutes. Remove and allow to cool thoroughly.

Pour the cream and coconut milk into a small pan, add the ginger and simmer for about 15 minutes over a very low heat. Strain through a fine sieve, discard the ginger and allow the infused cream and coconut milk to cool.

Cut the asparagus at a slight diagonal into 7.5 cm (3 in) pieces. Heat the oven to 200°C/400°F/gas mark 6.

Lay the asparagus on the cooked pastry. Combine the infused cream and coconut milk with the eggs, salt, pepper, sugar, spring onions, chives and desiccated coconut. Pour this mixture on top of the asparagus and cooked pastry.

Bake the quiche for 25 minutes or until the egg has set. Serve warm or at room temperature.

ⓋSTIR-FRIED RAINBOW VEGETABLES ≈

WHOEVER SAID VEGETARIAN FOOD HAS TO BE DREARY AND BORING WAS MANIFESTING A LACK OF IMAGINATION AND A DEFICIENCY IN THE ART OF COOKERY. FOR EXAMPLE, HERE IS A DELICIOUS VEGETARIAN TREAT, APPEALING TO THE EYE AS WELL AS THE PALATE.

THE VARIOUS COLOURFUL VEGETABLES CONSTITUTE THE 'RAINBOW', AND THEY ARE STIR-FRIED AND SERVED WITH CRISP LETTUCE AND HOISIN SAUCE TO CREATE AN UNUSUAL COMBINATION OF TASTES AND TEXTURES. I USE READY-BOUGHT PRESSED, SEASONED BEANCURD AS A TASTY MEAT SUBSTITUTE.

THIS DISH MAKES A LIGHT SNACK OR A GOOD FINGER-FOOD STARTER FOR A DINNER PARTY OR ANY FESTIVE OCCASION. THE RAINBOW VEGETABLE MIXTURE AND LETTUCE LEAVES ARE SERVED ON INDIVIDUAL PLATTERS, AND THE HOISIN SAUCE IN A SMALL BOWL. EACH GUEST PUTS A HELPING OF EACH INGREDIENT INTO A HOLLOW LETTUCE LEAF, RATHER LIKE STUFFING A PANCAKE OR A TACO, AND EATS THE FILLED LEAF WITH HIS OR HER FINGERS. AS AN OPTIONAL EXTRA, YOU CAN ALSO DEEP-FRY BEAN THREAD NOODLES AND SERVE THEM ON TOP OF THE RAINBOW VEGETABLES.

Soak the dried mushrooms in warm water for 20 minutes, drain them and squeeze out any excess liquid. Trim off the stems and shred the caps into 5 cm (2 in) long strips. Peel the carrots and cut into 5 cm (2 in) fine shreds. Cut the bamboo shoots, courgettes and pepper into 5 cm (2 in) fine shreds also. Finely shred the celery heart and pressed beancurd. Separate and wash the lettuce leaves, spin them dry in a salad-spinner and set aside in the refrigerator.

Heat a wok or large frying-pan over a high heat until it is hot. Add the oil and, when it is very hot and slightly smoking, add the garlic, shallots and spring onions and stir-fry for 20 seconds. Then add the carrots and stir-fry for another minute. Now add the remaining vegetables (except the lettuce), the soy sauce, rice wine or sherry, oyster sauce, salt and pepper and stir-fry the mixture for 3 minutes.

Turn onto a platter. Arrange the lettuce leaves on a separate platter, put the hoisin sauce into a small bowl, the bean thread noodles, if using, in another bowl and serve at once.

SERVES 4–6 AS A SNACK OR STARTER

15 g (½ oz) dried Chinese black mushrooms (page 18)
100 g (4 oz) carrots
100 g (4 oz) tinned bamboo shoots
100 g (4 oz) courgettes
100 g (4 oz) red or green pepper (about 1)
100 g (4 oz) celery heart
100 g (4 oz) pressed, seasoned beancurd (page 13)
225 g (8 oz) iceberg lettuce
1½ tablespoons oil, preferably groundnut
1 tablespoon chopped garlic
3 tablespoons finely chopped shallots
3 tablespoons finely chopped spring onions
2 teaspoons light soy sauce (page 23)
2 teaspoons Shaoxing rice wine (page 22) or dry sherry
3 tablespoons vegetarian oyster-flavoured sauce (page 22) or dark soy sauce (page 23)
½ teaspoon salt
¼ teaspoon freshly ground five-pepper mixture (page 21) or black pepper
4 tablespoons hoisin sauce (page 23), to serve
25 g (1 oz) bean thread (transparent) noodles (page 19), deep-fried, to serve (optional)

ⓋGRILLED VEGETARIAN SANDWICH ≈

MAKES 4 SANDWICHES

100 g (4 oz) cauliflower
100 g (4 oz) courgettes
100 g (4 oz) carrots
100 g (4 oz) aubergine
50 g (2 oz) French beans or
  runner beans
1 large onion
100 g (4 oz) small button
  mushrooms
Extra virgin olive oil or
  Tomato-flavoured Olive Oil
  (page 40), to serve
4 French bread rolls or
  chunks of baguette, slit
  open, to serve

For the Marinade:

1 teaspoon salt
½ teaspoon freshly ground
  five-pepper mixture
  (page 21) or black pepper
2 tablespoons light soy
  sauce (page 23)
2 teaspoons sesame oil
1 tablespoon extra virgin
  olive oil
1 tablespoon sugar
1 teaspoon chilli flakes
  (page 15)

THIS UNUSUAL TREAT – A PLEASANT SURPRISE TO THE PALATE FOR THOSE WHO THINK A SANDWICH *MUST* CONTAIN MEAT – WAS INSPIRED BY A SANDWICH I ENJOYED AT HONG KONG'S JOYCE CAFÉ. IT IS A TRENDY CAFÉ FAMOUS FOR ITS GOOD FOOD, WITH MANY OF THE MENU ITEMS BEING VEGETARIAN. THIS IS AMONG THE MOST POPULAR CHOICES.

THE STYLE IS A MIXTURE OF EASTERN AND WESTERN IDEAS, INCORPORATING CHINESE FLAVOURS INTO WESTERN COOKING TECHNIQUES. HAVE THIS SANDWICH WITH SOUP FOR A COMPLETE AND SATISFYING LUNCH.

Cut the cauliflower into small florets about 3.5 cm (1½ in) wide. Cut the courgettes, carrots and aubergine diagonally into thin 10 cm (4 in) slices. Cut the beans into 10 cm (4 in) pieces and slice the onion.

Blanch the cauliflower, carrots and beans in a large pan of salted water for 3 minutes. Remove with a slotted spoon, plunge into cold water and then drain thoroughly.

Combine the marinade ingredients in a bowl, add the blanched vegetables with the rest of the vegetables and mix well. Marinate for 30 minutes.

Soak some bamboo skewers in cold water for 30 minutes. Pre-heat the oven grill to high or make a charcoal fire in the barbecue. Thread the vegetables on the skewers, alternating the different sorts. When the grill is very hot or the charcoal is ash-white, cook the vegetables until they are tender and cooked through.

Drizzle olive oil or tomato-flavoured olive oil on the bread, top with the grilled vegetables and serve.

STIR-FRIED CUCUMBERS AND COURGETTES ≈

I OFTEN SPEND MY SUMMERS IN CATUS, FRANCE. WHILE I'M THERE, I MAKE SURE I VISIT MY FRIEND, ALAIN GASTAL. HIS MOTHER HAS A MAGNIFICENT GARDEN AND SHE USUALLY OFFERS ME SOME OF HER SUMMER HARVEST OF CUCUMBERS AND COURGETTES. ON ONE EVENING, I HAD INVITED FRIENDS FOR DINNER AND, WHEN MME GASTAL'S BOUNTY ARRIVED, I QUICKLY PUT TOGETHER THIS SIMPLE STIR-FRIED DISH, COMBINING THE TWO VEGETABLES IN AN UNUSUALLY DELECTABLE WAY. SALTING BOTH VEGETABLES BEFORE COOKING DRAWS OUT SOME OF THEIR EXCESS LIQUID AND GIVES THEM A FIRM, SLIGHTLY CRUNCHY TEXTURE THAT GOES WELL WITH THE SPICES I HAVE USED HERE.

Peel the cucumbers, slice them in half lengthways and, using a teaspoon, remove the seeds. Then cut the cucumber halves and courgettes into 2.5 cm (1 in) cubes. Sprinkle them with 2 teaspoons of salt and mix well. Put the mixture into a colander and let it sit for 20 minutes, to drain.

When the cucumber and courgettes cubes have drained, rinse them in water and then blot them dry with kitchen paper.

Heat a wok or large frying-pan over a high heat until it is hot. Add the oil and, when it is very hot and slightly smoking, add the garlic, ginger, the remaining salt and pepper and stir-fry for about 20 seconds. Then add the cucumbers and courgettes and continue to stir-fry over a high heat for 5 minutes or until the vegetables are cooked. Stir in the chilli-bean sauce, oyster or soy sauce and sugar and continue to cook for 2 minutes. Then add the sesame oil and serve immediately.

SERVES 4 AS AN ACCOMPANIMENT

750 g (1½ lb) cucumbers (about 1½)

450 g (1 lb) courgettes

3 teaspoons salt

1½ tablespoons oil, preferably groundnut

3 tablespoons coarsely chopped garlic

1 tablespoon finely chopped fresh ginger (page 17)

½ teaspoon freshly ground five-pepper mixture (page 21) or black pepper

2 teaspoons chilli-bean sauce (page 22)

2 tablespoons vegetarian oyster-flavoured sauce (page 23) or dark soy sauce (page 23)

2 teaspoons sugar

2 teaspoons sesame oil

ⓋFirecracker Corn ≈

SERVES 4 AS AN
ACCOMPANIMENT

275 g (10 oz) fresh
   sweetcorn kernels
   (about 2 cobs), or frozen
   sweetcorn kernels
1 tablespoon oil, preferably
   groundnut
2 small, mild fresh red chillies
   (page 16), seeded and
   finely chopped
½ teaspoon salt
¼ teaspoon freshly ground
   five-pepper mixture (page
   21) or black pepper
1 teaspoon sugar
2 teaspoons Shaoxing rice
   wine (page 22) or dry
   sherry
1 teaspoon sesame oil

ONE OF THE TRENDIEST RESTAURANTS IN SAN FRANCISCO IS BETELNUT, AN ASIAN BEER-HOUSE RESTAURANT WITH A VERY TEMPTING AND SATISFYING MENU. A PARTICULAR VEGETARIAN SIDE DISH I VERY MUCH ENJOYED AT BETELNUT IS THIS ONE. IT USES FRESH SWEETCORN, WHICH IS A RELATIVELY NEW FOOD IN CHINESE CUISINE, HAVING BEEN INTRODUCED BUT 300 YEARS AGO. THE DISH IS SIMILAR TO, BUT NOT AS EXPLOSIVE AS, A STIR-FRIED CORN DISH I HAD YEARS AGO IN SICHUAN, CHINA. SIMPLE TO MAKE, IT NEEDS THE FRESHEST, SWEETEST CORN.

If the corn is fresh, cut the kernels off the cob. Blanch frozen corn for 10 seconds in boiling water and drain.

Heat a wok or large frying-pan over a high heat until it is hot. Add the oil and, when it is very hot and slightly smoking, add the corn, chillies, salt and pepper and stir-fry for 1 minute. Then add the sugar and rice wine or sherry and continue to stir-fry for 2 minutes. Finally, stir in the sesame oil, mix well and serve at once.

VEGETABLES

ⓋSPICY ORANGE-FLAVOURED BEANCURD ≈

Le Cheval is a deservedly popular Vietnamese speciality restaurant in Oakland, California, but, as its name suggests, it also reflects a French *esprit de finesse* along with its native culinary inventiveness. It offers a wide variety of beancurd dishes, which are luscious and satisfying.

This spicy, orange-flavoured beancurd is among the most delectable on the menu, with an East–West fusion touch. The beancurd is lightly pan-fried in a little oil and then finished off with aromatic fresh orange zest, onions and rice wine, with dried chillies adding their own pleasant bite.

Cut the beancurd into 2.5 cm (1 in) cubes. Drain on kitchen paper for 20 minutes.

Heat a wok or large frying-pan over a high heat until it is hot. Add the oil and, when it is very hot and slightly smoking, add the dried chillies and stir-fry for 20 seconds. Push the chillies to the side of the wok or pan, turn the temperature down, add the beancurd cubes and brown slowly on all sides. When the cubes are golden brown on all sides, remove the beancurd and chillies and drain on kitchen paper. Add the onions, orange zest and garlic to the wok or pan and stir-fry for 3 minutes, until the onions are wilted. Now add the rice wine or sherry, soy sauce, pepper and sugar. Return the browned beancurd cubes to the wok or pan and stir-fry for 3 minutes. Add the sesame oil and turn the mixture gently several times to mix well. Serve at once or allow to cool, and reheat when ready to serve.

SERVES 4 AS A MAIN COURSE

900 g (2 lb) firm, fresh beancurd (page 13)
3 tablespoons oil, preferably groundnut
10 dried red chillies (page 15), halved
450 g (1 lb) onions, coarsely sliced
4 tablespoons shredded orange zest
2 tablespoons coarsely chopped garlic
4 tablespoons Shaoxing rice wine (page 22) or dry sherry
4 tablespoons dark soy sauce (page 23)
½ teaspoon freshly ground five-pepper mixture (page 21) or black pepper
2 teaspoons sugar
4 teaspoons sesame oil

ⓥBRAISED FUSION MUSHROOMS WITH HERBS ≈

SERVES 2–4 AS A MAIN COURSE

50 g (2 oz) dried Chinese
  black mushrooms (page 18)
50 g (2 oz) dried morel
  mushrooms
900 g (2 lb) button mushrooms
3 tablespoons extra virgin
  olive oil
4 tablespoons coarsely
  chopped garlic
2 teaspoons salt
1 teaspoon freshly ground five-
  pepper mixture (page 21)
  or black pepper
4 tablespoons Shaoxing rice
  wine (page 22) or dry sherry
4 teaspoons light soy sauce
  (page 23)
2 teaspoons sugar
50 ml (2 fl oz) double cream

To Garnish:
2 tablespoons finely chopped
  fresh chives
2 tablespoons finely chopped
  spring onions

MUSHROOMS CAN TURN A SIMPLE VEGETARIAN DISH INTO A LOVELY, SATISFYING MAIN COURSE. IN THIS EASY RECIPE, I COMBINE DRIED CHINESE MUSHROOMS, WHICH HAVE A RICH, SMOKY FLAVOUR, WITH BUTTON MUSHROOMS AND DRIED MOREL MUSHROOMS IN A MUSHROOM STEW.

Soak the dried Chinese and morel mushrooms in two separate bowls of warm water for 20 minutes. Then drain the Chinese mushrooms and squeeze out the excess liquid. Strain this mushroom liquid and reserve. Remove and discard the mushroom stems and cut the caps in half. Rinse the morel mushrooms, to remove any sand. Slice the button mushrooms.

Heat a wok or large frying-pan over a high heat until it is moderately hot. Add the olive oil and immediately add the garlic and stir-fry for 15 seconds. Then add the salt and pepper and all the mushrooms with the mushroom liquid and stir-fry them for 2 minutes. Add the rice wine or sherry, soy sauce and sugar and continue stir-frying for 5 minutes or until the mushroom liquid has been reabsorbed by the mushrooms or evaporated. Finally, add the cream and cook for 2 minutes. Give the mushrooms a few stirs, turn onto a warm platter, sprinkle with chives and spring onions and serve at once.

ⓥ POTATO AND CUCUMBER MASH ≈

SERVES 4–6 AS AN
ACCOMPANIMENT

1.5 kg (3 lb) cucumbers
2 tablespoons salt
900 g (2 lb) potatoes
250 ml (8 fl oz) double
 cream
10 tablespoons (150 g/
 5 oz) softened butter
1 tablespoon finely chopped
 fresh coriander
Freshly ground five-pepper
 mixture (page 21) and salt

THIS AMBROSIAL ALTERNATIVE TO HUMBLE MASHED POTATO IS EASY TO MAKE
AND WILL SURELY SURPRISE YOUR DINNER GUESTS AND FAMILY. THE
CUCUMBERS LIGHTEN THE POTATOES, AS WELL AS GIVING THE DISH AN
UNUSUAL TEXTURE.

Peel the cucumbers, slice them in half lengthways and, using a
teaspoon, remove the seeds. Then cut the cucumber halves into slices.
Sprinkle them with the salt and mix well. Put the mixture in a colander
and leave for 45 minutes to drain. This rids the cucumber slices of any
excess liquid.

When the cucumber slices have drained, rinse them in water to
remove the salt and drain well. Purée in a blender or food processor.
Then squeeze any excess moisture from the puréed cucumbers with a
clean tea-towel. Set aside.

Cook the potatoes, unpeeled, in salted water for 20 minutes, or
until tender.

When the potatoes are cool enough, peel them and pass them
through a ricer or food mill. Reheat them in a large, heavy pan. Bring
the cream to a simmer in a saucepan and whisk it into the potatoes.
Incorporate the butter and coriander, mixing well. Add salt and
pepper to taste and set aside.

Just before serving, reheat the potato mash, fold the cucumber
purée into it and serve at once.

ⓋGRILLED CORN WITH SPRING ONION AND GINGER BUTTER ≈

CORN IS PERHAPS ONE OF NORTH AMERICA'S GREATEST CONTRIBUTIONS TO THE WORLD OF FOOD. IT IS ESPECIALLY GOOD WHEN QUICKLY GRILLED AND SERVED WITH BUTTER. IN THIS RECIPE, I OFFER AN ALTERNATIVE TO PLAIN BUTTER, SPICING IT WITH ASIAN FLAVOURS FOR AN EASY, VEGETARIAN DISH.

In a bowl, mix the butter, spring onions, ginger, salt and Sichuan peppercorns together using a wooden spoon. Put the mixture in the refrigerator.

Pre-heat the oven grill to high or make a charcoal fire in the barbecue. Soak the corn cobs for 10 minutes in cold water but leave the husks on: the corn cobs will steam in their husks while on the grill. When the grill is very hot or the charcoal is ash-white, grill the cobs for 15 minutes. Remove and, when they are cool enough to handle, remove the husks and spread the cobs with the butter. Serve at once.

SERVES 4 AS AN ACCOMPANIMENT

6 tablespoons (75 g/3 oz) unsalted butter, softened at room temperature

5 tablespoons finely chopped spring onions

1 tablespoon finely chopped fresh ginger (page 17)

2 teaspoons salt

1 teaspoon roasted and ground Sichuan peppercorns (page 21)

1.5 kg (3 lb) fresh sweetcorn cobs, husks left on

Ⓥ Malaysian-inspired Vegetable Pancakes ≈

SERVES 2 AS A MAIN
COURSE (MAKES 5–6
PANCAKES)

100 g (4 oz) button
  mushrooms, thinly sliced
175 g (6 oz) spinach,
  washed, stems removed
2 tablespoons chopped fresh
  coriander
3 tablespoons chopped fresh
  basil
175 g (6 oz) onions, thinly
  sliced
175 g (6 oz) courgettes,
  thinly sliced
1 tablespoon finely chopped
  fresh ginger (page 17)
3–4 tablespoons groundnut
  oil, for frying
Salt, to serve

For the Batter:
300 g (11 oz) plain flour
1 teaspoon baking powder
2 teaspoons salt
1 teaspoon paprika
½ teaspoon freshly ground
  five-pepper mixture
  (page 21) or black pepper
750 ml (1¼ pints) ice-cold
  water
2 egg yolks

THIS RECIPE WAS INSPIRED BY THE WELL-KNOWN OYSTER OMELETTE FROM SINGAPORE AND MALAYSIA, WHICH IS MADE WITH SWEET-POTATO FLOUR. HOWEVER, INSTEAD OF USING OYSTERS, I USE FRESH VEGETABLES WHICH ARE PAN-FRIED AND HAVE A SLIGHTLY CHEWY TEXTURE THAT IS A TREAT. THIS DISH MAKES A WONDERFUL ACCOMPANIMENT TO ANY MEAT OR CAN BE A SUBSTANTIAL VEGETARIAN MAIN COURSE.

To make the batter, combine the flour, baking powder, salt, paprika and pepper and add the water. Stir, without mixing thoroughly. Then add the egg yolks and stir gently, again without mixing thoroughly. The batter will be slightly lumpy. Add the vegetables and ginger and stir to mix.

Heat a non-stick wok or large non-stick frying-pan until it is hot. Add a tablespoon of oil and, when it is hot, add some of the batter-vegetable mixture, tilting the pan so that the pancake becomes very thin. Cook for 1–2 minutes, until it is brown and crisp. Turn over and cook the other side. Remove to a warm platter. Cook the remaining mixture in the same manner.

Sprinkle with salt to taste and serve at once.

ⓥ Stir-fried Spicy Lemon Grass Vegetables ≈

SERVES 4 AS A MAIN
COURSE

450 g (1 lb) fresh broccoli
225 g (8 oz) carrots
225 g (8 oz) celery
2 lemon grass stalks
  (page 18)
1½ tablespoons groundnut oil
100 g (4 oz) shallots, finely
  sliced
2 tablespoons coarsely
  chopped garlic
1 teaspoon salt
½ teaspoon freshly ground
  black pepper
2 tablespoons Shaoxing rice
  wine (page 22) or dry
  sherry
1 tablespoon chilli-bean
  sauce (page 22)
1 teaspoon sugar
4–5 tablespoons water
2 tablespoons lime juice
2 teaspoons light soy sauce
  (page 23)
150 ml (5 fl oz) tinned
  coconut milk (page 16)

THIS IS A THAI-INSPIRED VEGETARIAN DISH THAT IS A PERFECT ACCOMPANIMENT TO ANY MEAL OR THAT CAN SERVE AS A GRATIFYING MAIN COURSE ON ITS OWN. IT IS AN EASY-TO-MAKE DISH THAT IS DELICIOUSLY AROMATIC.

Separate the broccoli heads into small florets and peel and slice the stems. Blanch the broccoli pieces in a large pan of salted, boiling water for several minutes; remove them with a slotted spoon and immerse them in cold water. Drain thoroughly. Peel and diagonally slice the carrots into 5 cm (2 in) pieces, blanch them in the same salted water as the broccoli and drain well. Cut the celery at a slight diagonal into 5 cm (2 in) pieces.

Peel the lemon grass stalks to the tender, whitish centres and slice the centres thinly into round pieces.

Heat a wok or large frying-pan over a high heat until it is hot. Add the oil and, when it is very hot and slightly smoking, add the lemon grass, shallots, garlic, salt and pepper and stir-fry for 1 minute. Then add the broccoli, carrots and celery and continue to stir-fry for 2 minutes. Add the rice wine or sherry, chilli-bean sauce and sugar. Stir-fry for a few seconds and then add the water, lime juice, soy sauce and coconut milk. Stir-fry at a moderate to high heat for 4 minutes, until the vegetables are tender and cooked. The vegetables are now ready to be served.

Ⓥ Ginger-leek Purée ≈

Growing up in a Chinese household, I only knew vegetables that were stir-fried or braised whole. Not until I lived in France did I discover the joys of puréed vegetables. I became particularly enamoured of leek purée; in this recipe, I enhance it with a touch of fresh ginger. It is easy to make and it goes extremely well as a side dish with roast or grilled fish, poultry or meat.

Trim the leeks and discard any yellow parts. Cut the leeks at the point where they begin to turn green and discard the green parts. Then split the white parts in half and cut them at a slight diagonal into 6 cm (2½ in) segments. Wash them well in cold water until there is no trace of dirt.

In a large pan, combine the leeks with the stock, ginger, salt and pepper and simmer for 15 minutes or until they are very tender. Allow the mixture to cool slightly and, when it is cool enough, purée in a blender or food processor.

Return the purée to the clean pan, add the butter and simmer for 3 minutes, then add the cream. Bring the mixture to a simmer again; it is now ready to be served.

Serves 4–6 as an accompaniment

1 kg (2¼ lb) leeks
475 ml (16 fl oz) Home-Made Vegetable (page 33) or Chicken (page 32) Stock
2 tablespoons finely chopped fresh ginger (page 17)
2 teaspoons salt
1 teaspoon freshly ground five-pepper mixture (page 21) or black pepper
2 tablespoons (25 g/1 oz) butter
3 tablespoons double cream

⒱Braised Aubergines with Mushrooms in Ginger Tomato Sauce ≈

SERVES 2–4 AS AN
ACCOMPANIMENT

15 g (½ oz) dried Chinese
    black mushrooms (page 18)

For the Sauce:
225 g (8 oz) tomatoes,
    peeled and seeded if
    fresh, drained if tinned
2 tablespoons extra virgin
    olive oil
1½ tablespoons finely
    chopped fresh ginger
    (page 17)
1 teaspoon salt
Freshly ground five-pepper
    mixture (page 21) or black
    pepper
2 teaspoons sugar

For the Aubergines:
450 g (1 lb) Chinese or
    ordinary aubergines
    (page 13)
75 ml (3 fl oz) extra virgin
    olive oil
5 garlic cloves, crushed
1 teaspoon five-spice
    powder (page 17)
2 teaspoons salt
½ teaspoon freshly ground
    black pepper
150 ml (5 fl oz) water

THIS APPEALING RECIPE IS THE INSPIRATION OF CHEF TAM AT THE CHINA HOUSE AT THE ORIENTAL HOTEL IN BANGKOK; EVERY YEAR HIS WONDERFUL RESTAURANT OFFERS THE THAIS A TWO-WEEK CELEBRATION OF VEGETARIAN MENUS. HE CREATED THIS SAVOURY TREAT BY COMBINING AUBERGINES WITH MEATY MUSHROOMS; THESE ARE THEN COOKED IN A SPICY GINGER TOMATO SAUCE – A FUSION DISH, IF EVER I SAW ONE. IT REHEATS WELL AND THIS MAKES IT IDEAL FOR PREPARING WELL IN ADVANCE.

I HAVE NOTED IN OTHER RECIPES THAT THE SMALLER, LONG, THIN CHINESE AUBERGINES ARE PREFERABLE TO THE THICKER EUROPEAN VARIETY BECAUSE OF THEIR SLIGHTLY SWEETER AND MILDER TASTE. HOWEVER, YOU CAN USE THE EUROPEAN TYPE, WHEN NECESSARY. LEAVE THE SKINS OF THE AUBERGINE ON. SOME PEOPLE MAY FIND THE GOING A BIT CHEWY BUT THE SKINS ARE NECESSARY TO ENHANCE THE TEXTURE OF THE DISH.

Soak the mushrooms in warm water for 20 minutes. Then drain them and squeeze out the excess liquid. Remove and discard the stems and finely shred the caps into thin strips.

If you are using fresh tomatoes, cut them into 2.5 cm (1 in) chunks. If you are using tinned tomatoes, chop them into small chunks. Heat a clean wok or large frying-pan over a moderate heat and, when it is hot, add the olive oil, ginger, salt and pepper and cook the ginger for 1 minute or until it is lightly browned. Add the tomatoes and sugar, reduce the heat and simmer for 15 minutes. Remove from the heat and set the tomato sauce aside.

Cut the aubergines into 5 x 1 cm (2 x ½ in) diagonal slices.

Heat a wok or large frying-pan over a high heat until it is hot. Add the oil and, when it is moderately hot, add the garlic and stir-fry for 30 seconds. Then add the aubergine slices, five-spice powder, salt and pepper and continue to stir-fry for 2 minutes.

Add the tomato sauce, mushrooms and water to the aubergines and continue to cook for 5 minutes. Turn the heat to low, cover and cook slowly for 15 minutes, until the aubergines are quite tender.

Serve at once, or allow to cool and serve at room temperature.

ⓥStir-fried Cauliflower with Fresh Coriander ≈

CAULIFLOWER, THAT SATISFYING VEGETABLE, IS NOT ONLY EASY TO PREPARE BUT IS ADAPTABLE TO ALMOST ANY TYPE OF SEASONING. HERE, I SIMPLY STIR-FRY IT WITH OLIVE OIL AND FINISH IT WITH A SHOWER OF FRESH CORIANDER.

Cut the cauliflower into small florets about 4 cm (1½ in) wide.

Heat a wok or large frying-pan over a high heat until it is hot. Add the olive oil and, when it is hot and smoking, add the garlic and stir-fry for about 20 seconds to flavour the oil. Quickly add the cauliflower florets and stir-fry them for a few seconds. Next, add the ground coriander, salt, pepper, lemon zest and stock or water. Turn the heat down and simmer for 10 minutes or until the cauliflower is tender.

Stir in the fresh coriander, turn onto a warm serving platter and serve at once, drizzled with curry-flavoured oil, if you wish.

SERVES **4** AS AN ACCOMPANIMENT

750 g (1½ lb) cauliflower
2 tablespoons extra virgin olive oil
4 garlic cloves, thinly sliced
1 teaspoon ground coriander
1 teaspoon salt
½ teaspoon freshly ground five-pepper mixture (page 21) or black pepper
2 teaspoons finely chopped lemon zest
150 ml (5 fl oz) Home-made Vegetable (page 33) or Chicken (page 32) Stock or water
3 tablespoons finely chopped fresh coriander
Curry-flavoured Oil (page 38), to serve (optional)

Ⓥ Corn Crêpes ≈

SERVES 4–6 AS AN
ACCOMPANIMENT
(MAKES 10–12 CRÊPES)

900 g (2 lb) fresh sweetcorn
cobs or 550 g (1¼ lb)
frozen sweetcorn kernels

2 eggs, beaten

2 tablespoons rice flour

1 tablespoon finely chopped
fresh coriander

1 tablespoon finely chopped
fresh chives

1 tablespoon finely chopped
spring onion

1 teaspoon sugar

2 teaspoons finely chopped
fresh ginger (page 17)

1 teaspoon salt

¼ teaspoon freshly ground
five-pepper mixture
(page 21) or black pepper

2 tablespoons olive oil

CORN IS ONE OF THE NUMEROUS VEGETABLES INTRODUCED RELATIVELY RECENTLY INTO ASIA AND IS NOW AN EXTREMELY POPULAR INGREDIENT OF THE AREA'S CUISINE. FUSION CHEFS USE IT EXTENSIVELY AND NO WONDER, IT IS A DELICIOUS FOOD. THIS RECIPE MAKES MAKES AN EXCELLENT STARTER BUT IS JUST AS GOOD SERVED AS A SIDE DISH WITH ANY GRILLED FOODS.

Remove the kernels from the cobs with a sharp knife or cleaver, if using fresh corn. You should end up with about 550 g (1¼ lb). If you are using frozen corn, thaw thoroughly. Set aside half the corn in a separate bowl. Combine the rest of the corn with the eggs, rice flour, coriander, chives, spring onion, sugar, ginger, salt and pepper. Purée the mixture in a blender or food processor, then fold in the reserved corn.

Heat a frying-pan, preferably non-stick, add the olive oil and, when it is hot, spoon in 2 tablespoons of the mixture to make a crêpe, tilting the pan in the usual way. Cook the crêpe over a medium heat for 2–3 minutes or until golden brown on one side. Using a knife or spatula, turn the crêpe over and cook the other side until crisp and golden. Put on a warm platter and keep warm in a very low oven. Continue until you have used up all the mixture. Serve the crêpes as soon as possible.

Ⓥ Vegetable Salad with Curry-soy Vinaigrette ≈

This is a delightful, warm vegetarian salad with a bold dressing. Although the idea is French-inspired, the flavours are exotically Asian and very enticing.

Make the curry-soy vinaigrette by combining the mustard, curry powder, soy sauce, salt, pepper and olive oil. Mix well and set aside.

Bring a pan of salted water to the boil. Drop in the tomatoes for 5 seconds, then remove, peel and seed them. Cut the tomatoes into 4 cm (1½ in) pieces and set aside. Now add the broccoli, French beans and cauliflower to the pan and cook for 3 minutes; then add the peas and cook for 1 minute. Drain the vegetables well, tip into a warm bowl and then add the water chestnuts and tomatoes. Drizzle in the curry-soy vinaigrette and add the shallots and chives. Mix well and serve at once.

Serves 4 as an accompaniment

For the Curry-soy Vinaigrette:
2 teaspoons Dijon mustard
2 teaspoons Madras curry powder (page 17)
2 tablespoons light soy sauce (page 23)
2 teaspoons salt
1 teaspoon freshly ground five-pepper mixture (page 21) or black pepper
4 tablespoons extra virgin olive oil

For the Salad:
225 g (8 oz) fresh tomatoes
100 g (4 oz) broccoli, cut in small florets
100 g (4 oz) French beans
100 g (4 oz) cauliflower, cut in small florets
100 g (4 oz) podded fresh peas or frozen peas
50 g (2 oz) fresh water chestnuts (page 24), peeled and sliced
3 tablespoons finely chopped shallots, squeezed dry
3 tablespoons finely chopped fresh chives

Ⓥ Ginger Vegetable Stew with a Herb Glaze ≈

Serves 4 as a main course

100 g (4 oz) red pepper
4 spring onions
2 tablespoons extra virgin
  olive oil
3 tablespoons finely chopped
  fresh ginger (page 17)
3 tablespoons finely chopped
  shallots
2 tablespoons chopped garlic
2 teaspoons salt
½ teaspoon freshly ground five-
  pepper mixture (page 21)
  or black pepper
250 ml (8 fl oz) Home-made
  Vegetable Stock (page 33)
3 sprigs of fresh thyme
175 g (6 oz) baby carrots
100 g (4 oz) baby sweetcorn
  cobs
175 g (6 oz) baby courgettes
225 g (8 oz) French beans

For the Glaze:

225 g (8 oz) tomatoes
1 tablespoon sugar
2 tablespoons (25 g/1 oz)
  unsalted butter
2 tablespoons finely chopped
  fresh chives
1 tablespoon finely chopped
  fresh coriander
3 tablespoons finely chopped
  fresh basil
Salt and freshly ground five-
  pepper mixture (page 21)
  or black pepper

Vegetables are as delicious as meat, especially when they are cooked with savoury ginger. In this dish, I use all the available spring vegetables and combine them in a stew finished with fresh, earthy herbs. The resulting fusion of flavours makes this tasty recipe a meal in itself. The tomatoes must be fresh and ripe.

Bring a large pan of water to the boil, quickly drop in the tomatoes, blanch for 5 seconds and remove them with a slotted spoon. Peel them and cut them in half widthways. Seed them by running your fingers round the centre. Save any juices, by draining them through a fine sieve. Discard all the seeds. Chop the tomatoes into 1 cm (½ in) cubes. Dust the chopped tomatoes with the sugar and let them drain in a stainless steel or plastic colander for 30 minutes, saving any juices.

Seed the red pepper and cut it into 5 cm (2 in) strips. Slice the spring onions diagonally into 5 cm (2 in) pieces.

In a wok or large frying-pan, heat the olive oil and add the ginger, shallots, garlic, salt and pepper and cook gently for 3 minutes. Add the stock, sprigs of thyme, carrots and sweetcorn. Cover tightly with a lid and cook over a high heat for 3 minutes until the carrots are partially cooked. Then add the courgettes, cover again and cook for another 2 minutes. Add the red pepper, French beans and spring onions. Cover again and cook for 4 minutes. Test the vegetables with a sharp knife to see if they are cooked.

In a separate pan, reduce all the tomato juices over high heat until only 1 tablespoon of glaze is left.

When the vegetables are cooked, remove them with a slotted spoon to a warm platter. To make the glaze, reduce the juices in the wok or pan by half, add the tomato glaze, the chopped tomatoes, butter, chives, coriander, basil and salt and pepper to taste. Cook for 1 minute and pour this over the vegetables. Serve at once.

ⓥ CURRY COUSCOUS WITH FRESH CHIVES AND APPLE ≈

2 tablespoons extra virgin olive oil

250 g (8 oz) onions, finely chopped

275 g (10 oz) couscous

475 ml (16 fl oz) Home-made Vegetable (page 33) or Chicken (page 32) Stock

1 tablespoon light soy sauce (page 23)

1 tablespoon (15 g/½ oz) unsalted butter

2 tablespoons Madras curry powder (page 17)

1 teaspoon sugar

2 teaspoons salt

½ teaspoon freshly ground five-pepper mixture (page 21) or black pepper

3 tablespoons finely chopped fresh chives

100 g (4 oz) peeled apples, finely chopped

ON MY FIRST TRIP TO MOROCCO, IN 1973, I FIRST ENCOUNTERED COUSCOUS, A CRUSHED WHEAT PRODUCT OF NORTH AFRICAN ORIGIN, WHICH CAN BE USED IN THE SAME WAY AS RICE AND PASTA. I ENJOYED THE TEXTURAL QUALITY OF THE GRAIN AND DISCOVERED HOW VERSATILE AND ADAPTABLE IT WAS. COUSCOUS HAS BECOME QUITE TRENDY, AND IS A PERFECT FOIL FOR FUSION COOKING BECAUSE IT IS SO ACCOMMODATING TO DIFFERENT FLAVOURS AND SPICES. THIS RECIPE TRANSFORMS IT BY COOKING IT IN VEGETABLE STOCK. IT MAKES A DELIGHTFUL ACCOMPANIMENT TO ANY POULTRY OR MEAT DISH.

Heat the olive oil in a medium-sized casserole, add the onions and cook them gently over a low heat for about 5 minutes, without browning. Add the couscous, mix well and continue to cook over a low heat for another 2 minutes. Now add the stock, soy sauce, butter, curry powder, sugar, salt and pepper and bring the mixture to the boil. Mix well and remove from the heat. Cover tightly and leave for about 20 minutes. Remove the lid, stir in the chives and apples and serve at once.

ⓥ GORDON'S CRANBERRY-GINGER RELISH ≈

This recipe comes from my chef-associate friend Gordon Wing, who is Chinese-American. An accomplished Chinese, as well as American, chef, he mixes cuisines, giving his food an exotic, personal touch. This relish is a delicious accompaniment to any meat or poultry dishes in this book. It can be made well ahead and keeps in the refrigerator for up to three weeks. Try it with Korean-style Grilled Beef (page 114).

Combine all the ingredients in a large pan and bring to the boil. Simmer the mixture for 15 minutes over a low heat. When the berries pop open, the relish is done. Let the relish cool to room temperature and then serve.

MAKES 450 G (1 LB)

350 g (12 oz) fresh or frozen cranberries

2 tablespoons finely chopped orange zest

175 ml (6 fl oz) fresh orange juice

8 tablespoons maple syrup or honey

2 tablespoons finely chopped fresh ginger (page 17)

RICE, NOODLES AND PASTA

ⓥThai-style Vegetarian Curry Rice ≈

This is my vegetarian interpretation of a delicious and glorious Thai rice dish, which uses spices and aromatics to transform the prosaic but congenial grain into a tasty and mouth-watering treat. Once the rice is made, the rest is quickly prepared. I find it reheats well in the microwave, which makes it a convenient dish, and it's one that is just as delectable cold as hot.

Cook the rice at least 2 hours before it is needed, or even the night before, according to the method for Steamed Rice on page 35. Allow it to cool thoroughly and put it in the refrigerator.

Heat a wok or large frying-pan over a high heat until it is hot. Add the groundnut oil, sesame oil and ½ teaspoon salt and, when very hot and slightly smoking, add the garlic, onion, ginger, the remaining 2 teaspoons salt and the pepper. Stir-fry for 2 minutes. Add the rice and continue to stir-fry for 3 minutes; add the curry powder and mix well. Finally, add the peppers, corn, peas and chilli oil and continue to stir-fry for 3 minutes. Sprinkle in the spring onions and coriander, mix well and continue to stir-fry for another minute.

Turn onto a warmed platter and serve hot, or cold as a rice salad.

400 ml (14 fl oz) long-grain white rice
600 ml (1 pint) water
2 tablespoons oil, preferably groundnut
2 teaspoons sesame oil
2½ teaspoons salt
2 tablespoons coarsely chopped garlic
1 onion, finely chopped
1 tablespoon finely chopped fresh ginger (page 17)
½ teaspoon freshly ground five-pepper mixture (page 21) or black pepper
1 tablespoon Madras curry powder (page 17)
175 g (6 oz) seeded and chopped red peppers
100 g (4 oz) fresh or frozen sweetcorn kernels
100 g (4 oz) frozen peas
1 teaspoon chilli oil (page 15)
3 tablespoons finely chopped spring onions
2 tablespoons finely chopped fresh coriander

Ⓥ Fragrant Fried Ginger and Spring Onion Rice ≈

SERVES 4 AS AN
ACCOMPANIMENT

400 ml (14 fl oz) long-grain
   white rice
600 ml (1 pint) water
2 tablespoons oil, preferably
   groundnut
3 tablespoons finely
   chopped fresh ginger
   (page 17)
100 g (4 oz) spring onions,
   finely chopped
2 teaspoons salt
½ teaspoon freshly ground
   five-pepper mixture
   (page 21) or black pepper
2 tablespoons finely
   chopped fresh coriander

GINGER ROOT HAS BEEN A MAJOR PART OF MY CULINARY LIFE — I MAY SAY, FOREVER, INASMUCH AS IT ALWAYS GRACED MY MOTHER'S KITCHEN. ALONG WITH SOY SAUCE, SPRING ONIONS AND GARLIC, GINGER IS THE FOURTH BASIC FLAVOURING OF SOUTH CHINESE CUISINE. AND FOR GOOD REASON: ITS ZESTY BITE CAN TRANSFORM EVEN THE MOST MUNDANE AND BLAND FOOD, SUCH AS RICE, INTO SOMETHING SPECIAL.

HERE IS A SIMPLE RICE DISH WHICH I OFTEN MAKE TO ACCOMPANY OTHER FOODS. THE GINGER IS SLOWLY STIR-FRIED SO THAT IT CARAMELIZES SLIGHTLY AND THUS GIVES OFF A TOASTY FRAGRANCE.

Cook the rice at least 2 hours before it is needed, or even the night before, according to the method for Steamed Rice on page 35. Allow it to cool thoroughly and put it in the refrigerator.

Heat a wok or large frying-pan over a high heat until it is hot. Add the oil and, when it is hot, add the ginger, turn down the heat and slowly stir-fry until the ginger has browned. Then add the spring onions, salt and pepper. Stir-fry for 2 minutes. Add the rice and continue to stir-fry for 5 minutes or until the rice is thoroughly heated through. Finally, add the coriander. Give the mixture several good stirs.

Turn onto a warmed platter and serve at once.

Ⓥ GREEN RICE ≈

RICE IS A MARVELLOUS FOOD THAT IMPARTS SUBSTANCE AND MILD CONGENIALITY TO ANY DISH. IT IS NOT NATURALLY A COLOURFUL INGREDIENT BUT IT DOES ABSORB THE COLOUR SPECTRUM AS WELL AS IT ABSORBS SPICES, SAUCES AND SEASONINGS.

I FIRST ENJOYED THIS COLOURFUL RICE DISH AT THE JOYCE CAFÉ IN HONG KONG. IT IS AN INTEGRAL PART OF THEIR POPULAR FUSION COOKING.

Cook the rice at least 2 hours before it is needed, or even the night before, following the method on page 35. Allow it to cool thoroughly and put it in the refrigerator.

Heat a wok or large frying-pan over a high heat until it is hot. Add the oil and, when it is very hot and slightly smoking, add the onions, garlic, shallots, spring onions, chillies, sugar, salt and pepper. Stir-fry for 3 minutes. Then add the rice and continue to stir-fry for 5 minutes until thoroughly heated through. Finally, add the coriander and mix well.

Turn onto a warmed platter and serve hot, or cold as a rice salad, with grilled foods.

400 ml (14 fl oz) long-grain white rice
600 ml (1 pint) water
2 tablespoons oil, preferably groundnut
225 g (8 oz) onions, finely chopped
2 tablespoons coarsely chopped garlic
3 tablespoons finely chopped shallots
6 tablespoons finely chopped spring onions
2 green chillies (page 16), seeded and finely chopped
2 teaspoons sugar
2 teaspoons salt
½ teaspoon freshly ground five-pepper mixture (page 21) or black pepper
4 tablespoons finely chopped fresh coriander

⒱ CHINESE MUSHROOM RISOTTO ≈

SERVES 4–6 AS A MAIN COURSE

50 g (2 oz) dried Chinese black mushrooms (page 18)

2 tablespoons (25 g/1 oz) unsalted butter

3 tablespoons extra virgin olive oil

1 small onion, finely chopped

3 tablespoons finely chopped shallots

2 teaspoons finely chopped fresh ginger (page 17)

300 g (11 oz) Italian arborio rice

1.2 litres (2 pints) hot Home-made Vegetable Stock (page 33)

Salt and freshly ground five-pepper mixture (page 21) or black pepper

Freshly grated Parmesan cheese, to serve

RISOTTO IS RICE THAT HAS BEEN SLOWLY COOKED TO A SMOOTH, CREAMY CONSISTENCY, SOMETHING THAT IS QUITE UNLIKE ASIAN STEAMED RICE. AS ITS NAME INDICATES, IT IS AN ITALIAN DISH. THE SLOW COOKING ENSURES THE RICE ABSORBS THE VARIOUS FLAVOURS, SEASONINGS AND SPICES. RICE LENDS ITSELF TO DIFFERENT FLAVOURS, AND MANY INGREDIENTS MAY BE BLENDED INTO THE ENSEMBLE. I HAVE EXPERIMENTED WITH A VARIETY OF INGREDIENTS AND FOUND THAT CHINESE MUSHROOMS, WITH THEIR SMOKY FLAVOUR AND PLEASING TEXTURE, ARE A DELICIOUS COMPLEMENT. PERHAPS MARCO POLO HIT UPON THE IDEA FIRST. CHICKEN STOCK IS USUALLY USED IN RISOTTOS BUT, IF YOU WANT A VEGETARIAN CENTREPIECE, VEGETABLE STOCK WORKS WELL TOO.

Soak the mushrooms in warm water for 20 minutes. Then drain them and squeeze out the excess liquid. Remove and discard the stems and cut the caps into thick strips.

Heat a wok or pan until it is hot and add the butter and olive oil. Then add the onion, shallots and ginger and stir-fry on a medium heat for 2 minutes, until the onions are translucent but not browned. Now add the rice and mushrooms and continue to stir-fry for 2 minutes until the rice is well coated. Turn the heat to low, add some of the stock and continue to stir until the rice has absorbed most of the stock. Continue to add stock, allowing it to slowly evaporate and be absorbed by the rice. Continue until you have used up most of the stock. This will take about 25–30 minutes. When the rice is cooked, add salt and pepper to taste and serve it on a warm platter with the Parmesan cheese.

Ⓥ Herbal Vegetarian Fried Rice ≈

400 ml (14 fl oz) basmati
rice
600 ml (1 pint) water
3 tablespoons extra virgin
olive oil
3 tablespoons coarsely
chopped garlic
2 teaspoons finely chopped
fresh ginger (page 17)
2 tablespoons seeded and
finely chopped fresh red
chillies (page 16)
2 teaspoons salt
1 teaspoon freshly ground
five-pepper mixture
(page 21) or black pepper
4 tablespoons sun-dried
tomatoes in oil, drained
and coarsely chopped
3 tablespoons finely
chopped spring onions
3 tablespoons finely
chopped fresh chives
3 tablespoons finely
chopped fresh coriander
3 tablespoons finely
chopped fresh flatleaf
parsley
3 tablespoons chopped fresh
basil

THIS IS A FUSION RICE DISH I DEVELOPED FOR MY VEGETARIAN FOOD PROMOTIONS AT THE ORIENTAL HOTEL IN BANGKOK, THAILAND. IT IS A TASTY AND AROMATIC DISH BECAUSE I USE INDIAN BASMATI RICE. THE HERBS GIVE THE RICE A TANGY BITE. IT MAKES A NICE COLD RICE SALAD.

Cook the rice according to the method for Steamed Rice on page 35, at least 2 hours before it is needed, or even the night before. Allow it to cool thoroughly and then put it in the refrigerator.

Heat a wok or large frying-pan until it is hot; then add the oil. Add the garlic, ginger and chillies and stir-fry for 15 seconds. Then add the rice, salt and pepper and stir-fry for 2 minutes over a high heat. Mix well, pressing on the cold rice to break up any lumps. When the rice is thoroughly heated through, add the sun-dried tomatoes, spring onions, chives, coriander, parsley and basil and stir-fry for another 3 minutes.

Ladle onto a warmed serving platter and serve hot or at room temperature.

ⓥLIGHT RICE NOODLES WITH FRESH HERBS ≈

IN THIS RECIPE, I USE FLAT RICE NOODLES, WHICH LOOK LIKE FETTUCCINE EGG PASTA. BECAUSE THEY ARE DRIED AND NEED LITTLE COOKING, THEY ARE VERY QUICK AND EASY TO USE. THEIR NEUTRAL AND LIGHT TASTE LENDS ITSELF TO A MORE ASSERTIVE FUSION FLAVOUR, IN THIS CASE A MIXTURE OF CHOPPED HERBS. THIS IS AN IDEAL RECIPE FOR SPRING OR SUMMER. IT CAN ACCOMPANY A MEAT DISH OR IS A PERFECT LIGHT PASTA DISH BY ITSELF.

Soak the noodles in warm water for 15 minutes, then drain thoroughly.

Heat a wok or large frying-pan over a high heat until it is hot. Add the oil and, when it is very hot and slightly smoking, add the spring onions, garlic, sun-dried tomatoes, shallots, salt and pepper. Stir-fry for 30 seconds then add the noodles and stir-fry for 2 minutes, letting the noodles brown slightly. Add more oil, if necessary.

Finally, add all the herbs and lemon juice. Mix thoroughly and serve at once.

SERVES 4 AS AN ACCOMPANIMENT

225 g (8 oz) dried flat rice noodles
3 tablespoons extra virgin olive oil
3 tablespoons finely chopped spring onions
3 tablespoons coarsely chopped garlic
3 tablespoons finely chopped sun-dried tomatoes
3 tablespoons finely chopped shallots
2 teaspoons salt
1 teaspoon freshly ground five-pepper mixture (page 21) or black pepper
4 tablespoons coarsely chopped fresh basil
3 tablespoons finely chopped fresh chives
3 tablespoons finely chopped fresh coriander
2 tablespoons finely chopped fresh tarragon
1 tablespoon lemon juice

ⓥ Vegetarian Nonya Laksa ≈

SERVES 2 AS A MAIN
COURSE OR 4 AS AN
ACCOMPANIMENT

1½ tablespoons oil, preferably
   groundnut oil
2 tablespoons coarsely
   chopped garlic
1 tablespoon finely chopped
   fresh ginger (page 17)
2 fresh red chillies
   (page 16), halved, seeded
   and finely shredded
225 g (8 oz) onions,
   finely sliced
1 teaspoon ground coriander
½ teaspoon ground turmeric
1.2 litres (2 pints) Home-made
   Vegetable (page 33) or
   Chicken (page 32) Stock
225 g (8 oz) rice noodles
   (page 19) or rice sticks
400 ml (14 fl oz) tinned
   coconut milk (page 16)
2 teaspoons Madras curry
   powder (page 17)
2 teaspoons chilli-bean sauce
   (page 22)
1 teaspoon sugar
2 teaspoons salt
½ teaspoon freshly ground five-
   pepper mixture (page 21)
   or black pepper

To Garnish:
3 tablespoons finely sliced
   spring onions
4 quail's eggs or 2 hen's eggs,
   hard-boiled and halved
Sprigs of fresh coriander

NONYA COOKING IS A MIXTURE OF CHINESE AND MALAY CUISINES, ALSO KNOWN AS 'STRAITS CHINESE' IN MALAYSIA AND SINGAPORE. THE WORD *LAKSA* DESCRIBES A ONE-DISH MEAL OF RICE NOODLES, TRADITIONALLY PREPARED WITH EITHER SEAFOOD OR CHICKEN. CLEARLY, THIS IS A VERSATILE DISH AND IT CERTAINLY ADAPTS WELL TO THE VEGETARIAN MODE. ITS MANY AROMATIC INGREDIENTS AND SPICY FLAVOURS ENSURE THAT IT IS AS TASTY AS THE ORIGINAL, NON-VEGETARIAN VERSIONS, BUT LIGHTER.

Heat a wok or large frying-pan over a high heat until it is hot. Add the oil and, when it is very hot and slightly smoking, reduce the heat and add the garlic, ginger, chillies and onions and stir-fry for 5 minutes. Add the coriander, turmeric and stock. Turn the heat to low, cover and simmer for 20 minutes.

Meanwhile, soak the rice noodles or rice sticks in a bowl of warm water for 20 minutes. Drain them in a colander or sieve.

Add the coconut milk and rice noodles to the simmering liquid. Season with the curry powder, chilli-bean sauce, sugar, salt and pepper and continue to cook for 15 minutes. Ladle the mixture into a large soup tureen and serve at once with the garnishes on the side or on top.

Neil Perry's Stir-fried Hokkien Noodles with Ham ≈

SERVES 2 AS A MAIN
COURSE OR 4 AS AN
ACCOMPANIMENT

225 g (8 oz) broad, flat,
dried rice noodles
(page 19)

2 tablespoons oil, preferably
groundnut

2 tablespoons coarsely
chopped garlic

1 tablespoon finely chopped
fresh ginger (page 17)

2 tablespoons coarsely
chopped black beans
(page 14)

50 g (2 oz) pickled mustard
greens (page 19), thinly
sliced

4 spring onions, shredded

2 tablespoons Shaoxing rice
wine (page 22) or dry
sherry

2 tablespoons light soy
sauce (page 23)

3 tablespoons oyster sauce
(page 23)

¼ teaspoon freshly ground
black pepper

1 tablespoon sugar

100 ml (3½ fl oz) Home-
made Chicken Stock
(page 32)

100 g (4 oz) smoked ham,
finely shredded

175 g (6 oz) fresh bean
sprouts (page 13)

A small handful of fresh
coriander

AUSTRALIANS HAVE TAKEN TO FUSION COOKERY LIKE DUCKS TO WATER. THEY HAVE ADAPTED ASIAN DISHES AND INFUSED THEM WITH EUROPEAN TOUCHES TO CREATE A UNIQUE CUISINE THAT IS UNRIVALLED IN THE WORLD. ONE OF THE BEST CHEFS IS NEIL PERRY, A TALENTED MAN WITH A TRUE LOVE OF GOOD FOOD. THIS IS ONE OF HIS DELICIOUS RECIPES FROM WOKPOOL, ONE OF HIS MANY POPULAR RESTAURANTS, WHICH I HAVE SHAMELESSLY ADAPTED. HOKKIEN IS A DIALECT LANGUAGE GROUP FROM SOUTHERN CHINA, WHOSE MEMBERS ARE AMONG THE MANY CHINESE WHO HAVE EMIGRATED TO THE MALAYSIAN PENINSULA AND THENCE TO AUSTRALIA. HOKKIEN NOODLES ARE A STYLE OF SINGAPORE NOODLES POPULAR IN AUSTRALIA.

Soak the rice noodles in a bowl of warm water for 25 minutes. Drain them in a colander or sieve.

Heat a wok or large frying-pan over a high heat until it is hot. Add the oil and, when it is very hot and slightly smoking, add the garlic, ginger and black beans and stir-fry for 30 seconds. Then add the noodles, mustard greens and spring onions and stir-fry for 2 minutes. Now add the rice wine or sherry, soy sauce, oyster sauce, pepper, sugar and stock and continue to stir-fry for 3 minutes. Finally, add the ham, bean sprouts and coriander and continue to cook for 2 minutes. Serve at once.

The Oriental Hotel's Stir-fried Noodles with Deep-fried Beancurd ≈

The Oriental Hotel in Bangkok is justifiably renowned as one of the best hotels in the world. Part of that reputation comes from the offerings of its wonderful kitchen, supervised by chef Norbert Kostner. His abiding interest in making vegetable dishes taste as good as any meat-based offerings makes him a pioneer in the culinary world. Here is his vegetarian version of the traditional Thai rice-noodle dish.

Soak the rice noodles in a bowl of warm water for 25 minutes. Then drain them in a colander or sieve.

Drain the beancurd, set it on kitchen paper and continue to drain it for 15 minutes. Gently cut the beancurd into 2.5 cm (1 in) cubes.

Separate the broccoli heads into small florets, then peel and slice the stems. Blanch the broccoli pieces in a large pan of boiling, salted water for 3 minutes and then immerse them in cold water. Drain thoroughly.

Finely shred the mangetout. If the French beans are large, slice them in half at a slight diagonal. If they are small, leave them whole.

Peel and thinly slice the shallots. Thinly slice the spring onions at a slight diagonal into 2.5 cm (1 in) pieces. Seed and finely chop the chillies.

Heat 450 ml (15 fl oz) of oil in a wok or deep frying-pan until it is hot and deep-fry the beancurd cubes in two batches. When each batch is lightly browned, remove and drain it well on kitchen paper. Drain off and discard the oil. Wipe the wok or pan clean.

Reheat the wok or pan and, when it is hot, add the rest of the oil; when it is very hot and slightly smoking, add the shallots, spring onions, garlic and chillies and stir-fry for 1 minute. Then add the rice noodles, broccoli, mangetout and French beans and stir-fry for 2 minutes. Now add the fish or soy sauce, lime juice, salt, pepper and sugar and continue to stir-fry for 2 minutes, mixing well. Finally, add the oyster-flavoured sauce or soy sauce and continue to cook for 4 minutes. Stir in the chopped coriander and beancurd cubes and cook for 30 seconds. Give the mixture a good stir and turn onto a warmed platter. Sprinkle with the peanuts and serve at once.

Serves 2 as a main course or 4 as an accompaniment

225 g (8 oz) broad, flat, dried rice noodles (page 19)
225 g (8 oz) firm, fresh beancurd (page 13)
175 g (6 oz) Chinese or ordinary broccoli
175 g (6 oz) mangetout
175 g (6 oz) French beans
100 g (4 oz) shallots
4 spring onions
3 fresh red or green chillies (page 16)
450 ml (15 fl oz) plus 2 tablespoons oil, preferably groundnut
2 tablespoons coarsely chopped garlic
2 tablespoons fish sauce (page 22) or light soy sauce (page 23)
1½ tablespoons lime juice
1 teaspoon salt
¼ teaspoon freshly ground black pepper
2 teaspoons sugar
3 tablespoons vegetarian oyster-flavoured sauce (page 22) or dark soy sauce (page 23)
3 tablespoons finely chopped fresh coriander
3 tablespoons coarsely chopped roasted peanuts, to garnish

ⓥ Jade Noodle Bowl ≈

Serves 2 as a main course

25 g (1 oz) dried Chinese
   black mushrooms (page 18)
350 g (12 oz) fresh or
   100 g (4 oz) dried spinach
   noodles or pasta
2 teaspoons sesame oil
1.2 litres (2 pints) Home-made
   Vegetable (page 33) or
   Chicken (page 32) Stock
½ teaspoon salt
1 tablespoon light soy sauce
   (page 23)
2 fresh red chillies (page 16),
   seeded and shredded
100 g (4 oz) ready-bought,
   pressed, seasoned beancurd
   (page 13), shredded
175 g (6 oz) fresh bean
   sprouts (page 13)

To Garnish:
3 tablespoons finely chopped
   spring onions
Sprigs of fresh coriander

This comforting, simple noodle treat found its inspiration in the Joyce Café in Hong Kong. It is a satisfying mixture of spinach ('jade') noodles with chilli, seasoned beancurd, mushrooms and bean sprouts in a hearty broth. Once the broth is made, jade noodle is easy to prepare for a perfect lunch or light supper.

Soak the mushrooms in warm water for 20 minutes. Then drain them and squeeze out the excess liquid. Remove and discard the stems and finely shred the caps into thin strips.

If you are using fresh noodles, blanch them first for 3–5 minutes in boiling water. If you are using dried noodles, cook them in boiling water for 4–5 minutes. Plunge the prepared noodles in cold water, drain them thoroughly, toss them in the sesame oil and put them aside until you are ready to use them. They can be kept in this state, if tightly covered with cling film, for up to 2 hours in the refrigerator.

Bring the stock to a simmer in a large pan. Add the salt, soy sauce, chillies and beancurd and simmer for 5 minutes. Then add the cooked noodles and simmer for 2 minutes. Now add the bean sprouts and cook for another minute.

Turn the contents of the pan into a soup tureen. Sprinkle on the spring onions and coriander and serve at once.

℣Lillian's Tasty Noodles ≈

Serves 4 as a main course

350 g (12 oz) fresh wheat
or egg noodles (page 19)

2 teaspoons plus
1 tablespoon sesame oil

450 g (1 lb) green
cabbage, shredded

1½ tablespoons plus
2 teaspoons salt

2 tablespoons groundnut oil

3 tablespoons coarsely
chopped garlic

½ teaspoon freshly ground
five-pepper mixture
(page 21) or black pepper

2 tablespoons light soy
sauce (page 23)

1 tablespoon dark soy sauce
(page 23)

2 tablespoons Shaoxing rice
wine (page 22) or dry
sherry

I always look forward to Sunday dinners at Lillian Robyn's home in El Cerrito, California. Sometimes she invites other Chinese friends and each of them brings a home-made dish for the others to enjoy. 'Pot luck' sounds so Chinese anyway. In any case, we all experience a delicious home-cooked Chinese banquet.

I recall with delight this very tasty noodle dish, which Lillian put together one evening – in a matter of minutes. Imaginative and yet easy to make, it is a good alternative to the usual rice.

Cook the noodles for 3–5 minutes in a pan of boiling, salted water. Drain and plunge them into cold water. Drain thoroughly and toss them in 2 teaspoons of sesame oil. (They can be kept in this state, if tightly covered with cling film, for up to 2 hours in the refrigerator.)

Meanwhile, soak the cabbage in cold water and 1½ tablespoons of salt for 1 hour. Drain the cabbage.

Heat a wok or large frying-pan over a high heat until it is hot. Add the oil and, when it is very hot and slightly smoking, add the garlic, the rest of the salt and the pepper and stir-fry for 10 seconds; then add the cabbage and continue to stir-fry for 2 minutes. Now pour in the soy sauces and the rice wine or sherry. Cook over a high heat for 10 minutes or until the cabbage is completely cooked. Add the cooked noodles and continue to cook for 4 minutes or until the noodles are heated through. Drizzle in the rest of the sesame oil and give the mixture several turns. Serve at once.

ⓋFRAGRANT COCONUT NOODLE SOUP ≈

A GREAT DISCOVERY FOR ME, AS WELL AS FOR MANY FUSION CHEFS AND COOKS IN THE PAST DECADE, HAS BEEN THAI CUISINE. WE LOVE THE SHARPNESS, ASSERTIVENESS, TANGINESS, SPICINESS AND RICHNESS WHICH, FOR ME, CHARACTERIZE THIS CUISINE. THESE SEEMINGLY CONTRADICTORY FLAVOURS WORK WELL WHEN COMBINED IN SOUP AND BRAISED DISHES. DESPITE THE RICH FLAVOURS, THE RESULTING DISH IS LIGHT, ESPECIALLY FOR SOUPS. HERE I HAVE COMBINED LESSONS LEARNED FROM THIS GREAT CUISINE INTO A LOVELY, HEARTY SOUP. SERVE IT AT ROOM TEMPERATURE DURING WARM WEATHER; IT WORKS WONDERS. IF YOU USE VEGETABLE STOCK AND SOY SAUCE INSTEAD OF FISH SAUCE, YOU CAN EASILY TURN THIS INTO A DISH SUITABLE FOR VEGETARIANS.

Soak the rice noodles in a bowl of warm water for 25 minutes. Drain them in a colander or sieve. Peel the lemon grass stalks to the tender, whitish centres and crush with the flat of a knife; then cut into 7.5 cm (3 in) pieces.

Heat a large, heavy pan over a high heat until it is hot. Add the oil and, when it is very hot and slightly smoking, add the onion, garlic and lemon grass and stir-fry for about 3 minutes. Stir in the stock, coconut milk and orange juice, turn the heat to low, cover and simmer for 10 minutes. Then add the tomatoes, chillies, orange zest, fish or soy sauce, sugar, curry powder, salt and pepper and stir well. Now add the drained noodles. Cover and continue to cook for another 10 minutes.

Remove the lemon grass with a slotted spoon, stir in the lime juice, then pour the noodles and soup into a large tureen and serve at once.

SERVES 4

100 g (4 oz) dried thin rice noodles (page 19)
2 lemon grass stalks (page 18)
1 tablespoon groundnut oil
1 small onion, finely chopped
2 tablespoons coarsely chopped garlic
1.2 litres (2 pints) Home-made Vegetable (page 33) or Chicken (page 32) Stock
2 x 400 ml (15 fl oz) tins of coconut milk (page 16)
150 ml (5 fl oz) fresh orange juice, strained
225 g (8 oz) tinned tomatoes, chopped
2 fresh red or green chillies (page 16), seeded and finely shredded
2 tablespoons finely chopped orange zest
1 tablespoon fish sauce (page 22) or soy sauce (page 23)
1 tablespoon sugar
1 tablespoon Madras curry powder (page 17)
2 teaspoons salt
½ teaspoon freshly ground five-pepper mixture (page 21) or black pepper
1 tablespoon lime juice

V COLD KOREAN-STYLE NOODLES ≈

SERVES 2–4 AS AN ACCOMPANIMENT

225 g (8 oz) somyun noodles (page 20) or thin Chinese wheat noodles (page 18)

2 teaspoons sesame oil

15 g (½ oz) dried Chinese black mushrooms (page 18)

2 tablespoons sesame seeds, toasted (page 23), to garnish

For the Sauce:

2 tablespoons finely chopped garlic

1 tablespoon oil, preferably groundnut

2 teaspoons sesame oil

2 tablespoons light soy sauce (page 23)

2 teaspoons sugar

2 tablespoons white rice vinegar (page 24)

1 teaspoon salt

½ teaspoon freshly ground five-pepper mixture (page 21) or black pepper

1½ tablespoons seeded and finely chopped fresh red chilli (page 16)

3 tablespoons finely chopped spring onions

WHILE I WAS WORKING AT THE HOTEL SHILLA PARKVIEW IN SEOUL, KOREA, I WAS DELIGHTED WHEN THE KITCHEN STAFF PUT TOGETHER THIS DELICIOUS COLD NOODLE DISH. UPON ASKING THEM FOR THE RECIPE, I DISCOVERED THAT IT INCLUDED A SPECIAL TYPE OF NOODLE, CALLED SOMYUN, MADE FROM A MIXTURE OF RICE FLOUR AND WHEAT FLOUR. WHEN COOKED, THE NOODLES ACQUIRE A PLEASING, TEXTURED CHARACTER. THIS REFRESHING NOODLE DISH MAKES AN IDEAL SUMMER LUNCH TREAT, OR IT COULD BE SERVED WITH ANY BARBECUE DISH. IF YOU COOK THE NOODLES IN ADVANCE, DON'T TOSS THEM WITH THE SAUCE UNTIL YOU ARE READY TO SERVE.

Bring a large pan of salted water to the boil and cook the noodles for 3 minutes. Drain the noodles, plunge them into cold water and drain well. Toss in the sesame oil and then chill in the refrigerator.

Soak the mushrooms in warm water for 20 minutes. Then drain them and squeeze out the excess liquid. Remove and discard the stems and finely shred the caps into thin strips.

When you are ready to serve the noodles, combine the sauce ingredients in a small bowl. In a large bowl, mix the noodles and mushrooms together; then toss the noodles with the sauce, mixing well. Sprinkle the sesame seeds on top and serve at once.

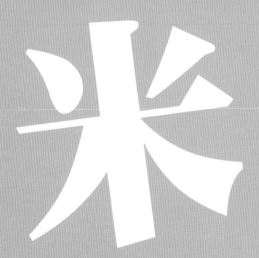

ⓋPENANG RICE NOODLES ≈

PENANG IS A MALAYSIAN CITY STRONGLY INFLUENCED BY CHINESE HISTORY AND CULTURE. THE CHINESE CULINARY INFLUENCE IS PARTICULARLY ROBUST. I MUST ADMIT THAT MY PARTIALITY FOR MALAYSIAN FOOD STEMS FROM ITS CLEAR AFFINITY WITH SOUTHERN CHINESE TRADITIONS.

I PARTICULARLY LIKE THE MALAYSIAN RICE NOODLE DISHES, AND HERE IS A SAVOURY VERSION WHICH IS EASY TO MAKE AND QUITE DELICIOUS.

Soak the rice noodles in a bowl of warm water for 25 minutes. Then drain them in a colander or sieve.

Heat a wok or large frying-pan over a high heat until it is hot. Add the oil and, when it is very hot and slightly smoking, add the onion, spring onions, garlic, Chinese greens and Chinese chives and stir-fry for 4 minutes. Then add the noodles, rice wine or sherry, light soy sauce, oyster sauce or dark soy sauce, salt and pepper and continue to stir-fry for 2 minutes. Add the bean sprouts and continue to cook for 2 minutes. Finally, drizzle in the sesame oil and give the mixture a good stir. Serve at once.

SERVES 2 AS A MAIN COURSE OR 4 AS AN ACCOMPANIMENT

- 225 g (8 oz) broad, flat, dried rice noodles (page 19)
- 2 tablespoons oil, preferably groundnut
- 1 large onion, thinly sliced
- 4 spring onions, cut diagonally into 2.5 cm (1 in) pieces
- 2 tablespoons coarsely chopped garlic
- 225 g (8 oz) Chinese greens such as bok choy (page 15), cut into 2.5 cm (1 in) pieces
- 175 g (6 oz) fresh Chinese yellow or green chives, or fresh chives, cut into 2.5 cm (1 in) pieces
- 1 tablespoon Shaoxing rice wine (page 22) or dry sherry
- 2 tablespoons light soy sauce (page 23)
- 2 tablespoons vegetarian oyster-flavoured sauce (page 22) or dark soy sauce (page 23)
- 1 teaspoon salt
- ¼ teaspoon freshly ground black pepper
- 175 g (6 oz) bean sprouts (page 13)
- 2 teaspoons sesame oil

✹MALAYSIAN CURRY MEE ≈

SERVES 2 AS A MAIN
COURSE OR 4 AS AN
ACCOMPANIMENT

450 g (1 lb) firm, fresh
beancurd (page 13)
225 g (8 oz) dried or fresh
Chinese egg noodles
(page 19)
1½ tablespoons oil,
preferably groundnut
2 dried red chillies
(page 15), halved
2 tablespoons coarsely
chopped garlic
100 g (4 oz) onions, finely
chopped
400 ml (14 fl oz) tinned
coconut milk (page 16)
½ teaspoon ground turmeric
2 tablespoons Madras curry
powder (page 17)
1 teaspoon salt
1 teaspoon sugar
2 tablespoons light soy
sauce (page 23)
225 g (8 oz) fresh bean
sprouts (page 13),
trimmed
A handful of fresh parsley
leaves, to garnish

MALAYSIA IS AN INTERNATIONAL COMMERCIAL POWERHOUSE SITUATED AT A GEOGRAPHICAL CROSSROADS. UNDERSTANDABLY, THEREFORE, IT IS ALSO A CULINARY CROSSROADS OF CUISINES, SPICES AND INGREDIENTS, WITH CHINESE AND INDIAN FLAVOURS, ESPECIALLY, MERGING INTO A DISTINCTLY NATIONAL STYLE OF COOKING – ONE THAT HAS BEEN INFLUENTIAL IN THE COOKING OF AUSTRALIA, WHICH HAS MANY MALAYSIAN IMMIGRANTS AND IS A POPULAR HOLIDAY DESTINATION.

A GOOD EXAMPLE OF A POPULAR MALAYSIAN DISH IN AUSTRALIA IS THIS SIMPLE BUT DELECTABLE EGG NOODLE DISH (*MEE* IS THE MALAYSIAN WORD FOR 'NOODLES'). IT COMBINES BEAN SPROUTS AND BEANCURD, STANDARD INGREDIENTS USED BY CHINESE COOKS, WITH A LIGHT CURRY SAUCE THAT MANIFESTS THE INDIAN INFLUENCE.

Cut the beancurd into 2.5 cm (1 in) cubes. Drain on kitchen paper for 30 minutes.

If you are using dried noodles, cook them according to the instructions on the packet or boil them for 4–5 minutes. Then cool them in cold water until you are ready to use them. If you are using fresh noodles, boil them for 3–5 minutes and then immerse them in cold water.

Heat a wok or large frying-pan over a high heat until it is hot. Add the oil and, when it is very hot and slightly smoking, add the dried chillies and stir-fry for 20 seconds. Push the chillies to the side of the wok or pan, turn the temperature down and add the beancurd cubes, browning slowly on all sides. When the cubes are golden brown on all sides, add the garlic and onions and stir-fry for 3 minutes, until the onions are wilted. Now add the coconut milk, turmeric, curry powder, salt, sugar and soy sauce and simmer for 4 minutes. Add the noodles and bean sprouts and cook for 2 minutes, mixing well. Garnish with the parsley leaves and serve at once.

ⓋSHANGHAI-STYLE WONTONS ≈

THIS SHANGHAI-STYLE WONTON DISH WAS INSPIRED BY A LIGHT, FLAVOURFUL SOUP I HAD AT THE TRENDY JOYCE CAFÉ IN HONG KONG. THE MENU FEATURES A MIXTURE OF EASTERN AND WESTERN INFLUENCES AND INCLUDES MANY VEGETARIAN OFFERINGS. I FOUND THIS ONE PARTICULARLY DELIGHTFUL TO THE EYE AS WELL AS THE PALATE. THE WONTONS ARE FILLED WITH CHOPPED FRESH CHINESE LEAVES MIXED WITH SPICY PRESERVED VEGETABLES, AND THEY ARE SERVED FLOATING IN A FRAGRANT SOUP.

WONTON SKINS CAN BE OBTAINED FROM CHINESE GROCERS, AS WELL AS SUPERMARKETS. THEY ARE YELLOWISH SQUARES PACKED IN SMALL STACKS AND THEY CAN BE BOUGHT FRESH OR FROZEN. BE SURE TO THAW THEM THOROUGHLY IF THEY ARE FROZEN.

Blanch the Chinese leaves for 1 minute in boiling salted water, remove with a slotted spoon and plunge immediately into cold water. Drain and squeeze all excess liquid out. Tip into a bowl, add all the other filling ingredients and mix well.

When you are ready to stuff the wontons, put a tablespoon of the filling in the centre of the first wonton skin. Dampen the edges with a little water and bring up the sides of the skin around the filling. Pinch the edges together at the top so that the wonton is sealed; it should look like a small drawstring bag. Repeat the procedure until all the filling has been used.

When the wontons are ready, bring the stock, soy sauce and sesame oil to a simmer in a large pan.

In another large pan, bring salted water to the boil and poach the wontons for 1 minute or until they float to the top (you may need to do this in batches). Remove them immediately and transfer them to the pan of stock. (This procedure will result in a cleaner-tasting broth.) Continue to simmer them in the broth for 2 minutes. Transfer to either a large soup tureen or to individual bowls. Garnish with spring onions and serve immediately.

SERVES 4–6 (MAKES ABOUT 20 WONTONS)

225 g (8 oz) wonton skins (page 25)

3 tablespoons finely chopped spring onions, to garnish

For the Filling:
350 g (12 oz) bok choy (page 14), coarsely chopped

50 g (2 oz) Sichuan preserved vegetables (page 23), rinsed and finely chopped

½ teaspoon salt

½ teaspoon freshly ground five-pepper mixture (page 21) or white pepper

1 teaspoon light soy sauce (page 23)

2 tablespoons finely chopped spring onions

1 tablespoon Shaoxing rice wine (page 22) or dry sherry

1 teaspoon sugar

2 teaspoons sesame oil

For the Broth:
1.2 litres (2 pints) Home-made Vegetable (page 33) or Chicken (page 32) Stock

1 tablespoon light soy sauce (page 23)

1 teaspoon sesame oil

Ⓥ Fusion Pasta with Chinese Greens ≈

SERVES 2 AS A MAIN
COURSE OR 4 AS AN
ACCOMPANIMENT

350 g (12 oz) dried Italian
   pasta, such as fusilli or
   farfalle
450 g (1 lb) Chinese greens,
   such as Chinese flowering
   cabbage or bok choy
   (page 14)
3 tablespoons extra virgin olive
   oil
3 tablespoons finely sliced garlic
1 teaspoon salt
½ teaspoon freshly ground five-
   pepper mixture (page 21)
   or black pepper
2 tablespoons light soy sauce
   (page 23)
1 tablespoon lemon juice
2 tablespoons finely chopped
   fresh chives
2 tablespoons finely chopped
   fresh coriander
Freshly grated Parmesan
   cheese, to serve

CHINESE GREENS ARE A NEW SOURCE OF INSPIRATION FOR FUSION CHEFS.
THESE TASTY, SLIGHTLY BITTER GREENS WITH A RICH CABBAGE FLAVOUR ARE
THE PERFECT FOIL FOR PASTA. HERE IS A DELECTABLE VEGETABLE PASTA DISH
THAT IS RAPID TO COOK AND DELICIOUS TO EAT.

Cook the pasta in a large pan of salted, boiling water, according to
the instructions on the packet. Drain well and set aside.

Cut the Chinese greens into 7.5 cm (3 in) pieces.

Heat a wok or large frying-pan over a high heat until it is hot.
Add the oil and, when it is hot, add the garlic and stir-fry for
30 seconds, until the garlic has browned. Then quickly add the
Chinese greens and stir-fry for 3 minutes or until the greens have
wilted a little. Now add the salt, pepper, soy sauce and lemon juice
and continue to stir-fry for 1 minute. Return the cooked pasta to the
wok and heat through, mixing well with the greens. Add the chives
and coriander and give the mixture a good stir. Turn onto a warmed
platter and serve at once, with Parmesan cheese.

ⓋPasta in Chilli Tomato Sauce ≈

900 g (2 lb) tomatoes,
  peeled and seeded if
  fresh, drained if tinned
150 ml (5 fl oz) extra virgin
  olive oil
100 g (4 oz) finely chopped
  onions
2 tablespoons finely
  chopped fresh ginger
  (page 17)
3 tablespoons coarsely
  chopped garlic
100 g (4 oz) carrots, finely
  chopped
100 g (4 oz) celery, finely
  chopped
3 tablespoons finely
  chopped spring onions
2 tablespoons seeded and
  finely chopped fresh red
  chillies (page 16)
2 teaspoons sugar
2 teaspoons salt
1 teaspoon freshly ground
  five-pepper mixture
  (page 21) or black pepper
1 tablespoon Sesame and
  Chilli Oil (page 39) or
  chilli oil (page 15)
450 g (1 lb) dried Italian
  pasta, such as spaghetti
Freshly grated Parmesan
  cheese, to serve

There is nothing simpler to prepare than pasta with tomato sauce and there is hardly anything more delicious: comfort food at its most satisfying. To add a spicy twist to this classic Italian dish, I have chosen a few Asian flavours that make it even more satisfying. This quick and easy dish is perfect for vegetarians, and serves as a light lunch or as a main course for an informal dinner party.

If you are using fresh tomatoes, cut them into 2.5 cm (1 in) cubes. If you are using tinned tomatoes, chop them into small chunks.

Heat a large pan and add the oil, then add the onions, ginger, garlic, carrots, celery, spring onions and chillies and stir-fry for 2 minutes. Then add the sugar, salt, pepper and sesame and chilli oil or chilli oil and continue to cook for 1 minute. Then add the tomatoes, turn the heat to low and simmer over a low heat for 30 minutes. The sauce can be made a day ahead to this point.

Cook the pasta in a large pan of salted, boiling water, according to the instructions on the packet. Drain well and put the pasta on a large, warmed platter.

Pour the sauce over the pasta and serve with Parmesan cheese.

DESSERTS

甜品

ⓥWARM MANGO COMPOTE WITH BASIL AND VANILLA ICE-CREAM ≈

THIS IS A SIMPLE DESSERT THAT I HAVE OFTEN MADE FOR MY FOOD PROMOTIONS AT THE ORIENTAL HOTEL IN BANGKOK. MANGOES ARE POPULAR AND ABUNDANT IN THAILAND. THEIR RICH, FLESHY AND SATIN-LIKE TEXTURE TRANSFORMS THIS RECIPE INTO AN EXQUISITE FINALE. VANILLA ICE-CREAM FOUND IN SUPERMARKETS IS OF HIGH QUALITY AND A GREAT CONVENIENCE. THE COMBINATION OF THE COLD ICE-CREAM AND WARM FRUIT IS UNBEATABLE.

SERVES 4

1 vanilla pod, split open
100 g (4 oz) granulated
    sugar
150 ml (5 fl oz) water
750 g (1½ lb) mangoes
    (2 medium)
2 tablespoons (25 g/1 oz)
    unsalted butter
6 fresh basil leaves, coarsely
    chopped
Salt
Vanilla ice-cream, to serve

Scrape the seeds of the vanilla pod into the sugar and mix well. Using a non-stick wok or pan, bring the sugar and water to the boil, add the vanilla pod and simmer for 10 minutes. Remove the vanilla pod, dry it thoroughly and save for future use by storing it in sugar. Peel the mangoes and cut the fruit into 5 mm (¼ in) thick slices.

Add the mango slices and a tiny pinch of salt to the syrup and simmer for 2 minutes, just enough to warm the fruit and not to cook it through. Remove from the heat and gently stir in the butter and the basil. Serve at once, with scoops of vanilla ice-cream.

ⓥ Orange Almond Cake ≈

Serves 4–6

175 ml (6 fl oz) fresh orange
  juice, strained
3 tablespoons finely
  chopped orange zest
1 tablespoon orange-flower
  water
120 g (4½ oz) dried
  breadcrumbs
90 g (3½ oz) whole
  blanched almonds, ground
2 egg yolks
150 g (5 oz) caster sugar
½ teaspoon salt
4 egg whites
Icing sugar, sifted, for dusting

The Chinese traditionally like to serve slices of fresh orange after a meal and this is a refreshing East–West variation on that theme. The cake is easy to make and quite delicious with vanilla ice-cream, plain yoghurt or crème fraîche.

Pre-heat the oven to 180°C/350°F/gas mark 4.

In a large bowl, combine the orange juice, orange zest, orange-flower water, 100 g (4 oz) of the breadcrumbs and the almonds. In a separate bowl, beat the egg yolks with half the sugar and the salt and gently fold into the orange juice mixture. In another bowl, beat the egg whites until they become stiff, then beat in the remaining sugar and continue to beat until the whites form stiff peaks. Fold the beaten egg whites into the orange juice mixture.

Lightly butter a 20 cm (8 in) square, non-stick baking tin and dust it with the remaining breadcrumbs. Pour in the cake batter and bake for 45 minutes or until done (a fine skewer should come out clean). Set aside to cool in the pan on a rack. Invert the cake onto a platter and dust with icing sugar to serve.

ⓥ Coconut Fruit Crumble ≈

Serves 6–8

1.25 kg (2½ lb) very ripe
  fruit, such as peaches,
  mangoes, cherries,
  raspberries and/or
  blueberries
200 g (7 oz) plain flour
200 g (7 oz) sugar
100 g (4 oz) desiccated
  coconut
9–10 tablespoons
  (135 g/4¾ oz) cold
  unsalted butter, cut in small
  pieces

Desserts are not a strong point of Asian cooking in general. Fresh fruit or jelly-like puddings are what you will find in many parts of Asia. However, I do find the English-inspired crumble quite appealing; using fresh fruit, with a touch of exotic eastern coconut, it is a perfect fusion dessert. The basic recipe is from Monique Pébeyre, who is a French Anglophile. She serves it often in the summer, when fruits are abundant and in season. It is an easy, quick and simple dessert to make. Although you can make it ahead of time, it is best served warm. You will find it quite delicious with vanilla ice-cream.

Pre-heat the oven to 180°C/350°F/gas mark 4.

If you are using peaches, stone them and cut into thick slices. If you are using mangoes, peel them, remove the stone and cut the flesh in thick slices. If you are using cherries, stone them and leave them whole.

In a large bowl, mix the flour, sugar, coconut and butter with your fingers until they are coarsely blended. Arrange the fruit in an ovenproof dish in one layer. Place the crumble mixture on top of the fruit and bake for 45 minutes or until the top is golden and bubbly. Allow to cool and serve warm or at room temperature.

ⓋCHOCOLATE CAKE WITH CANDIED GINGER ≈

CHOCOLATE IS RARELY FOUND ON ASIAN MENUS OR IN HOMES. HOWEVER, NOW THAT ASIANS HAVE TASTED THIS VERY WESTERN FLAVOUR, IT HAS BECOME VERY POPULAR. IN THIS CLASSIC CHOCOLATE CAKE, I HAVE COMBINED IT WITH CANDIED GINGER TO GIVE AN EASTERN ZEST TO THIS WESTERN DESSERT. SERVE IT WITH LEMON GRASS CRÈME ANGLAISE (PAGE 237). IT IS ALSO DELICIOUS WITH DOUBLE OR CLOTTED CREAM.

Pre-heat the oven to 180°C/350°F/gas mark 4.

Combine the chocolate, butter, sugar and candied ginger in a heatproof bowl; place this over a large pan of boiling water. Over a moderate heat, melt the mixture, stirring all the while, until the ingredients are thoroughly blended.

Allow the mixture to cool. Whisk in the egg yolks and then the flour. Mix thoroughly.

Whisk the egg whites until they form firm peaks.

Add one-third of the egg whites to the chocolate batter and mix vigorously. Then gently fold in the remaining egg whites.

Butter a 20–23 cm (8–9 in) cake tin. Pour in the cake mixture and bake until the cake is firm, about 35–40 minutes.

Allow the cake to cool thoroughly. Turn the cake onto a platter, dust with icing sugar and serve.

SERVES 6–8

350 g (12 oz) finest quality plain chocolate, broken in pieces
10 tablespoons (150 g/ 5 oz) unsalted butter
135 g (4¾ oz) granulated sugar
50 g (2 oz) candied ginger, finely chopped
4 egg yolks
40 g (1½ oz) plain flour, sifted
6 egg whites
Icing sugar, sifted, for dusting

Ⓥ GINGER CRÈME BRÛLÉE ≈

SERVES 8

1 vanilla pod
4 tablespoons caster sugar
500 ml (16 fl oz) double
  cream
6 tablespoons finely
  chopped fresh ginger
  (page 17)
4 egg yolks
1 egg, beaten
2 tablespoons dark
  muscovado sugar

CRÈME BRÛLÉE IS UNDOUBTEDLY OF FRENCH ORIGIN, BUT ENGLISH CHEFS ADDED CERTAIN FLAVOURINGS SUCH AS VANILLA, RUM AND ORANGE LIQUEUR TO CUSTARD SAUCE AND FROM THERE CAME UP WITH THE NOTION OF SIMILARLY SPICING UP THE TRADITIONAL CRÈME BRÛLÉE. THIS DESSERT MAY NOW BE FOUND ON ALMOST EVERY FUSION CHEF'S MENU ON EVERY CONTINENT. I SUPPOSE IT SHOULD BE CALLED CRÈME BRÛLÉE ANGLAISE. IT IS NOT SURPRISING THAT THIS RICH, SEDUCTIVE DESSERT SHOULD BE SO POPULAR. I THINK IT IS PERFECT FOR ENTERTAINING AS MUCH OF THE WORK CAN BE DONE AHEAD OF TIME — UP TO A DAY. IT IS ADAPTABLE TO MANY FLAVOURS AND HERE I USE MY FAVOURITE — FRESH GINGER.

Pre-heat the oven to 180°C/350°F/gas mark 4.

Slit the vanilla pod, lengthways, scrape out the sticky seeds and combine them with a tablespoon of the caster sugar. Set aside.

In a small pan, combine half the cream with the ginger and vanilla pod, bring to the boil, remove from the heat and leave to cool thoroughly, about 10 minutes. Strain the cream through a fine sieve, discarding the ginger. Save the vanilla pod, dry it thoroughly and put into your sugar jar. Mix the vanilla and caster sugar mixture into the ginger cream.

In a large bowl, combine the egg yolks, beaten egg and remaining caster sugar with the remaining cream; mix well. Finally, add the ginger cream mixture and mix thoroughly.

Arrange eight 6 cm (2½ in) ramekins in a large baking tin and pour in 2.5 cm (1 in) of hot water. Divide the mixture between the ramekins. Bake for 30 minutes or until the custard is set.

Allow to cool thoroughly and refrigerate. This recipe can be made one day ahead up to this point.

Just before serving, pre-heat the grill to hot. Sprinkle the muscovado sugar over each ramekin and grill until it has caramelized. Watch carefully, so that the sugar does not burn. Allow to cool for a few minutes so that the caramel can harden, and then serve.

ⓥ ROSEMARY AND THYME SHORTBREAD COOKIES ≈

MAKES 18–20 COOKIES

6 tablespoons (75 g/3 oz)
  unsalted butter, at room
  temperature
4 tablespoons sugar
160 g (5½ oz) plain flour
2 teaspoons fresh thyme
  leaves, finely chopped
1 teaspoon fresh rosemary,
  finely chopped
1 teaspoon edible flower
  petals, such as flowering
  sage or rose, finely
  chopped

THESE COOKIES WERE INSPIRED BY DARYLE RYO NAGATA, EXECUTIVE CHEF OF THE WATERFRONT CENTRE HOTEL IN VANCOUVER. HE IS A TRUE MIXTURE OF EAST AND WEST, WITH A SCOTTISH MOTHER AND A JAPANESE FATHER. THESE COOKIES MAKE GOOD USE OF HERBS FROM THE HOTEL'S HERB GARDEN AND FRESH HERBS ARE ESSENTIAL FOR THE BEST FLAVOUR.

Preheat the oven to 160°C/325°F/gas mark 3. In a large bowl, beat the soft butter and sugar together until smooth. With a spatula, slowly incorporate the flour, herbs and flower petals. Mix until you are able to gather the dough easily in one piece and then roll into a ball. Roll this out with a rolling pin to 5 mm (¼ in) thick, then cut into 18–20 cookies. Place them on a baking tray and bake in the oven for about 20 minutes or until they are slightly browned. Allow to cool and serve.

ⓥ GRANITÉ OF JAPANESE PLUM WINE ≈

SERVES 4–6

600 ml (1 pint) Japanese
  plum wine
100 g (4 oz) granulated
  sugar

INSPIRED BY AN ITALIAN SORBET, POPULARIZED IN PARIS IN THE NINETEENTH CENTURY, THIS DESSERT IS HALF-FROZEN WITH A GRANULAR TEXTURE.

JAPANESE PLUM WINE IS USUALLY MADE AT HOME FROM UNRIPE GREEN FRUIT SWEETENED WITH SUGAR AND THEN FERMENTED WITH RICE WINE. FORTUNATELY, IT CAN BE PURCHASED, READY-BOTTLED, FROM MANY ORIENTAL SUPERMARKETS.

YOU CAN MAKE THIS DESSERT WITHOUT AN EXPENSIVE ICE-CREAM MACHINE, AND ALTHOUGH THE SCIENTIFIC BASIS IS UNCLEAR, ALL WHO TRY IT AGREE THAT IT AIDS THE DIGESTION.

Combine the plum wine and sugar in a pan and boil the mixture for 1 minute. Remove and allow it to cool thoroughly.

Pour the cool mixture into ice trays and freeze for 4 hours, without stirring. When you are ready to serve, break up the *granité* with a large fork. It should have a granular texture.

Ⓥ Five-minute Orange Cream Pudding ≈

A fruit dish is the preferred close to most of my dinner parties; it is refreshing, easy to make and seems to be just what everyone craves after a tasty meal. This is an orange dessert that I have adapted from my experiences of eating in Hong Kong restaurants, and which I have modified to my taste by reducing the amount of gelatine. The result is a silky, custard-like dessert, only slightly firm but textured enough for me and, I hope, for you. A bonus is that it takes about 5 minutes to make, it can easily be doubled and can be made one day ahead, so it's perfect for entertaining.

Strain the orange juice, sprinkle the gelatine over the cold juice and leave for 2 minutes. Then bring the mixture to a simmer in a pan. Slowly stir and let the gelatine dissolve thoroughly. Place the hot juice in a blender, add the single cream and blend until smooth.

Add the sugar, orange zest and eggs and blend for 10 seconds. Finally, add the double cream and continue to blend for another 20 seconds.

Spoon into individual serving dishes or into a large gratin dish, cover with cling film and chill for at least 3 hours before serving. This recipe can be made one or even two days in advance. Be sure to cover tightly with cling film before storing in the refrigerator.

Serves 4–6

600 ml (1 pint) fresh orange juice
1 sachet of gelatine
120 ml (4 fl oz) single cream
8 tablespoons granulated sugar
2 teaspoons finely chopped orange zest
2 eggs
250 ml (8 fl oz) double cream

Ⓥ Apple and Lemon Grass Frangipane Tart ≈

Serves 6–8

For the Pastry:
300 g (11 oz) plain flour
12 tablespoons (175 g/
  6 oz) cold unsalted butter,
  cut in small pieces
A pinch of salt
1 teaspoon granulated sugar
4 tablespoons double cream

For the Lemon Grass and Almond Mixture:
3 lemon grass stalks (page 17)
100 g (4 oz) blanched
  almonds
120 g (4½ oz) sugar
1 egg
1 tablespoon (15 g/½ oz)
  unsalted butter, melted

For the Apples:
450 g (1 lb) Bramley apples
3 tablespoons granulated sugar
2 tablespoons (25 g/1 oz)
  unsalted butter, cut in
  small pieces

As a child in Chicago's Chinatown, I knew very little of European or American desserts. The one exception I remember very well is apple pie. For reasons that, even today, are unclear to me, the Chinese in my neighbourhood enjoyed apple pie and coffee. Not that apple pie is anything but an excellent sweet; it is just not very Chinese.

In my youth and while living in France, I discovered the joy of apple tarts, which are lighter, flakier and more buttery than traditional apple pies. And when I helped out in my friend's kitchen, I learned so much as I watched the family make the delicious almond paste that adds something really special to the prosaic apple. The Marquis Frangipane, who is credited with creating the original recipe in the sixteenth century, could not have been more pleased at the enjoyment his treat brought to our table.

In this fusion version, a touch of lemon grass adds a zesty, subtle Asian touch to this French classic. It is a delicious dessert when served right out of the oven, and perhaps even more delightful with vanilla ice-cream.

Combine all the pastry ingredients in a mixing bowl or in a food processor for a few minutes. Roll the dough into a ball on a lightly floured board. Cover with cling film and refrigerate for 30 minutes.

Pre-heat the oven to 200°C/400°F/gas mark 6. Peel the lemon grass stalks to the tender, whitish centres and finely chop. Grind the chopped lemon grass and almonds together in a blender; then add the sugar, egg and melted butter and mix until it is a smooth paste.

Roll out the pastry to 5 mm (¼ in) thick and press it into a 20 cm (8 in) greased tart tin. Spread the surface of the pastry with the lemon grass and almond mixture. Place in the refrigerator.

Peel the apples and cut them into 5 mm (¼ in) slices. Remove the pastry from the refrigerator and arrange the slices, overlapping, in circles on the top of the tart. Sprinkle with the sugar and evenly distribute the butter pieces over the top. Bake in the oven for 1¼ hours or until the pastry is cooked and the apples are tender. Remove and allow to cool slightly. Serve at once.

DESSERTS

Ⓥ Star Anise Crème Caramel ≈

Serves 8

For the Caramel:
150 g (5 oz) granulated sugar
3 tablespoons water

For the Custard:
750 ml (1½ pints) fresh milk
12 star anise (page 23), lightly crushed
1 vanilla pod
185 g (6½ oz) granulated sugar
12 egg yolks
1 egg, beaten

Chinese cuisine, indeed oriental cookery in general, has never featured sugar-sweetened desserts and, as I grew up in a Chinese household, I was not familiar with desserts. During my school days, I used to succumb to the temptations of cake, candy and ice-cream but it was only when I lived in France that I discovered the wonders of true western desserts. I especially remember how charmed I was when I experienced my first crème caramel. The silky texture of the custard and the contrasting caramel made a lasting impression on me. Here I offer a fusion version, one flavoured with star anise, a Chinese pod with a robust, liquorice-like taste. It imparts a lovely aroma to this classic dessert. For best results, make it the night before a dinner party.

Have ready a 1.2 litre (2 pint) soufflé dish or non-stick loaf tin. First make the caramel by putting the sugar and water in a heavy pan and heating them. Stir the liquid and cook until it turns an amber brown, then remove it from the heat and pour it immediately into the dish or tin. Quickly tip it around to coat the entire bottom.

Pre-heat the oven to 180°C/350°F/gas mark 4.

Pour the milk into a pan, add the star anise and simmer for 10 minutes. Meanwhile, slit the vanilla pod, spoon out the sticky seeds and combine the seeds with the sugar. The vanilla pod can be saved and put into your sugar jar.

Now whisk the egg yolks, whole egg and vanilla sugar together in a large bowl. Remove the star anise from the milk and discard. Pour the milk in a steady stream, while it is hot, into the egg and sugar mixture, whisking until thoroughly blended. Then pour the liquid into the soufflé dish or loaf tin. Place the dish or tin in a large roasting tin. Pour in enough hot water to surround it up to two-thirds in depth and carefully transfer to the oven. Bake for 1 hour 25 minutes or until a cocktail stick or fine skewer inserted in the custard comes out clean.

Remove from the oven and allow to cool. Refrigerate overnight.

Just before you are about to serve the crème caramel, gently free it by running a knife around the edges. Invert the dessert onto a serving platter.

ⓋLemon Grass Crème Anglaise ≈

There is nothing more satisfying than a velvety crème Anglaise or custard cream. In this recipe, the flavouring is the citrus fragrance of lemon grass. It is not difficult to make but you must be careful to keep stirring at a low temperature to keep the mixture from curdling. Once you have made this several times, you will find that it is a quick and easy dessert sauce that can enhance fresh fruit – or serve it with Chocolate Cake with Candied Ginger (page 229).

Serves 4

2 lemon grass stalks
   (page 18)
600 ml (19 fl oz) milk
5 egg yolks
75 g (3 oz) granulated sugar

Peel the lemon grass stalks to the tender, whitish centres and crush them with the flat of a knife. Then finely chop them. Combine the chopped lemon grass with the milk in a pan and simmer for 15 minutes over a low heat. Remove the pan from the heat and steep for 20 minutes.

Strain the milk through a fine sieve and discard the chopped lemon grass.

Whisk the egg yolks and sugar together until the mixture is a pale yellow colour. Then pour in the milk and mix well. Pour this mixture into a clean pan and simmer over a low heat, stirring all the while. When the sauce is thick enough to coat a spoon, it is done. Never let it boil. Strain the custard; it can be used immediately or cooled for use later.

INDEX